RURAL SMALL-SCALE INDUSTRY
IN THE PEOPLE'S REPUBLIC OF CHINA

MEMBERS OF THE AMERICAN RURAL
SMALL-SCALE INDUSTRY DELEGATION

Alexander DeAngelis, *Professional Associate, Committee on Scholarly Communications with the People's Republic of China*

Robert Dernberger, *Professor of Economics, University of Michigan*

Scott Hallford, *Deputy Director, Office of Chinese Affairs, Department of State*

Amir Khan, *Project Director, IRRI-PAK Agricultural Machinery Program, Pakistan*

Owen Livingston, *Director, Fertilizer Technology Division, International Fertilizer Development Center*

William Parish, *Associate Professor of Sociology and Director of the Center for Far Eastern Studies, University of Chicago*

Dwight Perkins, *Chairman, Director of Harvard Institute of International Development and Professor of Modern Chinese Studies and of Economics, Harvard University*

Thomas Rawski, *Associate Professor of Economics, University of Toronto*

Kenneth D. Simmons, *President, Eastern Division, Martin Marietta Cement*

Arthur Stinchcombe, *Professor of Sociology, University of Arizona, Tucson*

Peter Timmer, John D. Black, *Professor of Agriculture and Business, Harvard University*

Lyman P. Van Slyke, *Associate Professor of History, Stanford University*

RURAL SMALL-SCALE INDUSTRY IN THE PEOPLE'S REPUBLIC OF CHINA

THE AMERICAN RURAL SMALL-SCALE INDUSTRY DELEGATION

Dwight Perkins, Chairman   William Parish

Alexander DeAngelis   Thomas Rawski

Robert Dernberger   Kenneth Simmons

Scott Hallford   Arthur Stinchcombe

Amir Khan   Peter Timmer

Owen Livingston   Lyman Van Slyke

UNIVERSITY OF CALIFORNIA PRESS
Berkeley · Los Angeles · London

The views expressed in this report are those of the members of the Rural Small-scale Industries Delegation and are in no way the official views of the Committee on Scholarly Communication or its sponsoring organizations—the American Council of Learned Societies, the National Academy of Sciences, and the Social Science Research Council.

University of California Press
Berkeley and Los Angeles, California

University of California Press, Ltd.
London, England

Copyright © 1977 by
The Regents of the University of California

First Paperback Printing 1981
ISBN 0-520-04401-0
Library of Congress Catalog Card Number: 76-20015
Printed in the United States of America

1 2 3 4 5 6 7 8 9

Contents

List of Illustrations and Tables

TABLES

Travel route of the American Delegation on Rural Small-scale Industry in the People's Republic of China.

Preface

Our Rural Small-scale Industry Delegation was part of the exchange program between the Committee on Scholarly Communication with the People's Republic of China and the Chinese Scientific and Technical Association. The Committee is jointly sponsored by the American Council of Learned Societies, the National Academy of Sciences, and the Social Science Research Council. Since the 1972 signing of the Shanghai Communique calling for the establishment of cultural and scientific exchanges, the Committee's programs have been endorsed and supported by the governments of both countries. Our delegation was selected in accordance with the Committee's guidelines.

We flew to Peking from Tokyo on June 12, 1975, and left from Canton by train to Hong Kong on July 10, 1975. While in China we were guests of China's Scientific and Technical Association and of the People's Institute of Foreign Affairs. Within each region of China visited we were also guests of various foreign affairs, industrial, and water conservancy bureaus of the region. Everywhere we went we were shown courtesies too numerous to mention one by one. Leaders of revolutionary committees in factories and communes took hours and sometimes days of their time to help us understand what it was they were trying to accomplish, and what they had already achieved.

We are particularly grateful to the eight-member group, led by Mr. Li Cheng-jui of the Institute of Economics of the Academy of Sciences, which accompanied us throughout our journey. We were not an easy group with which to travel. Our viewpoint was that of American social scientists and engineers, and our endless supply of questions tended to reflect that viewpoint. Our hosts were Chinese Marxist-Leninists, who consistently interpreted their experience to us from that perspective. Seven of the members of our delegation spoke and read Chinese with varying degrees of skill, and the two interpreters who accompanied us, both of whom were professors at the Peking Foreign Language Institute, were consistently excellent in jumping from the terminology of economics to chemistry to mechanical engineering. Translation from Chinese to English, therefore, was not a problem. Understanding what the English meant in the Chinese context, however, was more difficult.

The chapters that follow are our attempt to interpret what it was we were told, and what we saw. In a fundamental way we all participated in the writing of each chapter. We traveled together, asked questions together, and discussed our findings at length over meals, and whenever we had a few moments of free time, which wasn't often. But particular individuals did have special responsibility for certain chapters.

Chapters II and III on administration and individual incentives were the responsibility of Art Stinchcombe and Bill Parish, our delegation's two sociologists, respectively. Our attempt in Chapter IV to reach conclusions about the economic efficiency of small-scale enterprises was the joint product of three of our economists: Bob Dernberger, Tom Rawski, and Peter Timmer. Amir Khan, Owen Livingston, and Kenneth Simmons, our three engineers, prepared the three chapters on farm machinery, chemical fertilizer, and cement, respectively. Chapter VIII on the role of these industries within the broader context of China's rural development program was also a joint product of Scott Hallford, Dwight Perkins, and Peter Timmer. Chapter IX on the social impact of small-scale industry was written by Bill Parish, and Chapter X on expanding knowledge and the transformation of values was written by Lyman Van Slyke. Alexander DeAngelis prepared the appendix lists of individuals met and places visited. The appendixes on prices and machinery were prepared by Thomas Rawski. Dwight Perkins wrote the introduction and conclusion and had overall editorial responsibility.

Chapter I

INTRODUCTION

No brief description or short systematic definition can do justice to the great diversity that characterizes rural small-scale industry in the People's Republic of China. Rural small-scale industry is not necessarily even rural (some of it is located in county towns), or all that small (the number of employees sometimes exceeds 500 per factory). And yet there are fundamental differences between large-scale urban plants and those that are termed rural and small-scale. All industries cooperatively owned by rural communes and brigades are classified as "rural small-scale." But state-owned enterprises also are included, provided that they are under the jurisdiction of a county and not some higher level administrative unit (district, city, province, or nation). Being under a county's jurisdiction usually means that the greater portion of the factory's outputs and inputs are sold or obtained within that same county. When an enterprise finds itself supplying a much larger area, it usually is transferred up to a higher level administrative unit.

Our delegation saw China's rural small-scale industry in June and July of 1975. These industries can be described as using greater amounts of "indigenous" as contrasted to "modern" technology, as being smaller in scale (from under 50 to around 600 employees), and as largely devoting their efforts to the service of agricultural production. But if anything came across clearly to our delegation, it is that these enterprises are continually in the process of change, and what is true today may no longer be valid a few years

1

hence. In many enterprises, for example, the scale and the ratio of modern to indigenous technologies are both steadily on the rise. Even the goal of serving agriculture has not always enjoyed the preeminence that it does today and the day may come again when subcontracting for urban factories receives a higher priority in the program.

Some visitors to China attempt to use their brief observations as a basis for a general appraisal of Chinese society. Our group will not even attempt a definitive statement about rural small-scale industry based on our four weeks of study. This report instead represents an attempt to describe what it is we saw and such conclusions as we thought we could reasonably draw from our observations. Our group included seven who could speak and read Chinese, among whom five had devoted their professional life to China-related scholarship. In addition, we had three engineers expert in the fields of cement, chemical fertilizer, and farm machinery. All twelve members of the group had had working as well as travel experience in other developing nations.

Against this relevant experience, however, must be put the vastness of the People's Republic of China. We visited 50 factories and 10 communes, a considerable number we felt at the time, considering the 95° F. heat. But these are only a tiny fraction of the hundreds of thousands of factories and tens of thousands of communes in China. What we saw was in no way any random sample of what China is doing in the area of small-scale industry. Our hosts wanted us to understand what they are trying to do as well as what they have already accomplished, and for that purpose model and advanced areas were deemed more useful than average or backward performers. As a result, all of the regions we visited were advanced in national terms and several were models to be studied not mainly by foreign visitors, but by millions of Chinese who were being encouraged to emulate their more successful brethren.

And even in the areas we did visit, our time was short and the amount of information we could gather varied widely. Much decision making in China has been decentralized to lower levels, and scientific and technical personnel from Peking, even if they were so inclined, cannot usually order factory and county revolutionary committees to divulge information that these revolutionary committees themselves, for whatever reason, are reluctant to give out. Thus in some regions we encountered a willingness on the part of the local people to answer most of the (very large number of) questions that our group could think to ask. In other areas officials were much more reticent.

Because of the limitations inherent in a 28-day visit, any attempt at a definitive statement of what we now know about rural small-scale industry in China, or could know, would have to involve prolonged research in the considerable quantities of material published on the subject. For those interested in pursuing further the issues raised by this trip report, there is no better place to start than with the works of Carl Riskin and Jon Sigurdson. Unless otherwise footnoted, however, all data used in this report were supplied to us by our hosts while we were in China.

What then did we see? Our detailed itinerary appears in Appendix B. We asked to and did visit small-scale enterprises in four kinds of settings: in rural mountainous areas of the north, on the North China Plain, in suburban (but still rural) regions of large cities, and in southern paddy rice regions. The greatest amount of time was spent in the Tai-hang Mountain area of north China and the least on the North China Plain. Except for the flight from Shanghai to Kwangchou, all travel was by car and bus or by train.

The pattern of small-scale industry development varies considerably between regions, but there are common themes. Central to all these themes is "self-reliance," the belief that all units in China (large or small, rural or urban) should not sit around waiting for outside help before setting out to improve their situation. Two of the principal models of self-reliance for all of China are Hsi-yang County in Shansi, which includes the Tachai Brigade, and Lin County in Honan. Both are in the Tai-hang Mountains, and we spent four days in each.

Rural self-reliance begins not with the creation of small-scale industry, but with efforts to raise the output of agriculture by the direct and massive application of labor combined with limited amounts of capital and simple tools (picks, shovels, hammers, carrying baskets, and blasting powder for the most part). In Tachai and now throughout Hsi-yang County, these efforts have been directed at converting small, low-quality fields where crops were washed away by rainy season flooding into what are now known throughout China as "Tachai-type fields." These new type fields are larger, more level, and underneath the fields run large drainage tunnels that divert rainy season floods away from the crops and, where possible, into newly built reservoirs for use in irrigation. Much of the soil for these fields was brought down with carrying poles and baskets from higher up on the mountainside. The tunnels, often several kilometers long, were built by chipping large rocks into the proper shape and then constructing the tunnel (building-block fashion) without benefit of cement and frequently without even the use of much mortar. It is difficult to imagine a more labor-intensive method of construction.

In Lin County the problem was not so much rainy season floods but a severe shortage of water at all times. The solution determined by the county, apparently with some resistance from higher authorities, was to tap the water of the Chang River at a point several ten's of kilometers away and in another province (Shansi). The effort began in 1960 and was completed in 1969. During the slack season the daily work force reached 30,000 (the number was much smaller during peak agricultural labor demand) and over the entire period the work put in totaled 40 million man days at a capital cost of only 47 million yuan, 78 percent of which was supplied by the communes of the county themselves. The end result was a canal network 1500 kilometers in length (including subsidiary channels) and the complete solution to Lin County's water shortage.

These efforts in Hsi-yang and Lin Counties were in a fundamental way preconditions for the small-scale industry program in China. As long as these regions stayed with the old ways, they had ample labor for cultivating, threshing and milling their crops. Nor would it have been easy to use many kinds of farm machinery even if they had such machinery. Power pumps must have water to pump and tractors don't work well on small, uneven, rocky plots.

With the advent of large-scale rural land development and water conservancy schemes, however, there is right from the beginning a demand for cement. And once there are supplies of water for the fields, it is possible to make much greater use of chemical fertilizers. The greater quantities of water and fertilizer lead to increases in crop output, and these increases in turn raise the demand for labor to do the threshing, milling, and moving of the surplus to market. Thus, where before during periods of peak labor demand the supply of workers may have been adequate, now there is likely to be a shortage and hence justification for using certain kinds of labor-saving machinery.

The term "labor shortage" must be used with care. Even in advanced areas such as Hsi-yang and Lin Counties, there is enough labor during slack seasons to continue highly labor-intensive and low-productivity occupations such as tunnel building. But during such peak periods as the harvest, there are no longer adequate numbers of people to perform the required tasks. Rather than cut back farm output, it obviously makes more sense to buy power threshers and milling machines and to transport food to market with a cart pulled by a hand tractor (rather than by a man).

The pattern on the North China Plain and in the rice growing regions we visited differs from the above model in certain key respects. The key difference is that the first stage of the process is more modest in scope and different in nature. Wuhsi County in Kiangsu Province where we spent five days was a comparatively well-off and advanced area even before 1949. There were ample supplies of water, and the drainage problem, although real enough, was not as difficult to deal with as that in Hsi-yang. Thus Wuhsi did not have to lift itself up by its bootstraps *before* it could make effective use of chemical fertilizer and farm machinery. It had a ready use for them as soon as they became available. Crop yields at Ch'i-li-ying Commune on the North China Plain, on the other hand, were quite low in the 1940s and early 1950s, and raising these yields depended not only on the Commune's own efforts, but also on larger-scale water conservancy projects carried out by higher level administrative units. Elsewhere on the North China Plain increased supplies of water have come in recent years from the sinking of tube wells using modern well-digging and construction materials, not indigenous labor-intensive methods. But once the water was available and yields rose, much of the rest of the sequence followed that of the model, particularly with respect to farm machinery.

If cement and chemical fertilizer contributed to an increase in agricultural output and this increase in turn created a demand for farm machinery, it does not follow automatically that the Chinese had to meet this demand through the construction of rural-based small-scale factories. Chemical fertilizer around the world, for example, is usually supplied by large-scale plants, and China itself has a number of large plants and is purchasing more. Cement is produced in smaller units even in the United States, but these "smaller" American plants are still many times larger than the largest of China's rural small-scale cement plants.

The rationale for the use of small-scale factories in rural areas begins with a recognition of the inadequacies of China's rural transport and marketing system. In most developing countries roads are poor, vehicles scarce, and commercial organizations inefficient with the result being that economic contact between rural areas and distant urban centers is limited. Transporting goods from urban to rural locations, or the reverse, is so expensive that the journey can be justified only for items of high initial price, low bulk, and easy transportability. For example, the cost of moving limestone from a rural location to a distant city where it can be processed into cement and then shipped back to the countryside is prohibitive. A similar situation prevails with respect to food processing and to a more limited degree to chemical fertilizers.

China's roads are improving. In the advanced areas we visited all or virtually all communes appeared to be connected to the main highways by good gravel or asphalt roads. But China is still extremely short of vehicles, particularly trucks, for use on those roads. In part this gap is being filled by tractors pulling carts, but human and animal-drawn carts are still very much in use. Even where trucks are available, the cost of moving bulky items is high. In Lin County, for example, the cost of transporting coal a mere 25 miles to the plant site raised its price by 50 percent (from 20 to 30 yuan a ton).

Reinforcing the effects of high transport costs is the nature of China's rural commercial system. Even when communes are prepared to pay the going price for some desired item, it won't necessarily be available. A commune, for the most part, is not free to go into the city and buy a tractor or more fertilizer. Individual commune members can do this with consumer items which are sold off the shelves at a price that usually clears the market.

But producer goods are allocated according to the plan. To purchase a truck, for example, a commune would have to get its request (as part of a proposed county-wide quota) on to the district, and from there to the province or to whatever level held principal responsibility for the distribution of trucks from the large domestic plants and from imports. Needless to say, such a procedure can involve long delays and the real possibility that the request will be rejected. Thus, even if a commune has saved up enough money for a piece of machinery, it may get it faster if it builds one on its own or persuades the local county authorities to build it. As long as local production doesn't draw heavily on higher level sources for scarce parts and materials, higher level planners are not likely to object.

Small-scale industries save time in at least three other ways as well. First, the time of construction (the time before the plant was put into operation) was held to be lower for small-scale plants. Many times in briefings at factories, the initiative of the workers for getting the plant into production in less time than planned was praised. Sitting and waiting for the government to solve local problems was the sort of thing that was overcome by the Great Leap Forward and the Great Proletarian Cultural Revolution. Second, especially in local agricultural machinery plants, but also in a plant producing spare parts for fertilizer plants, the downtime of machinery in repair was frequently mentioned as something being reduced by the plants' operations. Teams from local plants often went into the field at busy seasons, and inventories of spare parts were built up for busy seasons, with the clear intention of reducing downtime. Third, there was a rather confused argument about the time path of production, which had several elements. The basic idea is that you have to start somewhere, so why not start with what you can do now; if you can do something better later, you will be better off in lots of ways for having made investments in what will turn out to have been high cost operations. The most frequent formulation was that the small plant itself went from small to big, indigenous to modern, high cost to low cost, and implicitly that it would not be big, modern, and low cost in the future without the industrial experience, the chance to mobilize the masses in technical renovation, and the capital funds from profits in the meantime, that are the product of its first period.

Closely related to the limitations of transport and marketing is the question of the availability of local resources. If local resources are available at a reasonable cost, and these resources are not otherwise being exploited by large-scale enterprises, then local small enterprises can exploit these resources without cutting into priority projects elsewhere. The widespread availability of small outcroppings of coal and limestone too small for large-scale development, therefore, is a primary justification for the creation of local small-scale industries. And there are many other materials besides coal and limestone that would remain unused or undeveloped if no local demand existed. There is no incentive to develop the production of fruits and many other kinds of perishable foods beyond the needs of the locality, unless there exists a fruit processing plant that prepares the fruit for shipment to more distant points. Slag from a local iron and steel plant can be used to expand cement output if there is a cement plant nearby. This list of goods can be extended indefinitely.

A fifth major justification for rural small-scale industries is that they are closer to their markets than large urban enterprises, and hence can better understand and meet the needs of their customers. For standardized products, knowledge of the peculiarities of a particular market may not be essential, but for items such as farm machinery, this knowledge may make the difference between success and failure. A suburban Shanghai County farm machinery plant, for example, was making rice transplanters specially designed for local use. Transplanters produced elsewhere, it had been found, were designed for a slightly different cropping pattern.

A major shortcoming of state-owned and centrally-planned enterprises in many parts of the world has been their tendency to concentrate on production and to ignore the market for that production. In China too a factory's responsibility for its products often ends when the product passes out of the factory gate. On many occasions we were told that the lineup of new tractors or stacked crates of new machinery so much in evidence in or near the factory grounds was now under the jurisdiction of the county or city commercial bureau, not that of the factory. Placing the factory near to the end users of the product doesn't completely resolve this problem, but it at least removes the barrier of distance that stands in the way of effective market studies by large urban factories with nationwide sales. If a commune is dissatisfied with the product mix of the county farm machinery factory, or feels that output quality is too low, it can complain directly to the factory or to its immediate superiors (the county revolutionary committee) who are also the immediate superiors of the factory. More positively, if a factory wants to adjust production to local needs, all it has to do is form a team to walk a few miles down the road to talk with current and potential customers. Or the relevant county bureaus can do the job for the factory without having to pass their findings through several levels of bureaucratic red tape.

A sixth reason for emphasis on small-scale industry is that the location of enterprises in rural areas tends to narrow the gap between city and countryside. This narrowing has both economic and social advantages. The economic advantages include the elimination of expenditures on urban housing and public utilities. Factory workers continue to live in their old villages and hence have no need for much of the infrastructure that must be built alongside a large urban enterprise.

More important from the Chinese point of view is the elimination of the social gap between countryside and city. In commune and brigade enterprises workers usually continue to do some and often a great deal of work in the fields. Furthermore, in many cases, their wages are paid in the form of work points by their teams or brigades, and hence their incomes differ little if any from their farming neighbors. Workers in county-run enterprises are not integrated into the productive life of the commune, but they frequently live in their old villages and receive wages that are often similar to or only slightly higher than the incomes of those with whom they live. Rural small-scale industry, therefore, contributes to the Chinese goal of eliminating class barriers and preventing new ones from arising.

A closely related goal is the desire to bring modern technology to the countryside immediately rather than to wait until urban development has proceded to a point where its methods have begun to trickle out into rural areas. By locating factories in the countryside, instead of moving rural people into the cities, the countryside gains a cadre of personnel experienced in modern techniques, and millions not actually working in the new enterprises learn through observation something about the advantages and methods of modern engineering.

Surprisingly, the expansion of rural off-farm employment opportunities does not at present appear to be a major goal of China's small-scale industry program. These new factories do create employment opportunities, of course, but there is considerable effort expended to keep these enterprises from cutting heavily into the supply of labor available to agriculture. Agriculture has priority over rural industry, and rural industry's main priority is in fact to serve agriculture, and the Chinese appear to think of priorities more in absolute than in marginal terms. Activities that deprive agriculture of part of its labor force are, to that extent at least, not serving agriculture. Time and again we were told by factory representatives of the efforts they were making to eliminate manual, highly labor-intensive processes and to substitute mechanized methods. To some degree these modern methods seem to be desired for their own sake, but often the firm appeared to be under pressure to expand output without any major increases in employment. China's rural small-scale industries remain highly labor-intensive when compared to urban enterprises in China, and the contrast is even greater with similar industries in the United States. But most Chinese efforts at the moment appear to be directed not at exploiting the employment potential of labor-intensive techniques, but toward modernizing those techniques in a capital-intensive direction.

The rural small-scale industry program also is not conceived of as a substitute for urban-based large and medium-scale industrialization. The Chinese have attempted to freeze the population of many of China's large cities (neither Shanghai nor Cheng-chou among the cities we visited has grown much if at all during the past decade), but other intermediate cities have continued to increase in size (Hsin-hsiang grew from 320,000 to 420,000 between 1965 and 1975). More important, construction of large enterprises continues at a rapid pace, and by all appearances these enterprises continue to receive the lion's share of state funds. Between 1964 and 1974, for example, 1100 large modern enterprises were built in China. In a similar vein, the gross values of industrial output in Shanghai and Tientsin in 1973 were more than double the levels of 1965, and in Peking there was a tripling.

Finally, it is not at all clear that achieving a greater degree of equality of income between regions of the nation is a major goal of the small-scale industry program. No doubt Chinese leaders hope that greater equality will result, but the whole emphasis of the program is on self-reliance, not on using state funds to help lift up more backward areas. State funds from levels above the county are used, to be sure, and it may be that they are used in a way to promote greater equality, although we did not obtain any information on this subject. The fact that our travels were exclusively in advanced areas meant that we were not in a position to see directly how poorer areas were treated. But to a substantial degree, it would appear, a county or commune is expected to use its own funds and its own labor force. Rural areas with more funds for this purpose, with better leadership, and located near relevant natural resources, therefore, will naturally benefit more from the small-scale industry program than those lacking one or more of these characteristics. And there is no reason to believe that it is the currently more backward areas that are those best endowed for small-scale industrial development.

First and foremost, China is developing rural small-scale industry because this strategy is believed to be doing a better job of supporting agriculture than did the large-scale strategies of the past. There are many rural factories that do subcontracting work for urban enterprises, but these activities are clearly secondary to the main task of supporting agriculture in the rural industrial program as a whole. Furthermore, the rural enterprises that do subcontracting work that is not in support of agriculture appear to be doing only a small fraction of that kind of work. Industrial products designed for purposes other than the support of agriculture, and a substantial majority of all industrial products would appear still to fall into this category, continue to be made, for the most part, in and around urban centers and more often than not in medium- and large-scale factories.

The preceding discussion has attempted to list the objectives and advantages of China's rural small-scale industry program. The words, we believe, are a fair interpretation of many of the things we were told during our visit. Against these advantages must be put the question of the efficiency of these small-scale plants. Put differently, can these plants deliver farm machinery, fertilizer, and other products to agriculture at a cost that is competitive with alternative sources of supply and at a satisfactory quality level?

Our Chinese hosts were willing to discuss individual sources of cost savings, but they were consistently reluctant to add up the costs and benefits and consider the net result in a manner common to project feasibility studies, public as well as private, in much of the rest of the world. Thus our hosts would speak of low investment per plant and the speed with which plants could be constructed. And small-scale enterprises were also praised on occasion for accumulating funds for the state. In addition, as already mentioned, there were important savings in transport and in urban housing and public utilities.

The process of adding up these costs and benefits probably smacked too much of applying capitalistic profitability criteria to enterprises which, in their view, could not be judged properly by such methods. But the issue is really more complex than this. One way or another Chinese planners reach conclusions about the efficiency of small-scale enterprises. During the Great Leap Forward (1958–1960), efficiency criteria may have been ignored. But we saw no enterprises that were clearly irrational from the point of view of conventional cost–benefit analysis, and such a result could not have occurred by accident. To say that enterprises are not "clearly irrational," of course, is not the same thing as saying that such enterprises are efficient. Such conclusions as we were capable of reaching on the question of efficiency are presented in Chapter IV.

The concepts of engineering feasibility and efficiency are related to, but decidedly distinct from, the concepts of economic feasibility and efficiency. In determining whether rural small-scale industry is feasible in an engineering sense, the first question to be answered is whether the area has ample supplies of electric power. In certain of the areas we visited, electric power was obtained by tying the county or commune into one of the major grids. The suburban communes of Shanghai and Peking were obviously well-situated from this point of view, and Hsi-yang County was tied into the T'ai-yuan grid. But Lin County got much of its electric power as an additional benefit from the construction of the Red Flag Canal. And a commune in Kwangtung obtained power by building a dam across one of the tributaries of the Pearl River. Areas that do not yet have electric power presumably have little small-scale industry of a modern type, although we did not visit any such areas.

More difficult engineering questions concern such issues as whether the product being manufactured meets appropriate quality standards, and whether the processes being used make the most efficient use of key materials. These and related issues are discussed at length in Chapters V through VII for three of the types of enterprises visited: cement, chemical fertilizer, and farm machinery.

Before turning to questions of economic and engineering efficiency, however, it is important to understand how the Chinese have organized themselves to carry out their rural, small-scale industry program. How have the Chinese administered these programs, by elaborate rules or by moral example, and what is the role of the very present ideology? In many ways Chinese methods of handling such basic functions as the coordination of supply and demand and the promotion of innovation are similar in their structure to the way these functions are performed elsewhere in the world, but in other ways the Chinese approach is unique. These and related issues are the subject of Chapter II.

At the center of any program is the question of how to motivate the individuals responsible to implement it. Wages and promotions are only a part of the story. There are also non-material rewards for good performance, and the Chinese have made extensive use of praise and public recognition. Incentives, material or otherwise, are the subject of Chapter III.

Other chapters deal with the impact of small-scale industry on agricultural production (Chapter VIII) and on such key features of the Chinese countryside as the level of employment, the role of women, and the nature of rural administration (Chapter IX). Finally, there is the whole question of the role of education and training, both formal and informal. Rural small-scale industry is a source of technological education, but it is also to some degree a beneficiary of nationwide efforts to universalize education at the primary school and junior high school level, to send educated youth down to the countryside, to supply rural areas with practical technical publications, and the like. These and related issues are the subject of Chapter X.

Chapter II

SOCIALIST ADMINISTRATIVE SYSTEMS AND SMALL-SCALE INDUSTRY

The two principal administrative differences between socialism and capitalism are the relation of enterprise policy to state policy (or to put it differently, there are differences in the planning system), and differences in how the benefits of production are divided (or to put it differently, differences in the incentive system). This chapter is devoted to the first part of this administrative difference, the relation of the state to the enterprise.

The first section attempts to specify what the meaning is of Chinese "decentralization" of economic planning. Clearly it does not mean the same thing as the decentralization of capitalist firms responding autonomously to the market. It seems from our material that the central elements in the system of decentralization are county, city, subregional, and provincial planning authorities, *not* factories. We visited factories, which makes our analysis of what planners must have been doing largely a matter of elimination; since factories do not make their investment and marketing decisions, somebody else must. As far as we could find out from our questions on these matters, the "somebody else" is a different sort of body in more advanced technologies (larger, more urban industries) than in rural and small-scale industries. The administrative logic of the system gives a different meaning to the phrase "relying on our own efforts" in different factories. That is, the argument of this section is that decentralization, of which rural and small-scale industry is a reflection, is itself several different things. What things it is depends on the technical and administrative level of the factory one is talking about. Briefly, the planning system seems to be in part a nested or hierarchical system of rationing of technically advanced products in such a way that the demand for scarce, high-technology products in the production of products for rural life is minimized.

A closely related problem to "decentralization" is the problem of bureaucratic control by the state. If an administrative system tries to govern everything by regulation, and to control everything by policing conformity to regulations, then the ratio of "policemen" (auditors, bureaucrats of all kinds) to producers tends to increase. A stiff, top-heavy bureaucracy, where everything sensible violates some rule—this is the image an American gets if he imagines expanding a government agency into an organization for controlling a whole economy. The second section below explores the Chinese use of moral examples for communicating administrative purposes and standards. We were in a good position to observe this, because we were taken to model communes and factories that were proclaimed to be models, and were referred to as models when we went elsewhere.

In the third section we take up the functions of ideology in factory administration. That is, the Chinese state as a whole provides a language for discussing why what is done in factories is justified, ought to be the way it is, and ought to develop the way it is developing. This relation between socialist ideology and authority within the factory is not, of course, characteristic of the United States. Some speculations on what our informants used their ideology for, in the course of doing their jobs and explaining their jobs to us, is included in this section. The nature of the evidence is explained close to the conclusions it supports, because our evidence here is, if possible, weaker than in the first two sections.

THE COORDINATION OF SUPPLY AND DEMAND

In machinery production, either for capital equipment for factories or for capital outputs of industry to agriculture, there seems to be a hierarchy of what we might call parts and equipment brokers, made up of the planning office of the appropriate administrative level. This hierarchy corresponds roughly to that proposed by Vernon for international trade, with capital equipment of the heaviest and most technically advanced sort and serial (as opposed to batch) production of reasonably advanced machines (such as engines, automobiles, etc.) located in the traditional industrial centers (such as the Northeast, Peking, Shanghai, and some other newer major centers). Most such factories are either run by the ministries directly or are subject to city authorities of one of the three cities administered as provinces (Peking, Tientsin, and Shanghai).

Repair parts manufacturing, mass production of the simpler parts of machines with internal combustion engines (such as tractors) and their assembly, and some of the less sophisticated individual machines (e.g., simple forges and big electric motors or big pumps) are organized and distributed at provincial or subregional levels, mainly by coordinating through the city planning departments. That is, most such factories are in cities directly subject to the subregion or the provinces. These supply provincial governments with things that can be allocated to county level planners for supply to rural and small-scale industry.

One presumes that something like the same thing happens with consumer machines of high-income elasticity. Air fans with fancy controls, of very high-income elasticity, are produced in Shanghai; fancy designed cloth with medium-income elasticity is produced in subregional centers; plain cloth (sometimes) at county levels. That is, the higher the income elasticity of a good, the larger the advantage of traditional industrial and metropolitan centers. This is both cause and effect, since the largest markets for exports and luxuries are in traditional centers, and since the level of industrial differentiation of large centers facilitates producing goods with short production runs.

Some of the national level plants are clearly run directly out of the ministries, but I imagine probably most supply and demand coordination is done at the provincial or lower levels. At any rate, these levels are the most important for rural and small-scale industry. There seems to be a very great overrepresentation in smaller- and middle-sized plants of heavy machinery from within the province, rather than from Peking, Shanghai, the Northeast; of repair parts and simpler machines from within the subregion (rather than from provincial sources); technical help for new production lines also comes from within the province or subregion. Only the original chemical fertilizer plants and the heavy machines for national level industries (e.g. the precision grinding machines from the Shanghai plant) are evidently normally traded at the national level, coordinated by national ministries, and of the inputs or raw materials we have seen, only rolled steel ordinarily comes from above the provincial level.

What we can infer, then, is an organization along roughly the following lines. The internal supply system of the major industrial centers is either run on a city basis or by the national ministries. This applies especially for technically advanced products (e.g. machines that can grind to close tolerances or technically advanced processes, e.g., rolled steel, assembly line production of engines) or high-income elasticity products (e.g. fancy fans). At a national level these are allocated then to provinces, which form the main marketing channel for them, or to the national commercial agency, which allocates luxury consumer goods by price. The capital goods will usually be sold to subregional and provincial level factories.

Factories with provincial and subregional markets, whose supplies are allocated both from the national level through the provincial planning agency and are coordinated with suppliers from elsewhere in the province or subregion in the same provincial planning office, tend to be either producers of intermediate level machines on a mass production basis (e.g. Internal combustion engines, tractors, centrifugal pumps) or intermediate level, medium precision machine tools on a batch basis (e.g. lathes, compressor parts for chemical plants, large pumps). These factories tend to supply these products to other provincial and subregional factories and to county planning authorities. At the next lower level of technology, county authorities allocate to county factories and to communes both supplies from within the county and supplies from provincial or subregional authorities. The same happens at the commune and brigade levels. No doubt it is not as neat as this, and an advanced subregion near Shanghai may equal a province in Shansi, but it seems that the broad pattern is clear.

This means that the concrete meaning of "relying on our own efforts" changes with the level of the factory and its administrative authority. It means roughly minimizing the demands that depend on exchange at higher levels. Only in the ideal case does it mean producing one's machines in one's own factory. What it usually means is getting one's supplies and equipment from the factories and mines controlled by one's own planning authority.

The presumption of a one-way exchange downward is based on the notion that the products of more advanced technologies are the ones that are crucially scarce, that the inputs used by lower technological levels would not ordinarily (the main exceptions, I suppose, are rolled steel and stainless steel) be useful inputs at more advanced levels, but that the more advanced levels need each other's inputs. So a hierarchical system of market and supply spheres, with an arrangement which is in effect a protected local market for relatively inefficient producers of lower technology goods, economizes higher technology inputs for those activities that need them.

Further, such a system with prices set to give relatively large profits to inefficient producers of low technology goods, so as not to waste Shanghai talent producing small threshers for the whole country, encourages innovative attempts to move to the next higher level. We frequently saw trial production by lower level technology units of the next higher level technology, e.g., small-crawler tractors (but not their engines) at the county level in Shansi and small-wheeled ones in Hui County, large reciprocating compressors for ammonia plants at the subprovincial level in Hsin-hsiang.

Presumably each of these, if successful, takes some of the pressure off the next higher level, allowing then that level to produce more of what they alone can produce (e.g. in the first case, tractor engines, in the second case complete ammonia plants).

What we would expect under these circumstances is that over time the more efficient of such "one-step innovations" at lower levels could become producers at the next higher level, growing too big for their protected market. If these enterprises were collectively owned (e.g. as the now state-owned optical instruments factory in Peking had been), this rise to a higher level would produce ideological problems that then had to be resolved with a campaign of self-criticism. That is, the presumption that a collectively-owned factory should keep its own profits has to be criticized and overcome before the one making precision optical products, for example, can enter the national market for such products. But even if it is only turning over one's most successful factory projects to the next higher administrative level, there surely must be ambivalence about it.

Apparently when this happens, there is also a rapid infusion of new technology from sources at the next higher level. For example, soon after the mass production engine line was introduced in the Peking factory, which had previously made other things, they introduced air driven wrenches, which we did not see at any lower level. For another, there was continuing close relation between the T'ai-yuan tractor factory and the county factory, which was building a plant with a capacity of 1000 tractors a year near Tachai. For another, only the national level textile factory was proposing to experiment with electronically controlled looms. In short, it seems that inputs of technology are discontinuous, and tend to come in a big lump when a factory is about to, or has just, changed administrative level and (consequently) changed its supply and market range.

Another thing that such a hierarchical exchange system economizes, as has been at the core of theories of metropolitan dominance, is information and inventory costs. If information on the needs for repair parts for chemical fertilizer plants has to travel through seven bureaucratic levels to Shanghai, rather than through two to the subregional planning office and regional parts factory, it (1) takes longer, (2) takes more time of scarce administrative talent, and (3) overburdens the center with mass paper processing so it can't process the crucial pieces of information. The French scientific research establishment or American railroads are familiar examples of such inefficiencies of each small problem having to be decided by the central office. The inventories of engine parts held at the county level are more likely to be finely adjusted to the needs of the county than are massive, and locally unavailable, inventories at the center. Just as in the United States merchant wholesalers (decentralized planning) dominate the markets with diverse and variable demands (e.g. automobile parts), while manufacturers' branches (centralized planning) dominate flows of a few standard products (e.g. automobiles). Consequently a ministry of machines can directly administer the flow of a few standard engines from a mass production engine plant to a few large fabricators of tractors and automobiles, while the flows of many various engines to many small tractor and agricultural implement factories need decentralized coordination of supply and demand.

Note that the above analysis applies mostly to the production tractor and agricultural machinery industry among our industries, and to the supply of capital equipment for fertilizer and cement plants. Once the capital of the latter is in place, they normally have a regular flow of a few raw materials to manage, and a (normally local) reasonably steady and simple market to supply. A local coal mine, a local limestone pit, and a protected market in the county, is about all they need. The high technology is not in the activity of production, but is built into the plant.

When we consider this system of successive hierarchical administrative rationing from the point of view of economizing scarce resources, it gives a higher effective price to anything produced only at the higher levels. The cost in time, trouble, delay, and possible disapproval of an application, makes county level supplies more expensive in real terms than goods with the same cost of production made in one's own factory; the same administrative costs make provincial and subregional products effectively more expensive than those that can be produced at the same apparent cost in the county; the administratively most costly goods are those produced in national factories in Shanghai, Peking Liaoning. But these administrative costs are reduced by a small factory being in Shanghai, or being in the region of the lower Yangtze with its richer industrial tradition and its good water transportation.

Thus there are two contrary effects of the system. "Infant industries" in rural counties are protected by "administrative tariff barriers" that keep people in the county from buying tractors from Shanghai. They also are protected by the high national industrial prices, which give high profits for reinvestment to the national government and a high margin for inefficiency of small plants. But at the same time it gives tremendous cost advantages to factories in Shanghai, Peking, or the Northeast, especially advantages to factories that use many outputs of high technology industries, and luxury industries with complex inputs, while rapidly decentralizing the production of low technology industries. In short, it has much the same effect on the internal division of industrial labor among regions in China as tariff barriers and exchange controls have on the international division of labor among capitalist countries, preserving the advantage of advanced countries in high technology and high-income elasticity goods, while decentralizing simpler mass production industries. The remedy for the contradiction between the advanced coastal areas and the hinterland has its own ironic dialectic, tending to reinforce the contradiction in certain respects.

ADMINISTRATION BY MORAL EXAMPLE

The usual conception of administration in the United States is that one administers by setting standards, preferably in a regulation, and then checking on the meeting of those standards in an enforcement system. Of course a lot of administration in the United States does not go on that way: university graduate schools are mainly administered by professors setting examples of how to do research and helping students to follow the example. There is a constant battle with bureaucratic minds who think one can produce researchers by the numbers—(1) methodology, (2) theory, (3) substance, and (4) examination. The Chinese think of administration of industry much as we think of education for research, as a matter of mustering one's moral forces to follow an example. In some ways China is a very bureaucratic society, but it is a bureaucracy that seems to work very little by standards, very much by "exemplary prophecy," by showing the future to be aimed at by an administrative agency in the form of specifically exceptional examples in the present. Just as some Deans will explain graduate education by reading the rules of the graduate division, so most Americans expect to be shown a mass of examples of ordinary communes following the regulations. (On coming back home, perhaps the most common question is whether one saw a random sampling of places or whether one was shown Potemkin villages). But just as the average graduate department will talk about its Nobel Laureates rather than its examination regulations to tell what it is really all about, so the Chinese show Tachai to show what agricultural policy is all about. The crucial point here is that they not only show it to us, but also show it to the masses of leading cadres and students headed for the villages so they can see what they are supposed to do.

Thus the briefings we received at the model brigades, communes, and factories we saw, are idealized in the same general sense that regulations are an idealized view of an American organization. If you ignore the ideals stated in regulations in an American organization, you cannot understand the organization even well enough to keep from getting fired from it. Understanding the role of exemplary prophecy for propagating administrative standards is essential to understanding what we saw and were told. So we start here with a description of the standard form of the "story of this factory," which we were told in reasonable confidence that this is also what Chinese lower-level administrators of industry and agriculture were being told. Then by analyzing their response to our questions, (which had the general form of "that's nice, but how does it *really* work?"), we can get some clues as to what they were trying to do. But an appropriate comparison to what we were asking is to try to get a Dean who has just explained the regulations for graduate examinations to answer the question, "yes, but what are all the ways you can really get through the exam?."

If administration is to be by exemplary prophecy, rather than prophecy by doctrine and standards, then people have to be ready to produce the parables in which the principles are embedded. Since we saw the models, by and large, it is especially important that the people *we* saw be able to produce a transmissible story summarizing the experience. Roughly speaking, most of the stories we heard have the same structure and much of the language is formulaic. That is, production achievements enter both into the accounting system and into an oral literature as examples of communism in operation. The structure is roughly as follows (also extracted from two movies). Brackets indicate formulas as translated by the Chinese translators.

1. A brief introduction to the time span to be covered, old society to today, and to the causal agent, our following the revolutionary line of [Chairman Mao and the Chinese Communist Party], [maintaining independence, keeping initiative in our own hands, relying on our own efforts], [hard struggle].

2. A description of the old society, usually with one concrete local example, [under the yoke of imperialism, feudalism, and bureaucratic capitalism]. Selling children, leaving the area to beg in the cities, wages stopping because of sickness (with consequent death), and subjection to natural calamities such as drought, are the common themes.

3. The date of liberation for the area (the date of first communist control) starts the change.

4. The period of mutual aid teams and cooperatives for rural areas, or of first spontaneous organization by a few handicraftsmen with a few tools, brings the first accomplishments; yields go up or the workers start to build their own crude tools. This part of the story may be dated either in the whole post-liberation period up to the Great Leap Forward or may be dated in the Great Leap Forward. This is the "small and indigenous" period in [from small to big, from indigenous to modern].

5. [Liu Shao-ch'i and his revisionist line] tried to stop this development, but the masses objected, overcame difficulties by hard struggle, and by carrying out the [mass movement campaign to criticize Lin Piao and Confucius] (occasionally also Mencius is added) and to oppose [the revisionist line of reintroducing capitalism], and by following [the revolutionary line of Chairman Mao], Occasionally examples of capitalism (such as commune members working in the city) and occasionally opposition (by officials from the central government) to specific projects or investment are mentioned at this point, usually not.

6. A list of production, yield, capital investment, or product mix achievements are given, with a base year before the Great Proletarian Cultural Revolution and percentage increase to some recent year. For recent years very often the conquest of some natural disaster (drought or flood) is mentioned, overcome by [hard struggle], by [putting politics in command]).

7. In spite of these achievements, there are deficiencies to be remedied. Low level of mechanization, low or variable quality of the product, and high cost as compared with modern factories, are the most commonly mentioned.

8. But by keeping up mass campaigns and [following the instruction of Chairman Mao] to [take agriculture as the base and industry as the leading factor] or [to take grain as the key link and encourage all around development of sideline occupations], we hope to achieve further benefits.

The measures of success in Stage 6 vary according to the nature of the industry, but the following common themes are included.

6a. Amount of capital construction.

6b. Making capital equipment in the plant without outside funds or technical aid.

6c. [3-in-1 teams] (made up of technicians, workers, and cadres) consulting the masses about their needs.

6d. Making a [contribution to the state] or [the construction of socialism] as measured by grain sales in agriculture or by accumulation (profits) in industry.

6e. Technical innovation for labor saving, or even more often for capital saving by an innovation is highly praised. For example, doubling the output of a cement kiln is praised as an achievement, while they hope to be able to mechanize materials handling at some future time.

6f. New products.

6g. Advancing toward socialism by reorganizing the property system, e.g. by originating communes, by moving from team to brigade as the accounting unit, by abolishing private plots, by recruiting and training technicians from among the workers (or peasants) instead of being supplied from (implicitly privileged) outside sources of technical competence. This particular kind of achievement is analyzed in detail in the last section of this chapter under the heading of the function of ideology.

That is, Stage 6 is the core of the place where specialization of the general revolutionary lesson to the particular situation of the factory or commune takes place. In one place this may be almost entirely technical innovation (e.g. in a city textile factory in Hsinhsiang), in another increased yields per mu, or capital investment in water conservancy, or reorganizing the property system from collective to state, or team to brigade.

The formulaic content of this section on the standard story is generally much lower, and questions on the presentation of this section are generally answered in specific and concrete terms. Questions on the formulaic parts tend to be answered in very general terms: e.g. "How exactly do you organize the mass movement to criticize Lin Piao and Confucius; do people from the commune come to conduct study sessions in the brigade and teams, or at what levels is it organized?" get an answer "It's a national campaign, organized nationwide, at the provincial, commune, brigade, and team levels. You can't say it is organized at any specific level."

"What function do the more formulaic parts serve then?"

The first function is to provide a structure of causal adequacy for the whole historical development. This means that the assumptions of bourgeois scholars of causal variety in Stage 6 (Stage 6 is the real guts of the story) make them feel their message isn't getting across, that the delegation must have some concealed purpose of making fun of the Chinese, or collecting military intelligence, or must be limited in their analysis by trying to sum everything in numbers. That is, detailed questioning directed toward trying to find causes in a section of the story where the true causes are not supposed to lie indicates either evil intentions or incompetence. This is perhaps connected with Liu Shao-ch'i's sin of trying to administer by technical and economic standards and to reanalyze places like Tachai or the Red Flag Canal as technical systems rather than as moral examples, and to challenge the moral principles embedded in those examples. Conflict between good (socialist) and evil (capitalist) tendencies is supposed to be adequate to explain good and evil results. Thus the purpose of the facts in Stage 6 is to measure good results concretely, *not* to form a basis for a differentiated and chaotic analysis of concrete causes, after the bourgeois method of thought.

By and large, the more technically advanced the factory, the more "bourgeois" in this sense was the analysis (particularly in response to questions). But this correlation was (for our trip) reversed in agriculture, that the most advanced brigades and communes were the most ideological, the most offended by our bourgeois prejudices, and/or the most suspicious of our intentions.

But aside from explaining cross-cultural difficulties in understanding what people are up to, what does this complex of reactions tell us about the functions of these stories in their administrative context. One thing is clear, that not every brigade is expected to be Tachai, not every commune Ch'i-li-ying. Just as the Nobel Laureate's competence does not set examination standards, nor the Crucifixion of Christ set standards for the average parish priest, so the heroic rebuilding of clay hills into rich light loam in Tachai is not expected of each brigade.

The virtue of such stories is that they can teach at all levels. The yield-increasing effect of adding fermented chopped vegetation of clayey soils can be taught to those whose own brigade has clayey soils; the virtues of experimentation with seed strains in local conditions can be taught to the more general public of all agricultural collectives; the virtues of using slack season labor for capital construction can be taught to all economic enterprises; the virtues of combining theory and practice for everybody. Examples are much easier to adopt for local conditions than are regulations, because they are so vague. And whatever the interest of the listener, that interest is set in a causal context that makes loyalty to the policies of the regime a prime mover in his own future successes.

THE FUNCTIONS OF IDEOLOGY
IN ECONOMIC ADMINISTRATION

To an American, perhaps the most striking aspect of Chinese society is the level of "ideologizing." That is, discussions of all sorts of practical problems are couched in very general terms, and the frequency with which one is reminded of the general values of socialist society is that which would characterize a *fanatic* patriot in American society. Part of this impression is no doubt due to the structure of the exchanges, that one is taken to exemplary communes and factories, briefed by people used to public speaking in political leadership positions, and talks to people in a situation in which their political superiors are always present.

Even allowing for this, the level of ideologizing appears strident at first, though once a visitor finds that these are practical men and women concerned with concrete problems in a sane and sensible way, the ideology seems to fade into background noise. Our problem here is to explain how this general feature of ideologizing, characteristic of Chinese society, affects the administration of industry and agriculture.

There are three sources of information on the functions of ideology in economic administration in our experience on the trip. The first is the content of the ideology itself. The second is the occasional example given about what ideological mistakes were made, how they affected economic policies or performance, and how they were corrected. The third is the statistical variation in the density of ideological content in the speech of different people and in different situations.

This last sort of information on variations in ideologizing is the principal external check on one's speculative literary interpretation, correcting the "What would I have been thinking of if I had said that?" method of analysis. Unfortunately, it is also the information most contaminated by the exchange situation, by the fact that people were not talking to us "as human beings," but "as representatives of Chinese society under inspection by superiors."

First, then, to the variations among types of people that we met: Generally speaking, it seemed that officials of the central government had more ideological sentences per hour than people in other positions and could more readily produce an appropriate ideological response to varied situations. That is, their ideology was generally both more salient and more competent in the casuistic sense of being readily interpreted into a variety of concrete dicta on various situations.

Second, generally speaking the briefings in the agricultural communes had more ideological sentences in them than those in industry, and more in smaller and more technically backward industries than in larger or more modern ones. But also, generally speaking, the answers to concrete questions seemed to be significantly less ideological than those for officials of the central government. The ideology was high in salience, but lower in competence.

Third, there was a reverse variation in posters, with political posters being more common in larger factories.

Fourth, as far as we could tell the roles of the people talking, there were fewer ideological sentences among engineers and accountants than among political specialists. The highest frequency of ideological sentences was in a county in which people told us they got their production quotas from the party central committee, and in which an important official of the highways department told us that the reason a bridge could handle only a 13-ton tractor—but could, indeed, handle a 60-ton truck—was that trucks go faster. Offhand, this might suggest that ideology was a substitute for knowing what you are talking about, but for our purposes here it suggests that people whose position depends on political rather than technical competence have more ideological sentences.

Since the method of selection of places to visit presumably emphasized examples that our hosts thought would be impressive (and they certainly were), and since communes and brigades become impressive especially by being moral examples (while factories can be impressive by being modern) an implicit variation in the above variations is that the ideological content of exemplary organizations is higher.

The above report on variations in ideological sentences per hour consists of impressions of the central tendencies. There is probably more variation in the tendency to ideologize within these groups than between them—we made no systematic counts—and at any rate the situation in which we met people distorted the results. As far as they go, the following are the main checks on the speculations.

From the content of the statements interpreting the ideology concretely, we can suggest three main groups of functions of ideology in economic administration. The first group has to do with justifying the administrative structure of economic life, and especially justifying its continual reorganization. Economic development always involves changing the sizes of firms, deciding on prices for new industries, allocating new opportunities for economic return among various people, among authorities (to distribute the returns), and among various purposes those authorities might pursue. This reorganization always involves political tensions, as for example manifested in the antitrust laws in the U.S.. The second group of functions has to do with reforming people, by teaching them new principles (e.g. scientific experiment is good) or by holding up new ideal examples (e.g. learn after Tachai). The third group of functions has to do with the organization and justification of relations of the central government and its policies to local plants or specialized agencies with their concrete problems.

JUSTIFYING ADMINISTRATIVE ORGANIZATION

There are three main aspects of economic administration that play a large role in the ideological statements made to us: (a) the organization and reorganization of firms, especially smaller to larger, and of planning agencies (and the relations of firms to them) from commune to national—in short, the organization and reorganization of decision-making powers, (b) the policies followed by firms, especially their division of income and privilege among their work force, their investment (both size and allocation), and their demands on the economy for supplies and investment goods, and (c) the organization of technical innovation within the firm.

(a) Most American sociologists are inclined to take the formal organization of both industry and government as fixed, and to look for the informal organization that makes it work in spite of its rigidity. Consequently they are poorly prepared for the constant discussion in China of why things should be organized the way they are, and how they ought to be reorganized in the future. Why are communes more appropriate for mechanizing agriculture and introducing modern scientific agriculture? Because they can invest in maintenance shops or factories, concentrate investment funds, popularize the results of experimental plots. Why is a brigade (larger) a more rational accounting unit in agriculture than a team (smaller, usually part of a village)? Because they can more rationally allocate labor to the land and equalize returns for the same work between villages. Why should county industries be incorporated in the satate plan, but be self-reliant (i.e. get as much as possible of their equipment and supplies by their own efforts, either within the plant or from fraternal county plants)? Because unified planning must be combined with local initiative, and the scarce resources of the state husbanded. Why should the profits of county enterprises remain in the control of the county instead of being distributed to communes and brigades? Because further investment is needed to provide inputs to agriculture. In short, there is a pervasive sense that formal organization is a human creation—a recent and problematic one—and that the formal structure needs to be continually reorganized to pursue socialist aims more effectively.

This reorganization of decision-making power is inherent in economic development because development means undertaking new tasks and re organizing the flow of supplies as they increase in quantity and variety.

(b) Further, if development is successful, it creates large flows of income which are not already allocated to traditional purposes or to maintaining the socially established standard of living. In Veblen's phrase, these are "the advantages of backwardness and the penalty of taking the lead" that enabled the Japanese and German governments such flexibility and investment capacity. The purpose to which this new flow of "discretionary" income will be applied, its distribution between investment and consumption, and the distribution of consumption between social groups, are problematic. In Western countries the debate on this question provides much of the fuel of class conflict. The location of control over this "discretionary" flow of income is a crucial aspect of an administrative system, since it determines the range of policies that are politically and administratively feasible.

Much of the ideology is directed at this question. The campaign against Liu Shao-ch'i and the "revisionist line" seems to have most to do with the question of how much of this flow of income should go into the reward system (often discussed in terms of "material incentives"). An example of consequences of this campaign was given in one brigade, of calling back its city workers who were making up to 2000 yuan a year in "speculation" in the city, to persuade them to contribute to the commune agricultural economy. Another example was given of persisting in a policy of heavy investments in a county canal system rather than concentrating on immediate production. The principle seems to be that all rewards should be ideologically examined and the rewarded activities determined to be in the public interest, and particularly determined not to damage capital investment, before they can be considered legitimate.

(c) Economic development mainly consists of technical and organizational innovation. The ideology in China has a heavy emphasis on shifting the production function, so that the same amount of labor and capital produce more outputs. They often give as a measure of achievement the percentage of "designed capacity" that was produced last year. Regardless of how "designed capacity" is determined (we did not find out), this shows a constant concern with capital-saving innovations. The focus on yield per mu in agricultural performance reports shows an intense concern with land-saving innovations. There is less emphasis on labor-saving innovations, at least in the performance data given to us, but we were given many examples of reductions in labor force required for certain operations in industry. The mechanization movement in agriculture is usually justified on labor-saving grounds (for example, the symbols of mechanization are the tractor and the thresher, while probably the electric pump is in fact more crucial, as a "land-saving" capital investment).

What we are concerned with here is not so much the source and direction of flow of technical ideas, but the organizational readiness of the receiving unit to shift the social and technical arrangements of production into a new pattern. This was discussed by our informants under the heading of "consulting the wisdom of the masses," but the important point is that this consultation is systematically organized to reform the production process. There are institutionalized methods of forming task groups (3-in-1 groups, meaning groups of "senior workers," technicians, and cadres; or meaning users of the product, workers from the producing factory, and technicians from a higher level) to work out and institute innovations. There are fast and easy arrangements for visiting model communes, brigades, or factories.

The ideology emphasizes technical innovation in the models it chooses, in the doctrine, in the performance measures it uses, and in its administrative ideology justifying ad hoc non-hierarchical problem-solving groups. The ideology is, so to speak, a medium through which the flow of technical information, of operating models of innovations, and of administrative flexibility in receiving units, is speeded up.

At the administrative level then, the ideology is a common language for discussing the problems of creating formal organizations to fit the tasks of development. The language includes a vocabulary for discussing the reorganization of authority relations, the reorganization of allocations of flows of income, and the reorganization of technical systems.

MOTIVATIONAL AND MORAL FUNCTIONS

The most common notion of the functions of ideology in development is a motivational one, that heroic individual efforts are called forth by ideological enthusiasm, that "ideological rewards" substitute for "material rewards." As will be discussed in Chapter III, when the Chinese themselves make this argument, they usually mean two interlinked sorts of things: that exceptional individual performances are praised publicly, and that the ground for praise is contribution to socialist construction. That is, they do not usually expect people to be directly inspired by speeches or by reading Chairman Mao. They do praise exceptional self-sacrifice, but do not usually rely directly on political study for motivation.

There are two aspects of the ideology which do seem to bear on the motivational situation of individuals. The first is the campaign against fatalistic attitudes summed up in the popular image taken from Mao of the "foolish old man who moved the mountains." The notion is that if one does not regard nature (the mountains) as inevitable, but tries to change them, resources will be found (in the fable heaven intervenes to reward the foolish old man's efforts—in Mao the wisdom and enthusiasm of the masses will find a way). The conviction that men control their own fate, that pessimism is not a legitimate cognitive set, is manifested in stories of heroic accomplishment such as the Red Flag Canal, but also in critiques of "Western" marginal economics that takes the production function as fixed. (There is certainly that tendency in Western economics, but empirical development economists, such as were on the delegation, are not the worst sinners.) Roughly speaking, the psychological postulate for economic life is that more irrationality comes from incomplete exploration of the production possibility surface than from poor calculation of choices between known alternatives. By the campaign against Confucius and Lin Piao, by learning after Tachai and after Taching, by retelling the fable of the foolish old man who moved the mountains, the psychological costs of investment are reduced and the psychological promise of reward is rendered more certain.

A more general version of the same theme could be formulated as: "Do not take people's first impulses and analysis as the basis for action, but instead reform people until a better course of action appears." Or even, "Do not take human responses as fixed, for humans can transform their attitudes by the use of will and ideology." If we contrast the Western image of a market with fixed consumer tastes or an electorate with preferences among candidates manifesting their opinion in an election with the image of man in Chinese ideology, the difference is that the Chinese have a "future-oriented democratic" concept, that the masses *will* want what we collectively are getting for them when they have been transformed by the revolution.

The second motivational element is the preservation of the moral value of exemplary cases. Just as Alyosha's faith is somewhat shaken when saintly Father Zossima's body starts to stink in *The Brothers Karamozov,* so too close an examination of any exceptional advantages of Tachai or the Ch'i-li-ying commune undermines their value as moral models. Aside from the differences in approach to causal analysis outlined above, the combination of an itinerary including many models and our profane cost-accounting attitude toward those models created tensions. It was sort of like a geneticist inquiring of a theologian exactly which of Christ's chromosomes came from Mary, which from the Holy Spirit.

THE POLITICAL FUNCTIONS OF IDEOLOGY

The third set of functions seems to be specifically political and can be formulated in terms of the relation between the cosmopolitan national political system and the local systems, which run the details of the economy.

Many of these political ideological functions are resolutions of problems in the national system itself, so our observations do not bear as directly on them. Consequently, this section is a rather speculative sketch.

There seem to be three main political functions reflected in the content of the ideology. The first is legitimating the resolutions of national political conflicts and consequently setting out the main lines of policy, regarding who the enemies are, what the role of the party should be as compared to the Revolutionary Committees that run factories and local government, and so on. That is, we Westerners think of ideology as a weapon in a struggle which has yet to be resolved. When a discussion or an experiment of social reorganization *starts* in China, that is, just at the point where Western political talk is most ideological, it seems the Chinese are very leery of giving it a clear overall interpretation. Exactly what "eliminating the vestiges of the concept of private property" means in a commune is ordinarily not clear. But at the point when national policies are set, Mao's name and his sayings start to be used to explain why the policy is correct. Sometimes this is reflected in specific attacks on national level opponents, such as Lin Piao or Liu Shao-ch'i, but this is *after,* not before, these people's powers have been stripped from them. When one is taken to the place Mao said "communes are good," it is not the place he first advocated communes, which would be presumably buried in the minutes of national level meetings. It is rather the place where he proclaimed it as national policy.

The second function seems to be to formulate the authority of cosmopolitan (e.g. Peking) officials over local officials. It is hard to see in our observations what exactly this means, because most local officials show a good deal of independence and local autonomy, at least with respect to the Peking officials who traveled with us. That is, there is not an echelon relation in which all "officers" rank above all "enlisted men." Yet some local officials, in factories especially, seemed to be nervous about their performance in front of someone in the room. While we have little that is concrete and at the same time general to say about this authority relation of local to national levels, this itself shows that the relation is problematic, and that it is probably discussed in ideological terms, but not in front of visiting delegations. Chinese traditions of politeness in authority relations are sufficiently different from ours so that we could not read what was going on with any degree of accuracy.

A third function is apparently producing agents of the general national policy in local systems. On the average, in every kind of system we visited, someone could be produced from the leading cadres who could formulate the concrete policies and activities of his or her group in terms of the national ideology. These local people mentioned promotion of people by "political consciousness" many times (along with seniority and technical level). They used the phrase, "The masses of workers (or peasants) said . . ."; what the masses said generally fits nicely with the resolutions of political conflict at the national level. Being able to produce a leader who says the right thing from the point of view of national policy in every local system is a major achievement of the ideological system.

If we now take these functions and try to interpret the apparent distribution of ideological sentences, some of the connections are quite clear. The communes and brigades in the rural economy have had substantial reorganization of the property and reward system, substantial pressure to use the returns from industry for reinvestment rather than income, and structurally provide a conflicting answer to who is in charge of the flows of income and of authority. For example, commune industries must receive supplies from the state-operated system, yet the returns are supposed to be collectively owned. This gives the county (a state-operated industrial system) a chance to restrict supplies to those that contribute to agriculture rather than e.g. to supply communes with steel they might process and sell as consumer goods. Thus the leadership of commune industry (but perhaps not the peasants) have a substantial problem of justifying continual reorganization and reallocation of new flows of income. They also perhaps have more problems of the "modernization of personality." The larger factories, in contrast, have a stable and legitimately socialist organization, which does not have to be brought into congruence with a state system operated by different principles.

The principal problem of the leadership of a state-operated large factory is presumably not who owns the profits,, but rather justifying the "low wage policy," which allows the profits to grow as costs decline and provides more funds for national reinvestment. This means that the focus of ideology is on the wage system and the substitution of "ideological incentives" (praise) for "material incentives." Much of the wall poster ideology in larger factories is concerned with model workers and teams, with "socialist emulation," rather than with the justification of administrative and profit reorganization. Hence we visitors get less ideology at the level of factory organization discussion (except if we touch on the wage system when the 3–5 percent of income spent for rent, free medical care, maternity leave, stable and low prices, etc., are reliably produced), while the workers get a lot of "productivity ideology."

The high level of ideology among national officials is explained by the last set of functions of relating national policy to local activities. It is probably increased by the degree of decentralization since, when a national official's authority is problematic, perhaps ideological persuasion will work.

CONCLUDING COMMENTS

The themes of this chapter, themes of the relation of small-scale rural industry to the state, are central to the ideological disputes that divide socialists from the defenders of capitalism. Perhaps there is no way to discuss these questions free from ideological bias. But we were impressed by how often an apparently simple question (such as "Are they really decentralized as much as they claim?" or "Do people really believe the uniform and formulaic ideology that they use all the time?") turned out to be much more complicated than the ideological positions of either side would lead one to expect. Perhaps the chief value of our all too sketchy investigations on the relation of enterprises to the state is not the conclusions we have reached above, but the added complexity of the questions we are now inclined to ask. There is a complex human reality behind such formulas as "relying on our own efforts" or "bureaucratically planned economy." So questions that start with such formulas have to be made more complex first, then, conceivably, answered.

Chapter III

WORKER INCENTIVES

The structure of incentives in Chinese industry includes not only material rewards but also a structure of formalized praise, differential life chances, and collective benefits. The structure of these incentives is most highly elaborated in state industry. Though some county factories are classed as collective units, all or virtually all of the county factories we saw were in the state sector (see Appendix C), and the system of rewards and benefits in these plants was only a slightly simplified version of that offered in large urban enterprises. Accordingly, the bulk of this chapter examines the system of differential rewards for administrative cadres, technicians, and workers in state industry with only the note that the rewards in county industries are slightly less elaborate than those in large urban industries. With their much greater simplicity, rewards in small collective industries run by the commune and brigade are discussed much more briefly at the end of the chapter.

STATE INDUSTRY

Material incentives in state-owned industry include a wage system with grades for those of differential skill and experience, a promotion system to advance those who perform according to approved standards, and a system of fringe benefits including subsidized housing, medical care, accident

31

insurance, subsidized nurseries, and pension plans. Though the differences are not so extreme in county industries, in all state industries there is some differentiation between wages for cadres, technicians, and workers. That extreme differentiation in pay and prestige between these different kinds of personnel should be avoided was one of the most consistent themes of our trip.

CADRE WAGES

Administrative cadres comprise two to eight percent of the total work force in county factories that we visited. In large urban factories, we obtained less information on the number of administrative cadres, but from the great efforts to trim administrative staffs around 1968, we would expect the number of cadres in these plants to be fewer than ten years before. In 1965 Barry Richman toured 38 urban factories in China. From data gathered on his tour, Richman concluded that the administrative staff in Chinese factories was significantly larger than in comparable firms in the Soviet Union and the U.S.A.[1] The may have been good reason, then, to call for the reduction of these staffs in 1968.

The size of this reduction can be seen at Shanghai Machine Tools. In 1965 12.5 percent of all employees had been administrative cadres, and 7.5 percent had been technicians and engineers. By 1975 the number of technicians remained large (10 percent), but the staff on the cadre pay scale had been cut drastically to 3 percent.[2] We gathered information on administrative personnel in one other urban plant. At the Shanghai (Bumper Harvest) Tractor Factory in the suburbs of Shanghai, less than 10 percent of all employees were classed as administrators and technicians. This percentage places the plant below both the average and lowest examples found in comparable plants in 1965. The repetition of similar figures in the press suggests that this phenomenon is widespread.

The reduction in administrative personnel must have been in part just a paper change. In the original 30 grade wage scale for administrative personnel, the lowest grades were for janitors, clerks, and other support personnel. Today the reduction of the administrative wage scale to just 24 grades in many factories suggests that some of the lower grade scales were simply transferred over to the worker's pay scale with little change in pay or responsibilities.[3]

1. Barry Richman, *Industrial Society in Communist China*. New York: Random House, 1969, p. 759.
2. The situation with technicians at Shanghai Machine Tools is complicated by their use of an auxiliary research institute with an additional staff of 200.
3. For more information on wage scales for administrators, see Christopher Howe, *Wage Patterns and Wage Policy in Modern China 1919-1972*. Cambridge: Cambridge University Press, 1973.

There was plenty of room for a true reduction in administrative personnel, however. The administrative staff in the factory is restricted almost entirely to production matters. Many of the functions which the administrative staff handles in a Western factory are in China handled by government bureaus outside the factory. The head of the factory is really the Western equivalent of the vice-president for production. As early as 1961 in the government's Seventy Articles on Industrial Policy, it was specified that the factory was to keep its hands out of matters of marketing, price, and supply of factory goods. As it became painfully obvious to us when we kept asking questions about marketing and supply which the factory head could not answer, it is the commercial bureau and related bureaus in the county, special district, or province which must make the final decisions on these sorts of questions. Since the administrative staff of the factory is restricted to a rather specialized list of production questions, there should have been ample room for cuts in administrative personnel around 1968, and these cuts should have produced little subsequent degradation in performance.

It was probably also quite possible to reduce administrative staffs in the large urban factories around 1968 because of demand for these kinds of personnel outside their home plant. We were not told where the excess personnel had gone. With one exception, we were also not told where the new county and commune plants established in 1968 and 1969 had gotten their administrative and technical personnel. The implement repair and construction workshop in Red Star Commune outside Peking mentioned getting technicians from urban plants. It is our guess that many other county factories established around 1968, when urban factories were being pruned of excess administrators, got some of their senior leaders from the city. This would be consistent with the older age of some factory administrators. It would also be consistent with the close alliances between some city and county plants. Wu-hsi County personnel reported that when they had a problem they could just write a letter or send a telegram to a factory in Shanghai telling them that they were coming, and then pop down to visit in just a few hours. This case of visiting across a major administrative boundary is in some cases possible because the county plant happened to have gone to the Shanghai plant to learn the technology for its operation. In other cases, we speculate, the administrators in the county plant can visit easily because they are simply returning to their old home factory.

Regardless of their exact origin or number, the administrators in county and urban factories are on the national pay scale, which applies to all administrative cadres, regardless of whether they are working in factories, government, or elsewhere. This scale starts as low as that for the average worker, but goes considerably higher. It is rare that foreign visitors learn the salaries of top factory administrators. The highest salaries that they have heard of since 1972 have been in the range of 160 to 180 yuan per month.

This would be only about three times the average worker's salary in urban industry. Foreign visitors have been told that in the future, younger administrators will not be allowed to reach such high levels.

A more immediate approach to redressing the differential between administrators and workers are various methods to insure that administrators regularly meet and work with workers. Workers are represented on governing bodies and technical groups. Administrators are to spend at least a month per year working on the shop floor, thereby, it is hoped, gaining a clearer understanding of problems on the shop floor as well as a more humble demeanor.

TECHNICIAN WAGES

Technicians comprise only 1-2 percent of the labor force in six county factories for which we have data. In the larger urban factories controlled by provinces or cities, technicians are more numerous—3 percent at Hsin-hsiang Region Chemical Equipment and Accessories Factory, 10 percent at Shanghai Machine Tools, and 12 percent of the labor force at Hsin-hsiang City Water Pump Factory.

Several methods are being used to bring the rewards for technicians more in line with the rewards for workers. First, in county industries, there is a tendency to put technicians on the same eight grade pay scale as workers. The technicians start well above grade one and they advance rapidly into the upper middle ranks. Yet the top grade of some 100 to 110 yuan in the eight-grade wage system guarantees that they will not make much more than the average worker. Indeed, where we asked, technicians were considerably below the 100 to 110 yuan limit. At Hsi-yang County Tractor Factory, Wu-hsi County Iron and Steel Factory, Wu-hsi County Tractor Factory, and Nanhai County Cement Factory, all technicians were on the same pay scale as workers. At Nanhai Cement the top technician's salary was some 80 yuan. At the other factories, the top salary was only some 70 yuan. At Wu-hsi Tractor, the technicians' salaries began at some 50 yuan and advanced to only some 70 yuan per month. (See Table III.1.)

At the larger urban factories, information on the current situation with technicians' salaries is more muddled. As with administrative staff salaries, the state is reluctant to lower any existing wages. Usually the separate pay scales for technicians and engineers are still maintained with old engineers getting even higher salaries than top administrators. As first adopted in 1956, these pay scales start at only 20 to 30 yuan for technicians in training, but advance to between 250 and 350 yuan for senior engineers.[4] In the

4. State Council, "Notification on the Issuance of a Program of Wage Scales for Workers of State Organs," no. HSI-54, 1956, in *Compilation of the Laws and Regulations of Financial Administration of the Central Government*. Peking: 1956, pp. 226-47. Partially translated in

biggest industries, such as Peking Internal Combustion, senior engineers continue to get almost 250 yuan a month.[5] Since other visitors had been told that new technicians would not be paid as much as the old, we were surprised to note that in Peking, West City Optical Instruments Factory, which became a state (city) factory only in 1969, technician salaries ranged up to a high of 150 yuan per month. It may be that the technician earning 150 yuan transferred in from another plant and is therefore unrepresentative of technicians in most new plants.

A second way in which the gap between workers and technicians is reduced is by training technicians from among the workers. In county factories new technicians are simply trained on the job. We paid particular attention to this question in Wu-hsi County. The technically sophisticated Wu-hsi Electro-Chemical Factory, which makes polyvinyl chloride, had a total of nine technicians. Of the nine, six were university trained; three were trained on the job. At other plants in the county about half of the technicians in each plant were trained on the job. In urban plants, there were also some technicians trained on the job. In recent years this training has become formalized with the urban plants sending their workers to "workers' universities." The prototype of this sort of "university" is at Shanghai Machine Tools, which was publicly acclaimed by Mao Tse-tung on 21 July 1968. Accordingly, at Hsin-hsiang City Cotton Textile Factory and Shanghai (Bumper Harvest) Tractor Factory, we also found 21 July Workers' Universities. At Hsin-hsiang Textile, a class of about thirty workers were being taught calculus in order that they might become technicians. The largest factories have their own universities. Smaller factories send their workers to other nearby factory universities. In addition, those factories most in need of advanced technology, such as Shanghai Machine Tools, are sending a few of their workers to regular universities outside the plant.

The third procedure which narrows the gap between technicians and workers, as well as between administrators and workers, is the use of what are called "three-in-one" task groups. Instead of leaving innovations to technicians alone, "three-in-one" groups consisting of administrators, technicians, and senior workers are organized to attack technical problems and produce innovations in factory technology. Senior workers appear to be experienced workers who are either foremen or informal leaders who receive great respect from their fellow workers. The role of these groups seemed at times to be overstated. Some of the innovations reputed to be made by three-in-one groups at one plant was claimed for three-in-one groups at other plants as well, suggesting that the original source of innovation lay outside

Charles Hoffman, *The Chinese Worker*. Albany: State University of New York Press, 1974, Appendix A.

5. Also see Mitch Meisner, "The Shenyang Transformer Factory—A Profile," *China Quarterly*, 52 (1972): 731.

Table III-1

HIGH AND LOW WAGES BY TYPE OF EMPLOYEE

	Type of Employee	Lowest Wage	Highest Wage	Average Wage
Urban Factories				
Shanghai Machine Tools	Workers	42	124	68
	Technicians	—	200 +	70 +
Peking Internal Combustion	Workers	30 +	100 +	54
	Technicians	40	ca. 245	—
Cheng-chou Textile Machinery	Technicians	—	166	—
Peking Optical Instruments	Technicians	50	150 +	—
Foshan Ceramics and Porcelain	Workers & technicians	34	103	53
County Factories				
Nanhai Cement	Workers & technicians	40	80 +	57
Wu-hsi Iron and Steel	Workers & technicians	32	70 +	47
Wu-hsi Tractor	Technicians	50 +	70 +	—
Hsi-yang Tractor	Apprentices	23	29	—
	Workers & technicians	33	80 +	37
Hsi-yang Farm Tools	Workers*	38	60 +	40 +
Hsi-yang Chemical Fertilizer	Workers*	30	100 +	40
Lin Cotton Textile	Workers*	30	50 +	40 +
Commune Factories				
Peking Red Star (6 plants)	Workers & technicians	36	80 +	49

*Statistics for these three factories may include technicians.

the plant and that the role of the three-in-one group was more one of implementation than of invention.[6] Whether in implementation or invention, it
seems as though these groups might have some very practical functions. The
senior worker brings information about immediate problems on the factory
floor. And when a new procedure is developed with his participation, he
will be able to support its adoption on the factory floor—thus speeding its
application. Even when the technician has come from among the workers
and regularly spends time on the factory floor, the presence of the senior
workers in a task group should make the link between innovation and
practical problems even closer.

WORKER WAGES

In addition to the differentials in reward between administrators,
technicians, and workers, there are differentials in reward among the
workers themselves. The proper extent of this differential is now under active
discussion. The discussion of workers' wages was started in the Spring of
1975 when Mao Tse-tung, in his article on the Dictatorship of the Proletariat,
raised the issue of whether the society might begin to move a bit more
rapidly toward full communism, which would reward people not according
to their work but according to their needs. The issue was being discussed
in many factories, and this at times made it difficult to get information on
the wage systems. Some factories may have been reluctant to commit themselves until some more central decision on wages had been reached.

The eight-grade wage system for workers, ranging from a low of some
30 yuan a month to a high of around 100 yuan a month, was first adopted
in 1956. This system was still in effect in almost all factories we visited. The
only exceptions were one or two factories, which had raised workers out of
the lowest wage grade, and a few factories that used temporary laborers.

Instead of fixed wages averaging about 45 yuan per month in county
industry, temporary laborers get work points in their home production
teams. In the wealthier areas that we visited, these work points were worth
some 30 yuan per month. Temporary workers also were ineligible for health,
retirement, and other fringe benefits which usually equal some ten percent
of the factory's wage bill. Temporary workers that we encountered were in
county industry. Most of the 500 workers at Hui County Cement were
temporary. In that county's fertilizer plant, in contrast, none of the workers
were temporary. In the Lin County Cotton Textile Factory, 60 percent of
the laborers were temporary, while at the tractor plant only a very small

6. At textile plants we encountered multiple inventions or innovations to the electric
cart which was featured during 1975 in both *China Reconstructs* and *Peking Review*—see
China Reconstructs, Vol. 24, No. 3, March 1975, p. 5, *Peking Review*, No. 28, 11 July 1975,
pp. 22-23.

number were temporary. In the light bulb factory in that county, none were temporary. From these scattered observations, it is difficult to draw firm conclusions. Yet, from other reports, we know that temporary workers are frequently used where the need for factory labor is only seasonal. They are common in sugar plants, which only produce in the winter, and their large number at Lin County Cotton Textile Factory is likely to be in response to a high seasonal demand for spinning after the yearly cotton harvest. Also, it would seem that temporary workers are used for menial jobs, such as transport and stone quarrying, for which the factories are reluctant to pay high wages and fringe benefits.

Apprentice systems were used in the state factories that we visited. In the first year, apprentices get some 18-20 yuan per month. In the next year or two, they get slightly higher wages until they graduate to the lowest rung of the regular worker's scale, which is usually in the low 30s but 42 yuan in some Shanghai City plants.

Our information on average salaries is marred by several conditions: In urban plants, it is only the average salary for regular workers. Administrative cadre, technician, apprentice, and temporary worker (if any) salaries are usually excluded. In county plants, technicians' salaries may be included but not the salaries for other groups of workers. Even for workers, some factories give not a precise average but only the most common or model wage. And, we did not obtain wage data for all factories.

Nevertheless, the data in Table III.2 allow us to draw some conclusions about wage differentials among different factories. First, workers in county industries draw considerably lower salaries than those in urban factories. The average for urban factories run by the provinces or municipalities is 57 yuan per month while that for county factories is only about 45 yuan. As with technicians, then, it appears that county wages are kept intentionally low so as to not be too much higher than income in the surrounding countryside. There is already a great demand among young peasants to get into industrial jobs. Further income differentials would make this demand only more severe. In addition, in setting wages there is probably some consideration of cheaper costs of living around county factories, which are often situated in the countryside rather than in the county seat.

The second differential to be observed in Table III.2 is that between different regions. So as to allow for differences in costs of living, regional differentials were incorporated in the 1956 wage law. Large urban centers and some provinces were to have higher wages. In Table III.2 this can be seen clearly only in the instance of Shanghai where wages average 63 yuan per month rather than the usual 55 yuan for industries in other cities. This same regional differential was reported by Barry Richman from a larger sample of industries in 1965.[7]

7. Richman, op. cit., p. 803.

The third differential that we would expect from the 1956 wage law is one between heavy and light industry. Surprisingly, that differential does not appear in the industries we visited. Among urban industries in Table III.2 the first eight factories may be classified as heavy and the last six as light. Once Shanghai with its unusually high wages is excluded, the average wage for both heavy and light industry is 55. Barry Richman noted the same phenomenon in 1965 as did Carl Riskin from post-1971 visitors' reports.[8] Richman's explanation was that since much of the light industry started before 1949, it had more long-seniority, high-wage workers. This may be true in part. In county industries we were at times told that average wages were low because there was as yet no one with enough seniority to be in the top two or three salary grades. This is not the full explanation, however. Among the urban factories for which we have data, the nine started before 1960 have an average wage of 56 yuan per month, while the four started after 1960 have an even higher wage of 58 yuan per month. Among the county factories for which we have data, the four started before 1960 have an average wage of about 47 yuan, while the seven started later have an only slightly lower wage of 44 yuan per month. Age, it would appear, is not a major determinant of factory wages.

One might parenthetically note another implication of this observation. If by 1975 light industries pay salaries on the average no lower than heavy industries, then the salaries for females are more equal now than in the 1950s. There are neighborhood workshops where women are paid much less (about 30 yuan per month), but in the large state factories they may get about as much in the light industries (where they predominate) as the males do in heavy industry (where they predominate).

PROMOTION

For differentials in income to act as an incentive, there must be a publicly understood method of promotion. Promotion, it was reported, was based on seniority, skill, performance, and political attitude. The exact order of these criteria could not be ascertained, though it was frequently asserted that whether a factory had many workers in the top wage grades depended on whether it had many senior workers with many years of experience. According to other visitor reports, the nationwide promotions of 1971 were heavily dependent on seniority. Workers who had been at work before 1957, but had not risen above the third grade by 1971, had to be raised to the fourth grade; those who had been at work before 1960, but had not risen above the second grade, had to be promoted to the third grade; and so on.[9] Seniority is a major element in promotion.

8. Richman, op. cit., p. 803-04.
9. Joan Robinson, "For Use, Not for Profit," in Eastern Horizon, Vol. 11, No. 4 (1972), p. 6.

Table III-2

FACTORY CONDITIONS BY TYPE OF FACTORY

	Year Established	Personnel	Female %	Average Wage	Housing	Child Care	Praise Boards
Urban Factories							
Shanghai Machine Tools	pre1949	6,000	20	68	m	m	m
Shanghai Shaped Steel Tubing	1953	814	16	60	m	m	0
Shanghai (Bumper Harvest) Tractor	1963	1,300	35	60	m	+	+
Peking Internal Combustion	1964	7,000	34	54	+	+	+
Peking Capital Iron and Steel	pre1949	20,000	20	60	+	+	+
Cheng-chou Textile Machinery	1951	5,200	20	60	+	+	m
Hsin-hsiang Chemical Industry Equipment	1969	330	33	55	+	m	0
Hsin-hsiang Water Pump	1956	680	33	47	+	+	+
Peking Optical Instruments	1969	520	75	60+	0	+	m
Hsin-hsiang Cotton Textile	1956	1,400	64	56	+	+	+
Cheng-chou #3 Cotton Spinning	1954	5,600	58	—	+	+	+
Wu-hsi #1 Silk Filature	pre1949	1,700	85	55	0	0	+
Wu-hsi City Clay Figurine	1954	500	60	45	0	0	m
Foshan Ceramics and Porcelain	1952	500	65	53	m	+	0
County Factories							
Nanhai Cement	1958	549	14	57	+	+	0
Tachai Cement	1968	144	31	—	m	—	0
Hui Cement	1964	500	15	—	m	—	—
Wu-hsi Iron and Steel	1969	805	12	47	m	m	0
Wu-hsi Tractor	1969	661	15	40	+	m	+
Hsi-yang Tractor	1967	310	21	37	—	—	0
Tung-fang-hung Agricultural Machinery	1948	300+	—	—	—	—	0
Hsi-yang Farm Tools	1954	148	22	40+	m	—	m

Chia-ting Agricultural Machinery	—	450	30	40+	—	—	m
Wu-hsi Electric Motor	1958	340	5	42	m	0	0
Hsi-yang Chemical Fertilizer	1968	450	20	40+	—	—	+
Lin Chemical Fertilizer	1968	520	25	50	m	—	0
Hui Chemical Fertilizer	1968	536	9	—	m	m	0
Wu-hsi Electro-chemical	1968	600	20	46	—	m	+
Lin Fluorescent Light	1970	180	—	—	m	—	—
Lin Cotton Textile	1958	186	70	40+	—	0	0
Commune Workshops							
Red Star Implements	——	261	36	49	0	0	m
Red Star Grain Mill	——	183	ca.50	49	0	0	0
Yao-t'sun Agricultural Machinery	——	90	m	40+	—	—	0
Kao-chuang Agricultural Machinery	——	147	—	—	—	—	m
Ch'i-li-ying Agricultural Machinery	——	190	ca.33	—	—	—	0
Yang-shih Concrete Products	——	97	ca.27	—	m	m	0
Yang-shih Powder Metallurgy	1972	108	ca.27	—	m	m	0
Yang-shih Agricultural Machinery	——	192	ca.27	—	m	m	0
Mei-ts'un Agricultural Machinery	——	—	—	—	—	—	0
Ho-lieh Agricultural Machinery	——	—	—	—	—	—	0
Ma-lu Tractor Station	——	50	ca.20	35	0	0	0
Ma-lu Machine Plant	——	200	ca.20	35	0	0	0
Brigade Workshops							
Ta-ts'ai-yuan Grain Mill (in Lin County)	——	—	—	—	—	—	0
Chi-li-ying Grain Mill	——	—	—	—	—	—	0
Liu-chuang Carpentry & Tools	——	27	—	—	—	—	0
Urban Neighborhood Workshops							
Shanghai Toy Assembly & Packaging		270	90+	ca.30	—	—	—
Shanghai Vacuum Pump & Meter Assembly		150	80	ca.30	—	—	—

Note: "+" = present, "0" = absent, "m" = minimal, "—" = information not available. For further explanation, see text

Within the factory, the number promoted each year is subject to the state plan. Factories cannot on their own whim decide what proportion of their workers will be promoted. The Wu-hsi Electro-Chemical Factory reported that 40 percent of its work force was promoted in 1974. Since this included apprentices who had been promoted automatically after three years, the number of regular workers who had been promoted was somewhat smaller. At the Nanhai County Cement Plant no workers had been promoted in 1974, but 40 percent of the workers and apprentices had been promoted in 1973. Generally, one host suggested, large scale promotions had been written into the state plan only in 1971 and 1973. This same host could not recall when large numbers had been previously promoted though the widespread promotions in 1963 are widely known.

Generally, promotions seem to have been restricted so as to keep average salaries at about the same levels they were ten or even twenty years ago. This, it would appear, is part of a general program to reduce the gap between peasant and worker living standards. Average industrial incomes are kept constant in the hope that agricultural incomes will eventually catch up.

The average worker salary is dependent on both the salary scale used and how workers have been promoted within it. The scales used today appear to be almost exactly the same as adopted in 1956. In 1965 regular Shanghai Machine Tools workers began at 42 yuan a month.[10] They still begin at this level today. In 1965 Shanghai #3 Machine Tools Plant had salaries ranging from 42 to 120 yuan. In 1973 another group of visitors reported that this plant had salaries from 42 to 123 yuan.[11] In the northeast reported salaries have even longer continuity. In that area, 1972 visitors found the same wage scale at the An-shan Rolling Mill and Shen-yang Machine Tools plant as in the 1950s.[12]

The comparison of average salaries in 1975 with those of 1965 is confounded by the problem that 1965 salaries tend to include cadre and technicians' salaries, while 1975 data exclude them. Nevertheless, the comparisons that can be made suggest little or no rise in average salaries over the last ten years. The average salary at Shanghai Machine Tools was 70 yuan in 1965 and an only slightly lower 68 yuan per month in 1975. In 1965 at #2 Wu-hsi Silk Reeling Plant, the average salary was 52 yuan. At the Wu-hsi City Local (state owned) #1 Silk Filature Factory, which we

10. Richman, *op. cit.*, p. 800.

11. Carl Riskin, "Workers' Incentives in Chinese Industry," in *China: A Reassessment of the Economy,* (a compendium of papers submitted to the Joint Economic Committee of the Congress of the United States), Washington, D.C.: U.S. Government Printing Office, 1975, p. 217.

12. *Ibid.*, p. 216.

visited, average salaries were only slightly higher at 55 yuan per month. Stability of average wages is shown in other visitors' reports as well.[13]

Whether average income has changed depends in part on how bonuses, which prior to 1966 were 5-15 percent of the wage bill, have been handled. At some urban factories, other visitors have been told that the old bonus now serves as a wage supplement, which is divided equally among all workers. We did not explicitly ask, but at the factories we visited there was never any mention of such a supplement. Clothing allowances, allowances for working in high temperature areas (e.g. near ovens), free barbering, and other fringe benefits were discussed in some factories, but there was no across-the-board supplement that would substitute for the old bonus. Without precise information on the relationship between old bonuses and current wage supplements, it is difficult to make exact statements about changes in average wages over time, except to say that they have not changed greatly.

The stability of the average wage could conceal some significant changes in the distribution of workers among high and low wage categories. The Shanghai (Bumper Harvest) Tractor Factory reported that they had tried to promote those in the lower grades rapidly, while holding those in the top grades constant. This might not imply a very big change, for even in 1955 most workers were in the middle grades (three and four) while only a very small minority were in the lowest grade (one) or the highest grades (seven and eight).[14] More drastically, one or two factories implied that they had promoted everyone out of grades one and two. Anywhere from 10-25 percent of the labor force might have been thus promoted. This procedure alone would lead to a rise in the average wage. But combined with a reduction in higher paid administrators, the average wage could still have remained the same. The overall effect would be simply to narrow the wage span.

As true as this may be in some factories, it is our impression that in most urban factories, the wage distribution is about the same as in years past. In most places, new workers when they graduate from apprentice status continue to start the regular pay scale at some 30 yuan per month. The lowest two pay grades, however, do not include many workers, for young workers are within a number of years promoted to the middle grades three and four. After being promoted to rank three or four, the chances for moving further ahead in pay are drastically reduced. A worker can go for years without moving into the higher paying five to eight grades, and generally only a small minority of workers it would seem make it to the highest two or three grades before they retire. For the average worker aged 30 and above who has already advanced into the middle salary ranks, then, the hopes for wage

13. *Ibid.*, p. 217. Compare this with Richman, *op. cit.*, p. 800-02.
14. Hoffman, *op. cit.*, p. 99.

advancement may be less an incentive to work than the superior fringe benefits attached to the factory job as well as the system of formalized praise which operates through the small work group.

FRINGE BENEFITS

In state industries material rewards do not stop with wages, but extend to fringe benefits as well. At Peking's Capital Iron and Steel, fringe benefits were equivalent to between 10 and 13 percent of the total wage bill. Though our survey was less than complete, retirement, accident, and disability programs appear now to be universal in all state-owned plants. Gone are the distinctions of the 1950s when only the larger plants had adopted these programs.[15] With sufficient seniority, workers get 70 percent of their wages at retirement. Alternate jobs are guaranteed for the disabled. Though some smaller plants are without clinics, health insurance appears to be universal. Through an independent fund which it establishes, the factory pays all of the worker's medical expense plus 50 percent of his or her dependents' expenses.

The provision of housing, nurseries, and kindergartens is much more variable. In the housing column of Table III.2, a "+" indicates that the factory provides both single person and family housing for most of its workers. An "m" indicates minimal housing—usually single person housing for only a minority of all workers. A "zero" indicates no factory housing for workers. In Shanghai, factories provided only single person dormitories for a small number of their employees. Most employees were expected to commute daily from housing in the city where they lived with their families. As might be expected, in Shanghai and other major cities, much of the housing is of pre-1949 vintage such that workers from different factories are scattered throughout the city. Also in Shanghai, it would appear that new housing blocks are built by the city rather than by individual factories.

In county factories workers are provided with only minimal housing by the factory in which they work. Most workers live in private housing in their home village and commute to work daily. A small number from more distant parts of the county may live in single person dorms during the week and then return home to their family on weekends. When it exists, factory and city housing is reasonable. In the Shanghai neighborhood we visited, rent is designed not to recover building costs, but simply to provide for external painting, cleaning, and other maintenance costs. In Shanghai, in city built housing, two rooms for a family of four or five would include about 25 square

15. Audrey Donnithorne, *China's Economic System*. London: George Allen and Unwin Ltd., 1967, p. 213.

meters. Monthly rent plus utilities would come to about 11 yuan. Since two people are usually at work in each family, this 11 yuan would usually come to about ten percent of total family income.[16] Similar conditions were observed at Cheng-chou #3 Cotton Spinning Factory, which provided ample and convenient housing for its workers.

The provision of child care services is also highly variable. Since babies are still breast fed in China, large urban factories still provide nursing rooms for infants through the first year of life. When infants graduate from the nursing room, they may move into a nursery for two years and then into kindergarten at about age three-and-a-half. In the large urban factories, where these facilities are best developed, the costs for day care may range up to 9 yuan per month. A low-grade worker with several children would then have to turn to outside street nurseries that charge less. More commonly, most factories subsidize their nurseries and kindergartens so that the monthly fee for day care is only 1-3 yuan per month. A few charge no fees at all. Most commonly in county factories, it appears that child care is minimal. There is only a nursery for younger children or no care at all. Once they have passed the nursing stage, children spend the day at home with their grandparents or other female kin. A few others may spend their day in a village nursery or in a street nursery in the county seat. As with wages, then, fringe benefits in the county factory keep the worker in close contact with the countryside.

Before closing this section, we should say a word about the role of trade unions in handling welfare affairs. During the Cultural Revolution, because trade unions were accused of making excessive bourgeois demands for higher wages and welfare benefits, they were disbanded. It is only in the last few years that unions have been restored. They again have some responsibility for welfare funds—though this seems to be only a minor responsibility which they share with others in the factory. More generally, the union is to work hand-in-glove with the governing revolutionary committee of the factory in helping to organize the workers. The most complete description of the role of the union was given at the Shanghai (Bumper Harvest) Tractor Factory. There the role of the union was said to be to help the revolutionary committee mobilize the masses, raise their political consciousness, organize technical learning, and conduct socialist emulation in order that the factory could fulfill the state target. In other words, they said, the union was the revolutionary committee's assistant. On questioning, the factory managers further reported that the union was to organize recreation and see to the workers' livelihood. It was to take care of welfare funds. At Hsin-hsiang

16. Though they may exclude costs of utilities, many reports put the cost of housing nearer 5% of family budgets.

Water Pump the union took responsibility for political and technical study. At Wu-hsi Electro-Chemical the union was said to be in charge of political study and emulation campaigns. Their elaboration of this role could uncharitably be characterized as saying that the primary role of the union was to make the worker work harder. In contrast to the usual Western model which places management and the labor union in opposing roles, the Chinese union is to be but an arm of management. The union may act as an ombudsman, but it is to subsume the narrow interests of the worker to the larger goals of the state and society.

FORMALIZED PRAISE

As we have seen, the wage system provides strong incentives for young workers who may be promoted rapidly in a few years. For middle-age workers for whom promotion is less common, the wage system provides less of a work incentive. Prior to 1966, the material bonus system helped create incentives for the older worker. With the political destruction of the material bonus system in 1966, however, a system of formalized praise in factories became ever more important for singling out worthy workers and inspiring them to greater efforts.

It is impossible to miss the system of praise, political study, and emulation. The largest factories are a blaze of colors with banners hanging from the rafters, posters pasted on the wall, and multi-colored chalkboards standing about the floor. The banners and posters call for the workers to "Study Well," "Criticize Lin Piao and Confucius," "Go all out to speed production," and "Emulate Taching"—the oil field which is the industrial model for the whole nation. The often elaborate chalkboards spell out political lessons in greater detail as well as occasionally include lessons from economic theory. There are occasional letters of resolution on the wall written by the work group proclaiming what it will achieve during the year. Often in the largest factories, boards both on the floor and on the wall list targets for each worker and his or her performances to date. Banners and posters list workers who have exceeded their targets.

Workers are organized for study by work groups. In properly run places these groups will meet at least weekly for the study of political documents. In 1975 newspapers and bookstores were full of materials from the campaign to study Lenin's work on the Dictatorship of the Proletariat, which had been declared in the spring to be the nationwide study topic for the year. In the larger plants, workers not only absorbed lessons from this work, but also prepared commentaries on it which were published both in the local press and in the foreign language press for consumption abroad. In the urban setting at least, this sort of study is all pervasive, or as one of our hosts said, "Study is sort of like eating. We do it all the time."

At the end of the year the work groups, which are at the same time study groups, get together to evaluate their performance for the year. Individuals within the group are nominated as model workers. The larger workshift and workshop groups nominate model workers from the original list of nominees. The total factory selects not only all around model workers but also model work groups. These groups and individuals are no longer given material rewards, we were told, but praised by being held up for emulation by others. The largest factories have prominent glass-front cases, often at the entrance of the factory, where the photographs of the model groups and model workers for the year are displayed. Also in the workshops, there are often plaques on the wall from the factory administrators praising model work groups. The extent to which groups or individuals are held up for public emulation varies from place to place. From a quick glance at the glass cases at Wu-hsi Electro-Chemical Company, it appeared that about 80 percent of the pictures were dedicated to model groups rather than model individuals. This may be typical of machine paced processes where there is little room for individual worker variability. An equally brief glance at the glass cases at Peking Internal Combustion suggested that the majority of pictures there were dedicated to individual workers. Though in no place did we make an exhaustive count of plaques or pictures, most places with model worker displays seemed to praise individual workers more than groups.

Generally, public praise in smaller county industries appeared to be less than in large urban industries. Table III.2 presents a crude classification of plants according to whether they had a public display of individual worker target and performance boards and plaques or pictures of model workers. A " + " indicates that there was a large number of these displays in an open area such that all workers (and visiting delegations) could see them. An "m" indicates a minimal display of performance boards in one or two shops or possibly award plaques in only one or two shops. A "0" indicates the absence of public displays. On at least one occasion we were told that even when there were no public displays, there are still annual meetings to evaluate work performance. At these meetings model workers are selected and then later held up for emulation in public meetings.

Though we gathered no evidence for the conclusion, it is our suspicion that the impact of political study and formalized praise varies pretty much as its overt symbols do in Table III.2. In county and commune plants, where many workers return home nightly to their village, political messages may be buried amidst the day to day economic and family concerns of workers in their separate village existences. In the cities, where many workers go home to factory housing which is just adjacent to the plant, the political atmosphere generated at work may continue uninterrupted. Living amidst those with whom one works and studies, the group pressures toward social conformity are likely, one would conjecture, to be quite strong. In factory housing one's individual and family life are more exposed and more subject to social comment than when one lives in housing scattered throughout the city or in isolated villages.[17]

LIFE CHANCES

It is not only the structure of reward within industry that provides a strong incentive for work in state industry. There is also a clear differential in life chances between those within industry and those without. Though our hosts often spoke of their factory wage system as a low wage system, income and social benefits in state factories are greater and more secure than those provided in most villages. Except for a few prosperous vegetable communes in the suburbs of cities, average factory incomes remain stable from year to year regardless of weather or local harvests. Generally, factory workers are engaged in less physically taxing tasks out of the weather, and fringe benefits are much more abundant.

To the extent that workers are aware of the great rural-urban difference, it must make them more willing to work under conditions of moderate mobility and only modest increases in income over the last twenty years. There are several ways by which they are reminded of these differences. In large, urban factories some of the new workers are selected from among students who have been in the countryside for two or more years. Selected on the basis of their demonstrated commitment to serve the people in the village, or on the basis of their visible altruism, they should be highly committed, and they should be very conscious of how fortunate they are to get back to the city. In county factories lower wages are matched by an even closer contact with the countryside. Even in rich rural areas a wage of 45 yuan per month when combined with health and retirement benefits is likely to exceed that of nearby agriculturists.

Among middle-age workers in large cities that are further removed from villages, there may be more difficulty in sustaining this sense of superior life chances *vis-a-vis* peasants. Some of the older workers have gone for years with little increase in pay or material standard of living. Even when the government policy of holding urban wages constant while allowing peasant incomes to rise is explained to them, older workers may find it difficult to adjust expectations generated in the early 1950s that the rooting out of imperial capitalism and the introduction of communism would mean a steady improvement in life for everyone. Though everyone must be aware of the great improvement over 1949, the sense of almost constant income

---

17. For a nineteenth century example of the pervasive influence of ideology and social pressure in a company town within a capitalist setting, see Stanley Buder, *Pullman: An Experiment in Industrial Order and Community Planning, 1880-1930.* New York: Oxford University Press, 1967, Ch. 8.

since 1956 must be brought home to older workers by the absence of two phenomena common to workers in the West. The first phenomenon common to the West is the illusion of increasing salaries created by creeping inflation. In periods of rapid inflation the Western worker may know quite well that price increases have exceeded increases in salary. In more normal times of creeping inflation, the worker may be rather uncertain as to whether real income has actually risen or fallen. Unless the union very actively explains the exact relationship between prices and wages, the average worker may feel that real income has risen. The Chinese worker, in contrast, doesn't need any help from the union to calculate his or her real income or any help to conclude that real income has risen very little if any. There is no creeping inflation in China to delude the worker. The Chinese government takes great pride in its ability to hold prices constant. Except for a few increases in the early 1960s, prices for staple foods and consumer goods are about the same as they were 20 years ago. With no rise in prices, there also has been no need for wage increases. Except for a few seniority raises, which are very rare for the middle-age worker, wages have remained constant. From the viewpoint of the factory manager, then, we can conjecture that the control on inflation may have negative as well as positive consequences.

A related phenomenon which is common to the West, but rare among urban workers in China is what is known as the trickle-down effect.[18] In the West, new appliances and other consumer goods are generally introduced to the market at rather high prices and only later reduced to much lower prices as research and development expenses are recovered, as mass production lowers the costs of production, and as competitors making similar products force down sale prices. Recent examples are color television and electronic calculators. Earlier examples are the automobile, electric refrigerators, clothes washers, and automatic dishwashers. When these consumer goods are originally introduced they are so expensive that they can only be bought by the rich. But then as prices fall, the goods spread to the middle class and finally to the working class, creating the illusion among some people that the middle class and working class are catching up with the rich. What only the rich could buy a few years ago now everyone can buy. While in fact the rich are just as rich as ever and going on to buy even grander things, there is the illusion that class differences are narrowing.

In China, the prices of a few goods such as medical drugs have dropped in recent years. Yet, state policy is that the prices for most consumer goods will remain high in order that they can generate investment funds for heavy industry. A bicycle still requires about three months' salary for an urban factory worker to purchase. As long as the policy of high consumer prices for goods other than food, housing, and drugs is maintained, there will be

18. Lloyd Fallers, *Inequality.* Chicago: University of Chicago Press, 1974.

neither the reality of increasing living standards nor the illusion that the working class is catching up with anyone else. This is not to say that consumer goods are unavailable. Urban stores have an abundant supply of goods. Only, in China, because prices for consumer goods remain high, can we conjecture that there is less perception of progress among the older workers than among similar groups in the West.[19]

There are some offsetting features in the system. In time, the restrictions on salaries for new technicians and cadres in factories may partially compensate for the absence of a large trickle down of consumer goods from the more to the less affluent. Already the factory elite as well as the bureaucratic elite throughout the society are restricted in how they can flaunt their superior income. Though differentiated in cut and quality of material, the clothes of the average factory manager are not that distinct from those worn by the average worker. Private cars are unavailable and, to the extent that we could tell, company cars are not freely available either. Housing for factory managers and technicians is not all that different from that for the average worker in large urban plants. As for other consumer goods, the constant propaganda against bourgeois habits narrows the gap in ostentatious consumption, which is found in the West.

There are, then, likely to be contradictory tendencies in the life of the average urban worker. Among young workers there is likely to be both ideological commitment and a sense of how they have better life chances than other young people who have stayed in the countryside. Among this same group there are likely to be great expectations of upward mobility. Among the older workers in large city factories, there is likely to be little upward mobility and a strong sense of how incomes have remained constant for many years, tempered by a recognition that things are better than they used to be before 1949 and by the recognition that cadres and technicians do not openly flaunt their greater consumption of food, clothes, and other goods.

As for technicians and cadres, there is as yet little empirical evidence on which to evaluate the effects of the old restrictions on ostentatious consumption and the new restrictions on wages. On theoretical grounds, there is reason to believe that the negative effects will not be too great. Studies of worker motivation in the West consistently show that it is only workers who

---

19. The constancy of income should not be overstated. Even when individual incomes remain constant, family incomes may rise. Increasing female employment, especially in neighborhood factories, produces more multiple income families. The increasing seniority of workers allows more of them to retire on a full 70% pension, thereby relieving their children of the burden of supporting them. The increase in family income would be consistent with the report from visitors who return to China in successive years that urban food and clothing are continually improving.

are greatly concerned about the level of material reward.[20] Managers and professionals are much more concerned about their chances for creativity, independent action, and personal relationships on the job. The benefits of greater freedom of action provided by managerial and staff jobs, may, then, more than offset any restrictions on salary in China. The Chinese do not plan to eliminate all salary distinctions between technicians, administrators, and workers. If the technicians and administrators are not completely hemmed in by regulations or constantly subject to worker criticism and attack (as they were on occasion in the Cultural Revolution), then one may find them working just as hard as ever even with restricted material rewards.

COLLECTIVE INDUSTRY

The discussion to this point has been almost exclusively about incentives in state-run enterprises, which are controlled by the county and other higher level administrative units. The incentives in collectively-run commune and brigade industries are much simpler.

INDIVIDUAL INCENTIVES

For the most part, workers in commune and brigade industry get the same kind of rewards as temporary workers in state industry. It was only in two places that we found commune enterprise workers on a fixed wage. At Red Star Commune outside Peking all the enterprise workers were on a wage averaging a very high 49 yuan per month. At Yao-ts'un Agriculture Machinery Factory in Lin County, Honan, one-third of the workers were receiving a fixed wage. The rest of the workers at Yao-ts'un were getting work points in their home production teams. Throughout the rest of Lin County and in the five other counties we visited, the standard was for workers in collective industry to receive only work points in their home village. The goal of this procedure is to ensure that people in collective plants remain "both workers and peasants" (yi kung yi nung). This is most strongly symbolized in the practice of having workers in commune factories return to the fields each year for two to four weeks during the busiest harvesting and planting times.

When the commune factory makes payments through the production team, the worker's final income is determined as much by his neighbors in the village as by the factory. They determine how much of the payment from the factory will be kept by the team and how much passed on to the worker.

---

20. E. A. Friedmann and R. J. Havighurst, "Work and Retirement," in Sigmund Nosow and William H. Form, *Man, Work, and Society*. New York: Basic Books, 1962.

In Lin County, because commune factories try to set their payments at about the average level of income of surrounding production teams, there is likely to be little left over for the team. Practice, however, varies from place to place. The only constraint is that workers should make the same or only slightly more than the average able-bodied laborer in their home team. As a result, the worker's income might vary anywhere from 10–50 yuan per month in different parts of the country.

To the extent that the collective worker receives any fringe benefits, these must come through the production team. Except for a very small minority who live too far away to commute to work daily, collective workers live in private family housing. Even when they live in the factory, they will only stay in single person dorms during the week and return home to their family on weekends.[21] When their family house needs repair, they must pay for this out of their family budget. Health care is provided not by the factory but by payments out of the worker's own pocket into a village cooperative insurance program. At one or two yuan per year from each adult and child in the family, cooperative health insurance pays for visits to the village paramedic, occasional referrals to the commune hospital, and medicine. It is only in the more prosperous regions that the team will provide a substantial subsidy to health programs out of collective funds.[22] Retirement benefits, if they are paid at all, are paid by one's production team rather than the factory. The team pays for retirement only when the worker or peasant has no sons to rely on for support. Most workers, then, rely on their children for support in old age.[23]

The advantage of these restricted benefits is, of course, that commune industry can be started on a shoe string. It was explicitly stated in one briefing that one of the advantages of the "both worker and farmer" system was that the factory did not have to build housing. The worker-farmer system saved the factory money. All the extra costs which urban industry incurs

21. Even in urban industry there is a small number of workers without their families. If they came from the village and got their job after 1958, their family had to remain in the countryside. Workers with parents or spouse outside the city get two weeks paid vacation per year to return home. Except for these workers, the only rest from work urban employees get is one day off per week, plus about six national holidays per year.

22. We asked the vice-chairman of Liuchuang Brigade why it was necessary for such a rich brigade to require individuals to pay for medical insurance and to charge .05 yuan fees for hospital visits. She replied that the Brigade already paid two of the three yuan yearly insurance fees. However, they had not yet reached the point materially and politically where they could dispense with all fees. If there was free medical care, people would overuse its services. (On the problem of free medical care in 1958–59, see Michael Lampton, *The Politics of Public Health in China: 1949–1969,* Ph.D. dissertation, Stanford University, 1974, University Microfilms #74-13,653, Chapter V.)

23. The regulations on this are outlined in William L. Parish, Jr., "Socialism in the Chinese Peasant Family," *Journal of Asian Studies,* Vol. 34, No. 3, May 1975, pp. 613–630.

when industry provides housing, child care, health payments, and retirement benefits are avoided. This may not be an ideal policy, but it is a very realistic one fitting well the needs of the countryside at this time.

Even with these restricted benefits, the lure of industry is sufficiently strong that it can create contradictions between commune industry and agriculture. In Ma Lu Commune outside Shanghai, before 1972, it was found that the rapid growth of commune industry was drawing too many workers out of agriculture. The slightly higher pay, greater security, and better working conditions were attracting the youngest, most able-bodied workers into industry. Crop yields stagnated and ill feelings grew between those in industry and agriculture. We were told that it was only by more strictly limiting industrial salaries to an average 5 percent above agricultural salaries and by restricting the rate of industrial growth that these contradictions could be removed. Also, the commune had to remind itself that it could survive only by turning out products which would serve agriculture and increase agricultural income. Industry can grow only as fast as agriculture, or as they put it, "The boat can rise only as fast as the water."[24]

COLLECTIVE INCENTIVES

One reason that the commune and brigade must continually remind themselves about the close relationship between industry and agriculture is that the incentives for increasing industrial production are powerful. Industry provides a high rate of profit. The prices of industrial goods, whether produced by state or collective enterprises, are regulated by the state. The prices of some goods sold to agriculture, such as tractors, have been reduced in recent years. Likewise in the 1950s and early 1960s, the prices paid to the farmers for grain were raised to a certain extent. Nevertheless, prices for industrial goods remain sufficiently high for some local industry to make a handsome profit and to tempt commune leaders to emphasize industry.

Second, industry is one of the few sources of discretionary funds at the commune and brigade levels of administration. Since the Great Leap Forward in 1958–1960, communes have been kept from drawing funds from lower level brigade and team units. Brigades can only rarely ask for funds from their constituent teams. Communes get funds from the county above, but these are not only limited but also earmarked for special uses, such as education, hospitals, and administrative salaries. Industrial profits, then, provide commune leaders with much greater freedom of action. Even when their projects have to be approved by the county above, their proposals for

24. This case also is described in print: Editing Group, *Shanghai chiao-ch'ü nung-ye hsüeh Tachai* (Shanghai Suburban Agriculture Studies Tachai), union serial number 3144.96. Shanghai: Agricultural Press, 1974, pp. 52–67.

new projects must be far more forceful when they have their own funds to support them.

Finally, when commune industry becomes highly developed and commune accumulation funds grow, they provide the possibility for more extensive social services which will benefit all members of the commune. These themes will be developed at greater length in Chapter IX on the social effects of small industry.

Overall, the structure of incentives seems to respond well to the problems of different types of industries. Within the limitations of a tour, we felt the efficiency of the Chinese worker was quite acceptable. In Chinese factories, technical problems are confronted and solved, most machines are in working order, and goods are turned out at a steady pace. It was hard for us to judge the pace of work, because we saw a variable mix of technologies, where the appropriate measure of pace differs, and of course the workers saw us and their own superiors watching them. For what it is worth, it seemed to us that the pace varied around an average of steady but not pushing hard. On an earth-fill dam construction site, the pace looked very high, while some shops seemed to have a lot of people standing around— perhaps some were apprentices, perhaps some were technically necessary for an operation requiring bursts of concentrated activity.

If we can be allowed to speculate further in an already very speculative chapter, it is our guess that incentives are most acceptable in the small rural plants and somewhat less acceptable in the large urban plants. In the countryside even a commune plant paying only work points and providing few or no fringe benefits can be oversubscribed with potential workers. The possibilities of steady payment, work under a roof rather than out in the weather, a chance to learn and use a bit more technical skill, and only marginally higher rates of pay appear to assure a steady supply of young, committed workers. If one can judge from public display of signs and posters, in most of the commune plants we visited, there was little need to introduce additional ideological appeals to guarantee the cooperation of workers. The slightly greater material advantages of factory as opposed to agricultural field work, and possibly the importance of group social pressure in small work settings, were sufficient to insure committed workers.

In county plants as well, we would guess that incentives for the worker are not problematic. With many workers still having their family in the countryside, the higher wages and fringe benefits of factory work are sufficient to produce committed workers. For those factories which have begun operation in recent years, factory work has meant a rapid rise in income for former agriculturists. Though there are a few more overt signs of the use of ideological appeals and formalized praise in county factories, these appeals still tend to be minimally developed compared to those in large urban plants.

It is in the large urban plants, it would seem, that incentives are most likely to be problematic. Workers who have been in the city for many years, who have long gotten the same wage, and whose neighbors are all getting about the same wage are likely to have a rather different standard of comparison than the rural worker. The great elaboration of ideological appeals, study, and formalized praise in the large plants is in part simply the result of a specialized staff for political programs in large plants. The elaboration is also the result, one suspects, of the need to introduce additional appeals when material rewards are insufficient. For the purposes of socialist transformation of the work force, this may be all to the good. In the countryside, things are in some ways too easy. When comparative material rewards are adequate, workers and administrators are not forced to discuss socialist principles of work. When comparative material rewards are less adequate, people are forced to ask, "What do we work for? Is it for ourselves or for the whole nation? For our families or the world? For immediate consumption or for long term revolution?" The adequacy of the answers to these questions, their appeal or non-appeal to the workers, will have great consequences not only for the Chinese, but also for those everywhere who eagerly follow the Chinese model of development.

Chapter IV

THE ECONOMIES OF RURAL SMALL-SCALE INDUSTRY*

The purpose of our analysis in this chapter is to make an assessment based on what we observed and were told during our visit of the economic rationality and efficiency of rural, small-scale industry in China.[1] The analysis largely concentrates on an economic evaluation of these industries both as individual units of production and as essential components of the effort to solve the economic development problem in rural China. The broader social and political implications of the rural, small-scale industries are dealt with in other chapters in this report. Nonetheless, as will be shown in this Chapter, the rationale and benefits of these rural, small-scale industries can only be fully appreciated when they are evaluated in the context

---

*Our revision of this chapter for publication was greatly assisted by the comments of participants in a workshop in Washington, D.C., on December 13, 1975, which reviewed an earlier draft. A special expression of appreciation is due to Mr. Larry Westphal (World Bank) and Mr. Michael Field (CIA) for detailed, written critiques.

1. For other economic assessments of China's rural, small-scale industries, by Western economists, see Carl Riskin, "Local Industry and Choice of Techniques in Planning of Industrial Development in Mainland China," in *Planning for Advanced Skills and Technologies,* Studies presented at the Ad Hoc Meeting of Experts on the Role of Advanced Skills and Technologies in Industrial Development, New York, 22–29 May 1967, Industrial Planning and Programming Series, No. 3, United Nations Industrial Development Organization. Vienna: (1969), pp. 171–80.

of the rather complex, interdependent social, economic, and political system in rural China.

Thus, our economic analysis and assessment of these enterprises will emphasize the specific Chinese, developing-nation economic environment in which they operate. We do not intend to judge these enterprises against the benchmark of large-scale, modern enterprises in the industrialized countries of the West. The crucial question is not whether these enterprises are maximizing profits[2]—which is not their objective, nor how the productivity of labor employed in these enterprises compares with labor productivity in the United States. Although interesting questions, this approach is not the best means for determining the rationality or efficiency of small-scale industries in China. The question we hope to provide a preliminary answer to is much more important; how effectively are the Chinese utilizing the resources available to them to achieve their objectives. Specifically, we hope to provide some measure of how well, i.e., efficiently, the Chinese are mobilizing inputs of labor, capital, and raw material in the rural, small-scale industrial sector to produce the output mix assigned to that sector.

Furthermore, a very important consideration in our evaluation is the explicit recognition of the various constraints and conditioning factors that determine the actual possibilities available to the Chinese in pursuing their objectives. Thus, the effectiveness with which they utilize resources to achieve

---

Ibid., "Small Industry and The Chinese Model of Development," The China Quarterly, April–June, 1971, pp. 245–73.

Jon Sigurdson, "Rural Economic Planning," in Michel Oksenberg (ed.), China's Development Experience, Proceedings of The Academy of Political Science, New York, Vol. 31, No. 1, March, 1973, pp. 68–79; ibid., "Technology and Employment in China," World Development, Vol. 2, No. 3, March, 1974, pp. 75–85.

Ibid., "Rural Industrialization in China," in China: A Reassessment of The Economy, A Compendium of Papers submitted to the Joint Economic Committee, Congress of The United States, U.S. Government Printing Office, Washington (1975), pp. 411–35.

Carl Riskin, "Rural Industry: Self-Reliant Systems or 'Independent Kingdoms'?," in Victor Nee and James Peck (eds.), China's Cultural Revolution in Retrospect (tentative title), Pantheon Books, New York (forthcoming), and CIA, A(ER)74-60, China: Role of Small Plants in Economic Development, May, 1974.

In addition, Jon Sigurdson also has prepared an extensive monograph, "Rural Industrialization in China," which is to be published by the East Asian Research Center, Harvard University. Although these studies have contributed to our understanding, as indicated in the Preface and in the first sentence in this Chapter, our specific purpose in this Chapter is an attempt to interpret what it was we were told and what we saw during our visit to China, rather than present a research monograph on the subject which incorporates and appraises the arguments and findings of others. However, the findings of others are cited in this Chapter to help illustrate those impressions we obtained as a result of our trip.

2. Profits in the accounting sense of money revenue minus money costs to the enterprise, not in terms of the enterprises profitability to the economy as a whole. Determining these latter costs and benefits of Chinese rural, small-scale industries is one of the major objectives of this Chapter.

their objectives is not only not measured against the standards presently achieved in modern, industrialized countries, but also not measured against some hypothesized standard associated with a theoretical ideal type, which would assume the Chinese had complete access to, or there were free mobility of resources and technology, not only within China itself, but throughout the world as well. A true appreciation of the contribution and success of the rural, small-scale industrial program in China can only be obtained when one considers the actual circumstances in which that program is taking place.

As the following analysis will show clearly, the rural, small-scale industry program is greatly influenced by, in many cases dictated by, and in a real sense justified by the excess demand in the local rural areas for agricultural inputs produced in the modern sector; the poorly developed transportation network and the high cost of transportation in China; and the quantity and/or quality of raw materials, labor skills, producer's goods, and financial resources available at the local level, plus the difficulty of mobilizing these resources for use in the modern sector.

DEFINING EFFICIENCY

Any discussion of efficiency involves either implicit or explicit reference to some standard of what is best. Especially in situations where data for only a small number of productive factors are available, there is an understandable tendency to use very simple ratios to measure efficiency—the obvious example is value of output per man or tons of grain per hectare. It is well understood in principle that these measures can be extremely misleading and the reasons are most easily understood by referring to the standard production isoquant shown in Figure IV-1. In this figure, it is recognized that two factors of production, capital and labor, are needed to produce a standard unit of output, which is best measured in physical terms but can be measured in terms of value added.

Figure IV-1 shows four basic long-run manufacturing processes, each capable of producing a unit of output according to four techniques—labeled modern (M), intermediate-modern (I-M), intermediate-primitive (I-P), and primitive (P). Each technique has a fixed ratio of capital to labor used in the long-run process, and this ratio varies systematically from "low" for the primitive process to "high" for the modern process. By assuming divisibility (a questionable assumption in some circumstances, as will be noted later), it is possible to draw the unit isoquant relating the various amounts of capital and labor needed to produce a unit of output. This isoquant is shown as ABCDEF. The location and shape of this isoquant can, in principle, be determined from engineering data specifying the *best possible practice* for each type of manufacturing technique. That is, ABCDEF refers to the

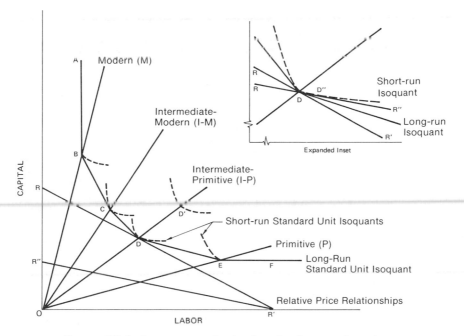

FIGURE IV-1. Long-run production function for manufacturing.

minimum amount of capital needed to produce a unit of output by each technique, for a *given* amount of labor (or vice versa). Thus, no firm can use a process that uses a capital-labor combination between the origin and the isoquant to produce a unit of output. These combinations are, for the moment, technologically not feasible. Any firm that uses exactly the amount of capital and labor indicated by the isoquant would be said to be "technically efficient," without regard to whether process P or process M is used. Thus, low output per worker, as in P, is entirely consistent with technical efficiency provided a sufficiently small amount of capital is also used (the lesson is generalizable beyond two dimensions). Four different firms, each using separate techniques, would *all* be technically efficient if they produced at points B, C, D, and E respectively. Which of these points minimizes the unit cost of production will depend on the cost factors of production, and, hence, choice among a set of technically efficient processes is an economic matter.

Production of a unit of output using factor combinations in the interior of the production possibility set defined by ABCDEF is inefficient. Many reasons exist that can lead to such inefficiency. If a firm produces a unit of output at D', instead of at D, it is *technically inefficient*—it uses *both* more capital *and* more labor than the firm at D to produce the same output. The reasons for such technical inefficiency are frequently grouped into three categories. Each type shows up as an interior point in the production set, but the means of improving the efficiencies in each category can be quite different:

1. *Engineering efficiency* refers to engineering and technical processes and how effectively these are operated relative to best practice for the type of equipment.

2. *"X-efficiency"* refers to organizational inputs, incentives, worker morale and the broad climate of worker-management-machine harmony.

3. *"Learning curve" efficiency* refers to the improvement in factory productivity as experience is gained in the operation of new machines or the production of new products. If experience is considered as a separate factor of production, then this category is not strictly a question of technical efficiency.

Allocative, or economic, efficiency refers to the static choice of processing technique when the firm is faced with a price line indicating the costs to the firm of capital and labor. Such a line, shown as RR' in Figure IV-1, can be thought of as a minimum cost line reflecting constant prices for the two inputs. The economically efficient process to use is the one that minimizes cost for the given level of output (economies of scale will be considered shortly—for the time being they are assumed away). In the figure shown, the *minimum cost technique* for producing a unit of output is I-P, and "a technically and economically efficient firm" would produce at D.

If all firms in a society face the same price environment, i.e., RR', then only one production technique can be economically efficient—using *process* I-P—but technically inefficient—using technique D'. But a single price environment guarantees a single long-run production process. Few societies can, or would care to, guarantee a single price environment, however. Introducing transportation costs into the analysis demonstrates why and the impact. If RR' is the (fixed) relationship between capital and labor costs in national manufacturing centers in China such as Shanghai, Peking, Tientsin, etc., the R'R'' might reflect the costs of nationally produced capital goods at the local level relative to local labor costs. The difference is a large transportation cost (either explicitly or implicitly in terms of waiting time for a state allocation to the local level of scarce nationally produced capital goods) that must be paid to transform national capital goods into local capital goods (substituting "raw materials" does not alter the argument). By the time the national level capital good actually arrives at the local level, its real price relative to labor is R'R''. More importantly, the new "real price" alters the choice of economically efficient technique *at the local level* from I-P to P. That is, high transportation costs will, as a general rule, raise the efficient level of labor intensity of production processes at the local level compared with national levels. Depending on the magnitude of transportation (and transfer) changes, which are certainly very large in China in an opportunity cost sense and probably in direct monetary costs as well for most products flowing *to* the countryside, a wide variety of production processes *for the same unit of output* might well be both economically and technically efficient. This is obviously an important, if elementary conclusion given the extent of diversity of manufacturing technique observed by our group in the agricultural machinery industry.

One last issue of principle must be treated before moving to impressions of efficiency in fact. The discussion so far has treated efficiency as a static concept, i.e., both the production isoquant and the relative prices are given for a point in time and no concern is given for what came before nor what is likely to come after. Since most capital equipment has a relatively long productive life, it is necessary to consider how both the isoquant and the price relationships are likely to shift over time and the consequent implications for point by point decision making. Thus, a static picture of a technical and allocative decision may look "wrong" relative to the immediate technical and price environment, but could be "right in the long run."

The production processes, whose fixed factor proportions are represented by the rays OB, OC, OD, and OE, involve investment in capital equipment that normally has a substantial life, especially for the more modern, capital intensive processes. Once such a basic process has been chosen, there are usually still a set of factor proportion decisions with respect to how the process will be operated. In economist's jargon, the world is at least partially putty-putty. The scope for varying factor proportions in the short run for each long-run process is shown in Figure IV-1 by the dashed isoquants for each process.

The effect of short-run factor variability is demonstrated in the expanded inset. In a rural environment where the effective price relationship is RR", static allocative criteria would call for investment in the primitive process at E. However, if this would involve installing equipment that might be completely obsolete in a few years as labor becomes more expensive, the actual process chosen might well be the intermediate-primitive one at D. But, since the effective short-run price environment is still RR", the I-P process should be modified along the short-run isoquant to point D" in the expanded inset. The impression this gives to the factory observer is of a surprisingly modern plant with more people working than seem necessary. This is a fair summary of our visits to a number of plants.

Figure IV-2 illustrates the impact of biased technical change. As in Figure IV-1, ABCDEF represents the efficient isoquant relating the minimum labor-capital combinations used in producing a unit of output. This isoquant now refers explicitly to the situation at a particular point in time,

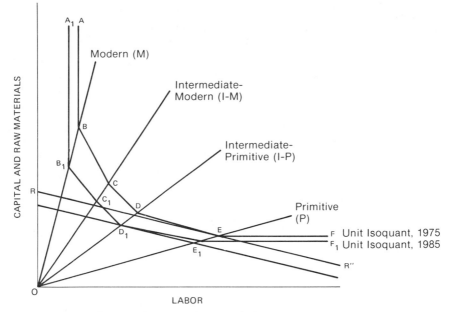

FIGURE IV-2. The impact of biased technical change.

say 1975. The given price line RR' indicates that the primitive process should be used with a technical minimum level of inputs at point E. The issue now is how the 1975 unit isoquant is likely to shift over time due to technological progress. It seems characteristic of modern technology that more progress is made in the capital intensive techniques than in the labor-intensive techniques, for the manufacture of a particular product. Thus, after 10 years of technical development, the original isoquant has shifted to $A_1B_1C_1D_1E_1F_1$, which was determined by lowering unit output costs for the primitive (P) technique by 10%, the intermediate-primate technique (I-P) by 15%, the intermediate-modern technique (I-M) by 20%, and the modern technique (M) by 25%. The net result is that the isoquant shifts toward the origin more quickly along the capital (and raw materials) axis than along the labor axis. Again, it must be remembered that these are alternative techniques for producing *the same* product, and that the capital-labor *ratio* remains the same for each process after technical change as it was before. Even if capital-labor costs remain the same during the 10-year period of technical change (a pessimistic assumption about real growth in labor income), the new isoquant touches the relevant cost line at D_1 instead of E. That is, this type of technical change results in a new production process (I-P) being economically efficient after the technical change, compared with the economically efficient process (P) before the change. If an investment decision is being made in 1975 between I-P and P, what is the economically rational choice? The answer obviously depends on the life of the equipment and its substitutability from P to I-P. If P equipment locks a firm into the D process for 20 to 30 years, I-P equipment might well be the rational long-run choice even though it appears inefficient in the short run. Short-lived equipment or high discount rates used to calculate net present value of future events would tend to make the P equipment preferable as the short-run choice even knowing that the choice will change sometime in the future.

The above general discussion of efficiency in a Chinese context serves mainly to explain the expectations of what we were likely to see in terms of manufacturing techniques in rural and urban areas. In summary, high transportation costs and high discount rates typical of capital-short societies should lead to a substantial difference in technique between urban and rural areas and an emphasis on labor intensity in both, but obviously more systematically in the rural areas. These expectations were only partly fulfilled, and then not in a uniform pattern, but that is the subject of the sections that follow.

CHARACTERISTICS OF OBSERVED INDUSTRIES

Our assessments of efficiency are biased by two equally important constraints: the need to rely on our own intuitive judgments about what we observed and were told, and the sample of rural, small-scale industries our hosts chose to show and tell us about—a sample that emphasized the models China hopes to emulate throughout the countryside, not a random sample of rural, small-scale industry in China today.

The definition of rural, small-scale industry in China is based on where any particular enterprise fits into the Chinese administrative system and is not defined by the plant's size or scale of operations. A complete list of the plants visited and the quantitative information we obtained concerning the scale of their activities is presented in Table IV-1. As pointed out in the Introduction, the Chinese definition of rural, small-scale industries includes those plants owned and operated by the countries, communes, and brigades. In general, the important distinguishing features of these rural, small-scale industries is that they do tend to be relatively small in scale, less advanced in technology, and are primarily financed with local funds. Nonetheless, due to this organizational and administrative definition of rural, small-scale industries, the plants we visited in the rural, small-scale sector varied greatly in size.

Within the category of rural, small-scale industries, our hosts had arranged for us to see more examples of the county-run plants, i.e., those that were largest in scale, more modernized and better equipped. The extent to which our sample is biased in favor of these county-level plants is indicated by the data given us in a briefing on rural, small-scale industry in Lin County, which clearly shows the significant correlation between the organizational level to which the plant belonged and its size. Of the 65 rural,

Table IV-1

INDUSTRIAL PLANTS VISITED BY THE DELEGATION ON RURAL, SMALL-SCALE INDUSTRY, JUNE 12-JULY 9, 1975 (CHRONOLOGICAL LIST)

Location	Name of Plant	Produce	Level	Annual Output 1974	Employment	Construction Costs
Peking Municipality	Red Star Peoples Commune: Farm Machinery and Production Shops	Produces threshers and rice transplanters; repairs	Commune	575,000 yuan	261	n.a.
Peking Municipality	Red Star Peoples Commune: Grain and Food Processing Mills	Wheat flour, feed grain, husked rice	Commune	n.a.	183	n.a.
Peking Municipality	Capital Iron and Steel Factory	Rolled steel	National	One million tons	40,000[1]	n.a.
Peking Municipality	Peking Internal Combustion Engine Factory	Gas and diesel engines	National	About 100 million yuan	7,000	n.a.
Peking Municipality	Peking West City Area Optical Instruments Factory	Optical instruments	National	n.a.	520	n.a.
Hsi-yang County	Hsi-yang County Tractor Factory	Water pumps, threshers, tractors	County	1,044,000 yuan	310	n.a.
Hsi-yang County	Hsi-yang County Chemical Fertilizer Factory	Ammonium nitrate, synthetic ammonia	County	2,700,000 yuan	450	7.5 million yuan
Hsi-yang County	Tachai Cement Plant	Cement	County[2]	763,800 yuan	144	350,000 yuan
Hsi-yang County	Hsi-yang County Farm Tools Factory	Cornshuckers, water pumps, furniture, threshers	County	2000 water pumps 150 threshers	148	n.a.
Lin County	County Hydroelectric Power Station	Electric power	County	2500 kw. capacity	43	1.46 million yuan
Lin County	Commune Hydroelectric Power Station	Electric Power	Commune	250 kw. capacity	n.a.	n.a.
Lin County	Brigade Hydroelectric Power Station	Electric power	Brigade	40kw. capacity	4[3]	17,000 yuan

Location	Factory	Products	Level	Output Value	Number	Investment
Lin County	Lin County Chemical Fertilizer Factory	Nitrogenous fertilizer	County	1,260,000 yuan	520	6 million yuan
Lin County	Lin County Cotton Textile Factory	Cotton cloth, handkerchiefs, towels	County	Over 1,00,000 yuan	186	500,000 yuan
Lin County	Tung-fang-hung Agricultural Machinery Factory	Threshers, sluice gates, small and medium agricultural machinery, repairs	County	Over 1,000,000 yuan	300	1.5 million yuan
Lin County	Lin County Fluorescent Light Factory	Fluorescent light bulbs	County	700,000 yuan	180	300,000 yuan
Lin County	Commune Agricultural Machinery Factory	Threshers, motors, choppers, pumps, crushers	Commune	450,000 yuan	90	n.a.
Lin County	Brigade Flour Mill (operates part-time)	Winnowers, repairs	Brigade	300 kw./hr. capacity	about 4	n.a.
Hui County	Hui County Cement Factory	Cement	County	50,000 tons	500	n.a.
Hui County	Hui County Chemical Fertilizer Factory	Synthetic ammonia[4]	County	10,510 tons Synthetic ammonia	536	n.a.
Hui County	Commune Agricultural Machinery Workshop	Water pumps, threshers, plows, grain bagger[5]	Commune	n.a.	under 100	n.a.
Hsin-hsiang City	Commune Agricultural Machinery Factory	Tractors, mainly repairs	Commune	n.a.	190	n.a.
Hsin-hsiang City	Brigade Agricultural Machinery Repair Workshop	Makes spare parts and does repairs	Brigade	n.a.	27	n.a.
Hsin-hsiang City	Brigade Food Processing Mill	Processes grain for members of 34 teams in brigade	Brigade	n.a.[6]	n.a.	n.a.
Hsin-hsiang City	Brigade Repair Shop	Makes wooden wheat seeders, spare parts, repairs	Brigade	n.a.	23	n.a.

Table IV-1 Continued

Location	Name of Plant	Produce	Level	Annual Output 1974	Employment	Construction Costs
Hsin-hsiang City	Hsin-hsiang Water Pump Factory	Water pumps	City	7,100,000 yuan	680	n.a.
Hsin-hsiang City	Hsin-hsiang Cotton Textile Mill	Undyed and printed knit cloth, towels and washcloths	City	n.a.	1,400	n.a.
Hsin-hsiang City	Hsin-hsiang Region Chemical Fertilizer Industry Equipment Factory	All major spare parts for small-scale chemical fertilizer plants	Region	1.3 million yuan	330	n.a.
Cheng-chou	Cheng-chou No. 3 Cotton Textile Factory	Cotton cloth, dacron, corduroy, taffeta, etc.	City	85 million yuan	5,600	n.a.
Cheng-chou	Cheng-chou Textile Machinery Factory	All types of machinery for textile factories	City	n.a.	5,200	n.a.
Wu-hsi County	Wu-hsi County Iron and Steel Factory	Steel rods and ingots	County	Over 9 million yuan	805	n.a.
Wu-hsi County	Commune Concrete Products Factory	Cement telephone poles, slabs	Commune	450,000 yuan	97	n.a.
Wu-hsi County	Commune Agricultural Machinery Manufacturing and Repair Factory	Presses, transformers, lathes, fabrication and repairs of vehicles	Commune	1.6 million yuan	192	n.a.
Wu-hsi County	Commune Powder Metallurgy Factory	Oilstone, grinding wheels, and parts of pressed powdered metal	Commune	600,000 yuan	108	n.a.
Wu-hsi County	Wu-hsi County Tractor Factory	East wind 12-walking tractor	County	3,000 units	661	n.a.
Wu-hsi County	Wu-hsi County Electric Motor Factory	Electric motors	County	145,000 kw.	340	n.a.

Wu-hsi County	Wu-hsi County Electrochemical Factory	Polyvinyl chloride, caustic soda, lime, calcium carbide	County	9.8 million yuan	600	3.8 million yuan
Wu-hsi City	Wu-hsi Clay Figurine Factory	Clay figurines	City	3 million yuan	Over 500	n.a.
Wu-hsi City	Commune Agricultural Machinery Repair Workshop	Overhauls agricultural machinery[7]	Commune	n.a.	n.a.	n.a.
Wu-hsi City	Wu-hsi Silk Filature Factory	Silk thread	City	n.a.[8]	1,700	n.a.
Wu-hsi City	Commune Agricultural Machinery Factory	Were making 4-h.p. rice transplanters, aeraters (for fish ponds)	Commune	n.a.	n.a.	n.a.
Shanghai Municipality	Shanghai (Bumper Harvest) Tractor Factory	4-wheel, 35-h.p. tractors and sets of auxiliary equipment	City	80 million yuan	1,300	n.a.
Shanghai Municipality	Shanghai Shaped Steel Tubing Plant	Shaped steel tubes, seamless aluminum tubes	City	15 million yuan	814	n.a.
Shanghai Municipality	Shanghai Machine Tool Factory	Grinding machines	National	2500 grinders	6,000	n.a.
Shanghai Municipality	Commune Rice Mill	Mills rice	Commune	50,000 Cattie per day capacity	Over 30	n.a.
Shanghai Municipality	Commune Agricultural Machinery Factory	3½-h.p. diesel engines, makes and repairs small agricultural equipment, wooden buckets and furniture	Commune	n.a.	200	n.a.
Shanghai Municipality	County Agricultural Machinery Manufacturing and Repair Factory	Rice transplanters	County	1.8 million yuan	450	n.a.
Shanghai Municipality	Street Processing Workshop	Toy assembly and packaging	Cooperative Unit[9]	n.a.[10]	270	n.a.
Shanghai Municipality	Street Processing Workshop	Vacuum pump and meter assembly	Cooperative Unit[9]	n.a.[10]	150	n.a.

Table IV-1 Continued

Location	Name of Plant	Produce	Level	Annual Output 1974	Employment	Construction Costs
Hsun-te County	Tidal Hydroelectric Project	Electric power	County	12 million kw.h.	96[11]	9.7 million yuan
Foshan City	Foshan Pottery Factory	Pottery and porcelain	City	1.5 million yuan	500	n.a.
Nan-hai County	Nan-hai County Cement Factory	Cement	County	103,000 tons	549	8 million yuan

Summary[12]

| | | State Enterprises | | Collectively-Owned | | |
| | | Urban Large-scale | | Rural Small-scale | | |
	Total	National-Provincial-Municipal	County	Commune	Brigade	Street
Factories in Sample	52	14	18	13	5	2
Percent	100	27	35	25	10	4
1. Average Gross Value of Output (Million yuan)		36.6(8)	2.9(10)	0.74(5)	n.a.	n.a.
Standard Error		21.6	1.1	0.2	—	—
2. Average Employment		5110(14)	379(18)	145(10)	15(4)	210(2)
Standard Error		2759	51	22	6	60
3. Average Capital Construction Costs (yuan)		n.a.	3,900,000	n.a.	17,000(1)	n.a.
Standard Error		—	3,900,000	—	—	—
Capital/Output Rates (3/1)		n.a.	1.34	n.a.	n.a.	n.a.
Labor Productivity (1/2)		7162	7652	5103	n.a.	n.a.

1. Includes 10,000 employed in iron mine owned by the factory and 10,000 employed in full-time capital construction.

2. This factory appeared to be run by the county, but we were not told directly that this was the case.

3. Employment in all brigade-operated factories was seasonal, these plants frequently being closed during periods of high-level activity in the fields.

4. This factory began to produce ammonium nitrate and ammonium bicarbonate in 1975.

5. This workshop also was engaged in making their own ballmill for a cement factory that the commune was constructing.

6. Charges processing fee of .01 yuan per kilogram of grain.

7. Workshop also had a foundry and was making turret lathes.

8. Factory supplied cocoons by, and provides silk thread to, the Commerce Department of the City, being paid a processing fee of approximately 10,000 yuan per ton, depending on quality of product.

9. These street processing workshops were part of a large urban housing development; the workers in all shops belonging to the same unit (not clear if unit meant the entire housing development or a lower level grouping) sharing equally in the earnings of all shops.

10. Processing fee paid by factory providing items for processing.

11. This project included navigation and flood control functions in addition to its hydroelectric power generation; only 96 of the 230 employees at this project were engaged directly in the electric generating functions of the project, the others working on operating the locks and in river dredging and maintenance.

12. Number in parenthesis refers to number of factoories used to calculate relevant estimate.

EXPLANATORY NOTES:

The three national plants in Peking were, in varying degrees, also under the jurisdiction of the municipality. The exact extent of the municipal authorities' participation in direction and control (vs. National Ministry direction and control) appeared to be greatest for the optical instruments factory and least significant for the iron and steel factory.

The employment data for these factories includes the entire staff. Not only does this mean that the use in this Chapter of these employment data for calculating worker productivity probably is downward biased due to the inclusion of administrative personnel, but more importantly—as will be pointed out later on in the text—the staff in these factories often included a significant share of the workers who are assigned to construction and maintenance (renovation) work. In other words, unlike many factories in the West, Chinese factories have their own construction crews and workshops producing and repairing fixed capital for the plant. These workers, of course, are not directly engaged in the production of the factories' product and should not be included in calculations of worker productivity for the factory for the purposes of cross-country comparisons.

small-scale industries in Lin County, employing 8500 workers with an annual gross value of output of 41 million yuan, 20 were state owned, i.e., run by the county, and they employed an average of 210 workers with an average annual gross value of output of 1.25 million yuan. Thus, they accounted for 31% of the number of plants, but for 60% of the total output. A second category, described to us as collectively owned, i.e., *owned* by the communes and brigades, but *run* by the county (as mentioned earlier, possibly referring to commune and brigade-operated hydroelectric power stations that had been integrated into the county's electric power network), included 19 plants which employed an average of 137 workers with an average annual gross value output of 579,000 yuan, i.e., they accounted for 29% of the number of plants and 26% of the output. Finally, there were 26 commune-owned and operated, i.e., collectively owned, plants (probably including the brigade-level plants), which employed an average of 62 workers with an average annual gross value output of 192,000 yuan, i.e., accounting for 40% of the number of plants, but only 27% of the output. In Wu-hsi County, the difference in scale between the county-run plants and the collectively owned and operated plants was even more pronounced, the county-run plants accounting for less than 5% of the total number of rural, small-scale industries in the county, but for approximately 50% of the county's gross value of industrial output.

Production teams, of course, also operated sideline "industrial" facilities but these were explicitly not included within the category of rural, small-scale industries for a variety of reasons. Unlike those factories included in the rural, small-scale category, these production team sideline "industrial" facilities are not included in the state plan, and their production is not subject to the states' allocative mechanism, i.e., they are an integral part of the production team's production and consumption activities. As far as the higher administrative levels are concerned, we were told, the production team is not assigned any industrial production responsibility. Its primary function is agricultural production and husbandry, although it is also called upon to provide its quota of labor for construction projects and industrial plants undertaken at higher levels.

Our sample also must be seen in the context of the historical development of small-scale industry in China. China's small-scale industries fall into three groups: enterprises whose origins lie in handicraft workshops established prior to 1949; enterprises founded during 1958–60 under the impetus of the Great Leap Forward policy of encouraging local industrialization particularly in iron and steel, but also in other sections as well; and finally, units established during the resurgence of small-scale industrial growth, which began around 1963 and has continued to the present time.[3]

3. Although the policy decision to reactivate the small-scale industry campaign occurred in 1963, the actual resurgence of small-scale industries on a broad scale occurred in 1968 and 1969.

With these diverse origins, it is natural to expect wide variation in the timing, pace, and pattern of industrial development in different localities. Some areas enjoy the advantage of proximity to regions of considerable pre-1949 industrial development. Different localities attained unequal success in establishing new industries during 1958-60 and in maintaining them during the subsequent period of restriction, which saw many small plants shut down, often permanently. During the past decade, emphasis on local self-reliance has favored areas with substantial industrial experience, natural, technical, and entrepreneurial resources and agricultural surpluses.

At the enterprise level, there is similar scope for variation based on historical background, resource conditions, the degree of specialization permitted by local market conditions, and the presence or absence of various forms of external assistance.

The regions and enterprises which we visited varied widely with regard to past industrial experience, ranging from Shanghai and Canton, where machine shops and other small workshops appeared before 1900, to northern Honan, which developed little industry before 1949. On the other hand, it seems reasonable to assume that the localities and units visited are well endowed with material resources and entrepreneurial initiative.

Except for large, urban factories, the overall industrial development of the localities which we visited appeared to be closely linked to the local farm economy. Most of these areas inherited agriculturally linked handicraft cooperatives, but output expansion of this section was not a significant facet of economic policy, and these small, rural enterprises were largely isolated from the centrally-directed industrial economy prior to 1957. Finally, the industrial aspects of the Great Leap of 1958-60 can be viewed as a premature effort to link large and small-scale industry which, despite its failure, achieved further consolidation of existing handicraft production, established some enterprises and provided industrial training and experience, which has contributed to the subsequent success of small-scale plants.

AGRICULTURAL MACHINERY INDUSTRY

Of all the industries surveyed by our delegation, none begin to approach the complexity of the agricultural machinery industry in three fundamental dimensions of economic analysis: (1) level of organizational control, (2) diversity of products, and (3) mode of operation. In just 28 days, we visited two plants at the Provincial (Special Municipal) level, five at the county level, eight at the commune level, and two at the brigade level (See Table IV-1). In general, the level of organization closely mirrored the level of product distribution, but it was not always a reliable guide to either diversity of products being manufactured, nor to sophistication of manufacturing capability and technique. We observed a commune workshop trial-producing a 10 h.p., 4-wheel tractor with techniques not unlike those used in a county factory producing 10 h.p. crawler tractors. We saw a commune "agricultural" machinery workshop producing 5600 kw. oil-cooled transformers in one building, large rotary presses in a second building, and a mini-van in a third!

Even with comprehensive data on a consistent basis and adequate time for econometric analysis, this industry would not lend itself to formal judgments about economic and technical efficiency. In the present context, all that will be attempted is a set of summary impressions "documented" by examples. Some of these impressions are strong and likely to withstand the observations of previous and subsequent visitors. Others are offered as plausible hypotheses.

The multi-tiered organizational structure of the agricultural machinery industry has been consciously fostered by encouragement and permissiveness from the top and adopted with considerable enthusiasm from below. Perhaps more than any other industry, it typifies the desired characteristics in a small-scale, rural industry: (1) It is specifically designed to serve agriculture and to be served by agriculture in turn. At all levels our briefers emphasized this orientation, and by and large the products being manufactured were well adapted to assisting mechanization of the local agriculture. (2) The principle of "walking on two legs" was constantly, almost stereotypically, visible. It was the rule in all plants at the city level and below to see very large, complex machine tools—some imported, but most of domestic manufacture—being used in the same room where a blacksmith would be pounding out small parts on an anvil, or a row of workers would be sitting on the dirt floor assembling parts with an adjustable wrench. If a complex machine tool from above the organizational level was required to make the machine, it was somehow provided. But if a primitive technique would suffice, at the lower levels it was almost invariably used. (3) The degree of "self-reliance" was high, but not absurd. Especially at the county level, it was very common for factories to equip themselves with nearly all the basic machine tools; they quite literally made their own lathes, milling machines, rotary presses, and so on. But if a sophisticated inclined rotary gear cutter or a high-tolerance finish grinder was required, a way was found to bring one in from outside the factory, although surprisingly often such items came from within the county or district. One county tractor factory actually had a subsidiary production line making hydraulically controlled semiautomated lathes to be put on their own production line. This "making your own machines to make machines" theme, although usually not carried to such a sophisticated level, was constantly seen at all levels of production. (4) The agricultural machinery industry has been the major diffuser of technology to the countryside via both a direct training effect and a considerable demonstration effect. Indeed, a reasonably strong argument can be made that the major contribution of the agricultural machinery industry to Chinese society has not been through any direct impact on agricultural production, but has been through an indirect process of "scientification" of the rural masses. A hand tractor imported from Japan would have the same physical productivity as one made in China, but it would certainly not have the same impact as one made in a brigade or commune machine shop where every peasant knows someone who helped build it. By pushing the production of particular agricultural machinery all the way to the brigade level, China has removed the "foreignness" from new technology. Not only will this speed adoption of the technology, but the presence of the factory and machine shop locally means spare parts, and repairs are readily available. The level of utilization of machinery produced locally is thus likely to be far higher than of machinery imported from higher levels or from abroad for which no such capability exists. (5) A mirror-image of the technology-to-the-masses feature of the industry is that the masses can more easily make known their technological requirements. In a country as large and diverse as China no research institute in Peking will be able to design machines suitable for all environments and conditions. Local production facilities coupled with design inputs from two directions have largely alleviated this problem. Assistance from above for basic designs is readily available—e.g., for 12 h.p. diesel engines—or for electric motors and pumps. From below comes a flow of comments and suggestions as to how trial machines perform and what tasks need to be mechanized. The local factories, especially the commune level machine shops, seem ideally suited to wed these two inputs into locally adapted machines. (6) Finally, partly as a consequence of a number of the above aspects of the industry, an enormous flexibility exists at the county level agricultural machines plants and below. It is possible to stop producing high-pressure pumps and start producing crawler tractors, because none of the equipment is specialized. With a single example and a little patience in the foundry, almost any casting can be produced. Standard lathes, milling machines, etc., can produce a wide variety of machined parts, and workers with an adjustable wrench are remarkably flexible in their assembly capability. Some comments about the efficiency of this approach are made shortly, but there can be no question that flexibility is a highly desirable trait when producing for a local market that is fairly quickly saturated with any single piece of simple machinery.

SUMMARY OF DATA

Table IV-2 provides a rough summary of the enterprises we visited and an evaluation of the level of technology employed in various activities. (When available, employment and gross value of output data for these plants are presented in Table IV-1 and wage data for these plants are presented in Table III-1.) The number of workers was seldom a sensitive issue although seasonality in the work force in the lower-level operations presents serious problems of comparability. Gross value of output figures were frequently unavailable, and average wages were available only for those operations paying cash wages instead of workpoints, which basically means county level plants and above. The level of manufacturing technique was judged impressionistically for four sub-categories of agricultural machinery manufacture (and repair): foundry, machine shop and metal processing, fabrication and forming, and final assembly. Four levels of technique were used in the assessment corresponding to (1) "modern," (2) "intermediate: modern," (3) "intermediate: primitive," and (4) "primitive." We had no quantitative basis for assigning these values—they were impressionistic only and based on comparative personal experience.

The table bears out a number of observations noted in the previous section, especially the increasing diversity of products as the level of organization moves from national to production brigade (although there is significant variation around this trend). Commensurate with the increasing specialization at higher levels is an increase in modernness of manufacturing technique. Only at the highest level is foundry technique modernized—all other levels maintained considerable flexibility in their foundry at significant short-run cost in terms of labor, fuel and raw materials (the static and dynamic efficiency of this approach will be considered shortly). Similarly, machinery and metal processing did not achieve modern standards until a relatively high degree of product specialization also was achieved. Even in sophisticated county- and city-operated plants, the rule was to see banks of machine tools of varying sophistication, such as lathes, milling machinery, shapers, gear cutters, and grinders, machining individual parts to man-controlled tolerances. Automated and semiautomated machining occurred only rarely, and then usually in combination with a considerable nonautomated machining capability as well. Fabrication techniques were always the least advanced of the four categories in any factory. They never achieved modern standards and were frequently crude and makeshift. This area especially demonstrated the "two legs" principle. Fabrication seldom needed to be to close tolerances and consequently labor intensive methods sufficed. Where close tolerances were required, as in many machine parts, modern and even semiautomated machine tools were used, even at the lowest organization level. Similar things can be said about assembly techniques. Although three plants are listed as "modern" in this regard, none of them would be considered as advanced by current Western standards. These three were placed in this category to indicate moving assembly lines with air wrenches and similar modern assembly devices.

Table IV-2 shows a fairly strong tendency for techniques across the board to become more modern as organizational and market level rises. The tendency is not uniform, however, and certain processes, especially machine processing and fabrication techniques, do not fit well at all. Machine processing technique was more uniform than expected, with relatively sophisticated equipment at low levels and surprisingly unsophisticated equipment at some (but not all) higher levels. Here dynamic efficiency considerations about long-lived (and relatively flexible) machines must have played a role in choice of technique. Fabrication, on the other hand, requires great flexibility if product mix is going to change. Modern fabricating techniques require large investments in highly specialized machines, which in the Chinese context would probably be used a short time only (relative to the physical life of the machine). These the Chinese evidently felt they could do without.

A more general impression was that the rural agricultural machinery factories, especially below the county level, used somewhat more capital and considerably more raw materials than expected based on the reasoning outlined above. The capital was primarily in the machining stage and, as noted, a good deal of it was locally produced. The large, perhaps excessive, use of raw materials was due to the relatively primitive techniques being used in the foundry and fabricating stages. Fuel consumption in particular seemed likely to be high by modern standards. But there are plausible explanations for apparent inefficiencies, and Figure IV-3 attempts to present an analytical framework for the discussion.

The basic assumption underlying Figure IV-3 is that a minimum feasible scale exists for industrial production of any significant type of output. Although it is perhaps possible to build a tractor in the backyard with a hammer and chisel, in fact some minimum scale is necessary, perhaps a trial production of 50 or so, to make the effort worthwhile. Thus, the partial isoquant shown in Figure IV-3a–d, is the same as in Figure IV-1, except that the modern technique is off the scale, and the quantity of industrial output is now defined to be the *minimum* feasible scale of output instead of a unit of output. Higher isoquants are possible and would simply mean greater output than the feasible minimum. They would not imply technical inefficiency. Indeed, if the minimum feasible isoquant represented 100 tractors, for example, the isoquant for 200 tractors would be twice as far from the origin (measured along any ray) as the 100 tractor isoquant, if there were no economies of scale. This is, of course, quite unlikely, and for at least a certain range of possible output, the isoquants for equal increments of tractors would probably nest closer and closer together, until all economies of scale were realized. Beyond this the isoquants would space out again if diseconomies of scale set in.

The point of the argument is merely to emphasize that in Figure IV-3a, only combinations of capital/raw materials and labor that reach or exceed the isoquant make the production of industrial output possible. If the state allocates a locality capital and raw materials equal to C' and the available labor is L' (as in Figure IV-3a), then production of the desired industrial output is no problem. The minimum feasible isoquant could be reached using technique I-M (with some labor left over), or alternatively a higher level of output might be achieved by using I-P and more of the available

Table IV-2

SUMMARY EVALUATION OF TECHNICAL LEVEL IN THE AGRICULTURAL MACHINERY INDUSTRY

Organization	Name of Facility	Products	Foundry	Machine Shop	Fabrication	Assembly
State or Municipal	Peking Internal Combustion Engine Factory	4-cylinder diesel and gasoline engines	M	M	I-M	M
	Shanghai (Bumper Harvest) Tractor Factory	35-h.p., 4-wheel tractors	—	I-M	I-M	I-M
County	Hsi-yang County Tractor Factory	10-h.p. crawler tractors; high-pressure pumps	I-P	I-M	P	P
	Hsi-yang Country Farm Tools Factory	Threshers, concrete pipe, miscellaneous agricultural implements	P	I-P	P	P
	Lin County Tung-fang-hung Agricultural Machinery Factory	12-h.p. walking tractors, drop-hammers, agricultural implements	I-P	I-P	I-P	P
	Wu-hsi County Tractor Factory	12-h.p. walking tractors	—	M	I-M	I-M
	Chia-ting County Agricultural Machinery Manufacturing and Repair Factory	Rice transplanters, 2 cyl., 18-h.p. diesel engines (trial)	None	I-M	I-P	I-P
People's Commune	Red Star Commune Farm Machinery Manufacturing and Repair Shop (near Peking)	Large threshers, miscellaneous repairs	—	I-P	I-P	P
	Yao-ts'un Commune Agricultural Machinery Factory (Lin County)	Threshers, electric motors and pumps, miscellaneous implements	I-P	I-P	I-P	P

	Products				
Kao-chuang Commune Agricultural Machinery Manufacturing and Repair Factory (near Hsin-hsiang)	Water pumps, threshers, ball mill for cement plant	I-P	I-P	I-P	F
Ch'i-li-ying Commune Agricultural Machinery Manufacturing and Repair Factory (near Hsin-hsiang)	Agricultural implements; 10-h.p., 4-wheel tractors (trial)	I-P	I-P	P	F
Yang-shih Commune Agricultural Machinery Manufacturing and Repair Factory (near Wu-hsi)	Oil-cooled transformers, rotary presses, and mini-van	I-P	I-P	I-P	I-P
Mei-ts'un Commune Agricultural Machinery Factory (near Wu-hsi)	Rice transplanters; miscellaneous agricultural implements; lathes	—	I-M	I-P	I-P
Ho-lieh Commune Agricultural Machinery Factory (near Wu-hsi)	Rice transplanters; agricultural implements; parts for assembly	I-P	I-M	P	P
Ma-lu Commune Agricultural Machinery Factory (near Shanghai)	Rice transplanters, 3.5-h.p. diesel engine (trial); small implements	P	I-P	P	P
People's Communes Production Brigades — Liu-chuang Brigade Agricultural Machinery Manufacturing and Repair Factory (Ch'i-li-ying Commune)	Small agricultural tools and implements	P	I-P	P	P
Ho-lieh Brigade Agricultural Machinery Repair Station (Ho-lieh Commune, near Wu-hsi)	Agricultural repairs, small implements	—	—	—	—

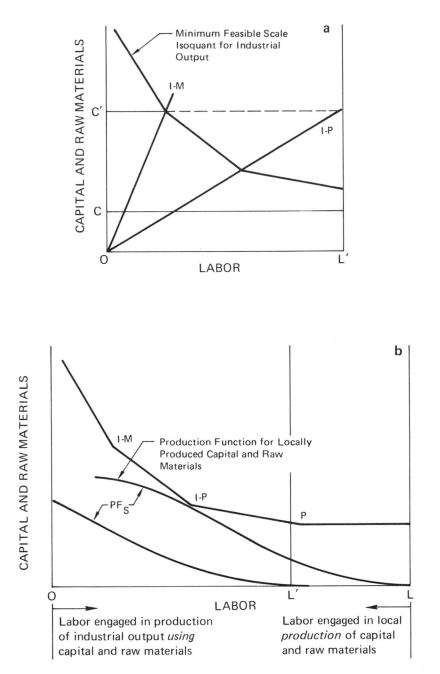

FIGURE IV-3. Production functions for agricultural machinery plants.

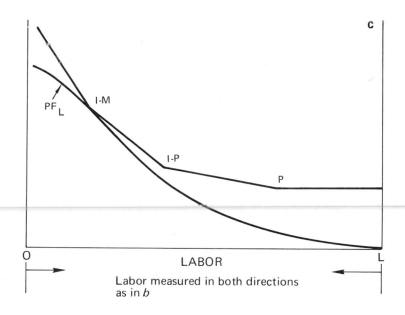

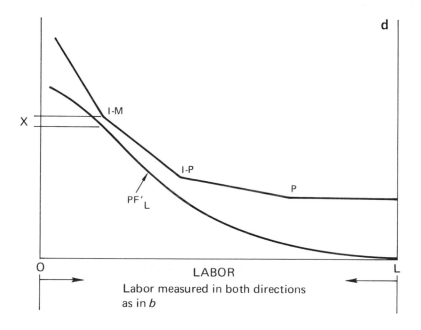

labor. But what is the locality to do if the state can allocate only C of capital and raw materials, which might be its "fair" share if the nation's national resources were equally divided, or even provided no capital and raw materials at all on the grounds that the national industries can make more effective use of nationally available resources? This is the question Figure IV-3a–d is primarily designed to answer. Most localities have been strongly encouraged by national policy to emphasize self-reliance in industrial expansion. This means finding local sources for the capital and raw materials that might otherwise have been allocated by the state, since a local labor supply already exists. Depending on the local natural resources and initiative, some production function for locally produced capital and raw materials will exist using primarily local labor as an input. One such local production function is shown in Figure IV-3b as L'PF$_S$. The output of capital and raw materials is read on the left vertical axis, while the labor input is measured from L' toward the left. It is clear that with only OL' total labor supply and local resources providing a production function such as L'PF$_S$, that even maximum local production of local capital and raw materials will be insufficient to reach the minimum feasible industrial isoquant, assuming both production functions are operated simultaneously.

The solution in this instance is to somehow expand the labor force available locally. Although this sounds almost foolish given much of rural China's factor endowment, the actual fact is that primary attention in agricultural mechanization has been placed on precisely those tasks that are inordinately labor absorbing and which could free large quantities of productive labor if mechanized or semi-mechanized. Thus, grain processing—wheat, rice, and corn milling—tends to be the first task mechanized. A single example can illustrate the gains in labor potentially available for other productive tasks: hand-pounding rice was reported to take two hours for 5 kg. per person, or 400 man-hours per ton. A simple pedal operated device can do 25 kg. in three hours, or 120 man-hours per ton. A commune-run rice mill produces 25 tons per eight-hour day with 30 workers, which works out to about 10 man-hours per ton. And larger mills can reduce that even further. Thus a 25-ton-per-day rice mill, operating 200 days per year, requires 50,000 man-hours compared with 2,000,000 that would be required to mill the rice by hand.

The effect is substantial and becomes even more so when mechanized threshing and spinning are added to the list. In fact, since Liberation, many millions of man-days of (mostly female) labor have become available for more productive work than primitive agricultural processing. This would be a hollow gain if no productive opportunities existed for these workers, but Figure IV-3b demonstrates how a goodly proportion of them have been put to productive use. By shifting the total labor supply from OL' to OL, the capital/raw materials production function also shifts to the right. And although nothing has happened to increase local natural resources *or* the productivity of labor, the additional *quantity* of labor has a dramatic effect. The production function LPF$_S$ now touches the minimum feasible industrial isoquant at technique I-P, and so it now becomes possible for the locality to produce its desired industrial output, e.g., tractors, by relying on its own resources and with no assistance from the state (perhaps apart from the engineering knowledge implicit in knowing about the industrial production techniques and possibly about the ways to exploit local raw materials as well).

Thus, Figure IV-3b can explain how labor intensive exploitation of local natural resources can lead to local labor intensive production of industrial output while maintaining full self-reliance. But other possibilities exist also and they are perhaps even more interesting. Consider a locality with somewhat greater natural resources, but which are harder to obtain. Thus, production function LPF$_L$ in Figure IV-3c shows more capital/raw materials being potentially available, but at a substantially greater cost in labor than in the previous example. That is, labor productivity may be lower in LPF$_L$ than in LPF$_S$, but more labor can be productively utilized before zero marginal productivity sets in (the production function becomes flat on top), and more capital/raw materials can be produced. The apparently paradoxical result is that this locality can, and should, use the *more* modern, capital/raw material intensive industrial process precisely because it *saves labor,* labor which is needed to produce the very capital/raw materials it needs in more abundance than in the I-P process. Of course, other functions can be drawn with other lessons—even contradictory to these. But, the lessons of LPF$_L$, I-M and LPF$_S$, I-P were demonstrated in concrete terms in the local industries the group saw.

Lastly, Figure IV-3d, also illustrates the often critical contribution made by the state to local industrial production. While the rhetoric of self-reliance and keeping the initiative in local hands is clear, powerful and by and large effective, no agricultural machinery factory visited at any level made *all* its own equipment. Critical pieces of sophisticated, close tolerance machinery somehow found their way to the appropriate place. On the other hand, we never saw entire factories supplied by the state either. The situation is perhaps best summed up by the production function labeled PF$_K$'L in Figure IV-3d. Here the local capability to produce capital/raw materials from their own resources falls just short (by the amount "X") of the amount needed to reach industrial capacity at I-M. At such a point the state seemed entirely willing to provice the critical "X" input (usually after being paid) and thus make the difference between production and no production. It may even be that the state finds such a situation entirely desirable.

AGRICULTURAL PROCESSING

Agricultural processing in urban centers is vastly different from agricultural processing in the rural areas. The differences are most obvious in scale of operation and technologies used, both for grain and textiles, but the differences go much deeper than that. The ultimate source of the differences lies in the nature of the market served and the primary role of each factory in the local economy.

Rural agricultural processing is based, as earlier arguments have indicated, on the need to generate substantial surpluses of (mostly female) labor that were previously trapped in the very low productivity tasks of hand spinning and weaving and hand pounding or milling of grain. Our observations, although limited, tend to confirm a number of hypotheses about this sector:

1. The equipment used is "low technology." That is, the machinery is small-scale, usually produced within the county or district. The quality of the finished product is only slightly higher than that of the hand-produced version.

2. The process is labor intensive by Western standards for these products, but is still enormously labor saving relative to the primitive hand methods for which the substitution was made. The labor time freed for the entire country must now total in the hundreds of millions of man days. In Lin County alone, for instance, a spinning facility saved 800,000 man days of labor compared to the traditional hand-spinning.

3. The rural grain processing facilities operate almost exclusively to meet local needs. There seems to be very little marketing of *processed* grain from rural areas to urban centers. Somewhat more interchange of processed fiber seems to take place, with spun cotton going up the marketing system, and woven cloth coming back down.

By contrast, the large-scale processing facilities were exclusively in the urban centers and were more "modern" by Western standards.

4. That is, the urban facilities were much more capital intensive with more sophisticated equipment capable of producing a much higher quality and more uniform product.

5. The sophisticated machinery is made in national centers or imported.

6. Perhaps most importantly, the markets served by the modern, high technology mills are almost exclusively urban or export, with only small amounts of textiles returning to the rural areas and almost no milled grain.

To the extent that these hypotheses are valid, they argue that competition between the small-scale rural processing facilities and the large-scale urban facilities is very limited at the present time. Although they both produce the same type of output—milled grain or flour and spun fiber—the lack of common markets reduces competitive pressures. (In the Chinese context, of course, these pressures would show up in losses for rural mills if urban products were priced on a cost basis.) The shortage of transportation facilities and their consequent high opportunity cost reinforce this conclusion.

But in a more fundamental sense the two basically different sectors are or shortly will be competing with each other for scarce resources. Manpower productivity is higher in the more sophisticated facilities; so is the technical conversion rate. As back-transportation to rural areas becomes cheaper and more available, the larger urban mills will find it possible to offer a consistently higher quality product at lower cost than the rural facilities will be able to offer. At this point local self-sufficiency and initiative will have visible economic costs relative to centralization. Their continuation will require conscious decisions on the part of China's planners so that the benefits of rural small-scale processing facilities outweigh the costs and thus should be protected. Otherwise they will wither away as in all other modern societies.

It is not difficult to identify these benefits. It is nearly impossible to quantify them. Local self-sufficiency in a country as large and diverse as China should have positive effects even after transportation and communications integrate the country much more thoroughly than is now possible. It is not clear that the higher and more consistent quality of sophisticated mills has any significant welfare contribution even if their products tend to command higher prices in international markets. Such markets are not perfect and tend to reflect the purchasing power of Western consuming countries whose values the Chinese reject anyway. High extraction un-bleached flour characteristic of the village mills contains more nutrients than the flour typically produced by more sophisticated mills. Cotton material from rural looms may not be smooth and fine count, but it may be just as durable as that from high-speed looms in urban factories. In short, the higher labor productivity and technical efficiency of large-scale urban mills may not be sufficient to offset the political and social advantages of small-scale rural mills. If this is the case, then the dual structure of China's agricultural processing industry will exist indefinitely. Because of China's ability to separate productivity from personal income there is no consequent implication that rural incomes, or more particularly rural industrial workers' incomes, must also lag significantly behind urban industrial workers' incomes. It is this capability, of course, that will make it possible for China to prevent the extinction of the rural agricultural processing industry in the face of the technical superiority of the urban industry.

While reasonable and supported by our observations, discussions and prior and subsequent reading, these hypotheses and conclusions are based on a very small sample of actual facilities inspected (see Table IV-3). Based on our observations in the plants shown in the table and other discussions, we have a fairly strong impression that mechanized rural grain milling is almost universally done in very small facilities on a fee basis. The proportion of agricultural output still processed more or less by hand is hard to judge but our impression is that grain milling is one of the very first processes to be mechanized, along with cotton spinning where this is important. The scope for raising labor productivity by eliminating these hand tasks is

Table IV-3

AGRICULTURAL PROCESSING INDUSTRY

Organization	Location	Type of Product	Extraction Rate	Capacity (tph)	Processing Charge (yuan/kg.)	Technology
Red Star Commune	Peking	Milled animal feed	—	6.25	—	I-M
Ta-ts'ai-yuan Brigade of Ch'eng-kuan People's Commune	Lin County	Wheat, flour	87.5%	1.00	0.02	I-P
Lin County Cotton Textile Factory	Lin County	Cotton	—	—	0.02 (spinning)	I-P
Ch'i-li-ying Brigade of Ch'i-li-ying Commune	Hsin-hsiang	Corn, wheat, flour	85.0%	0.40	0.02	I-P
Hsin-hsiang Cotton Textile Factory	Hsin-hsiang	Cotton, synthetic woven and knitted goods	—	—	—	I-M
Cheng-chou #3 Cotton Textile Factory	Cheng-chou	Cotton, yarn and cloth	—	—	—	M
Cheng-chou Wheat Flour Mill (from road only)	Cheng-chou	Wheat, flour	—	16.70	—	—
Wu-hsi City Silk Filiature Factory	Wu-hsi	Silk thread	—	65.00 kg./hr.	10.00	I-M

NOTE: Where available, employment, investment, and gross value of output data for these plants are presented in Table IV-1.

enormous. Even carrying rocks and dirt with shoulder poles for irrigation ditches or rebuilding farmland is more productive than hand-pounding or milling grain. Also, grain milling is part of the stream of final consumption while carrying dirt, etc. is part of investment.

By virtue of this reasoning plus our own observations we feel that a sizeable proportion of production brigades seem to have mills for the primary food grain raised locally while a single commune mill would process the "secondary" grain, as in the Red Star Commune near Peking. Where a single grain such as rice predominated, the following situation on a suburban commune near Shanghai may be typical: The commune operated one rice mill with a capacity of about 3 TPH, requiring thirty workers per shift. Five of the fourteen Production Brigades also operated smaller rice mills, each with a capacity of about 1/3 to 1/2 TPH. Brigades without rice mills took their grain to the Commune for processing, or to the other Brigades on a space-available basis. Presumably a fee was charged for this service.

The rationality of this type of arrangement is obvious. Excess capacity is a chronic problem when investment in small-scale milling facilities is accomplished through private market incentives. The Commune and Brigade milling centers seem able to avoid this problem by suitable sharing of the harvest. Further, the higher level of technology possible with a Commune mill, because it has a larger guaranteed source of supply, enables a gradual approach to modernization and technical sophistication to be taken. As experience and technical expertise are gained with the 3 TPH mill, for instance, it should be possible to develop larger and more sophisticated mills, and to phase out gradually the small, technically inefficient Brigade mills or return to them for peak periods only.

The Cheng-chou wheat flour mill shown in Table IV-3 was observed only from the road, and was the only urban grain processing facility for which any information was obtained. A six-story milling facility was attached to thirty-six concrete storage silos, each about 6 m. in diameter and 20-25 m. height. The complex was located on a major rail siding in Cheng-chou, which is itself a major rail intersection of North-South and East-West traffic. Inquiry revealed that the daily milling capacity was 800,000 chin, or 400 tons, in 24 hours. Since the population of Cheng-chou was reported to be about 800,000, and an approximate estimate of daily per capita wheat consumption would be about 0.5 kg. (1.0 chin), the daily wheat flour consumption of the city would be exactly the listed capacity of the plant. If we assume that one cubic meter of wheat weighs about 0.8 tons, then the storage capacity of the silos is between 16,000 and 20,000 tons—40 to 50 days milling requirements if the mill runs at full reported capacity (as it would need to in order to supply the city). These calculations thus imply substantial up-country storage capacity (or flow of imported wheat from the coastal port), since the entire silo storage capacity must be turned over eight to nine times per year for this mill to meet the city's consumption requirements. If this reasoning is approximately correct, it further confirms the hypothesis that there is at present little real competition between the large, modern urban processing facilities serving the urban population and the small rural processing facilities serving the local population.

RURAL, SMALL-SCALE CEMENT PLANTS

Rural, small-scale cement plants have been an important feature of China's efforts to develop rural, local industry ever since the late 1950s.[4] At the time of our visit there were 2800 rural, small-scale cement plants located in 80% of China's counties and accounting for more than half of China's total output of cement. We were able to visit three of these cement plants, all at the county level, too small a number for definitive conclusions, but enough to get a general picture of some of the goals in this sector.

The case for the economic rationality of these rural, small-scale cement plants is simple and overwhelming. The widespread effort to develop and harness sources of water for the purpose of irrigation, the prevention of floods, for rural electrification, and for all types of construction work in the agricultural sector, has generated a tremendous demand for cement in the rural areas of China. This demand has not only exceeded the supply made available by the output of large-scale cement plants in the modern sector, but the transport costs involved in shipping this cement to many rural areas would be prohibitive.[5] To take an example given to us, a major irrigation project in Shansi Province, which was undertaken for the purpose of irrigating a large area of cultivated, but dry and drought-susceptible fields, was estimated to require 20,000 tons of cement. The cost, including transport costs, of this cement, if supplied by the nearest large-scale, modern

4. Estimates prepared within the U.S. Government for the share of rural, small-scale cement plants in China's total output of cement are listed here:

Year	Percent	Year	Percent	Year	Percent
1957	Negligible	1963	27	1969	30
1958	13	1964	20	1970	30 (40)
1959	14 (14)	1965	26	1971	40 (44)
1960	25	1966	26	1972	48 (48)
1961	25	1967	25	1973	50 (50)
1962	26	1968	27	1974	52

Source: CIA, *Peoples Republic of China: Handbook of Economic Indicators*, A(ER)75-72, August 1975, p. 12. The percentages in parentheses are those presented by Jon Sigurdson in "Rural Industrialization in China," *op. cit.*, and are said to be based on figures and percentages published in the Chinese news media.

5. In his discussion of the rationalization for creating rural, small-scale cement plants, Sigurdson argues, "There can be no doubt that the high transport costs, in the absence of

cement plant, would have been over 1.6 million yuan. To significantly reduce
build a rural, small-scale cement plant with a capacity of several thousand
tons. The cost per ton of the cement produced by this local plant was
approximately 25% below the delivered cost of cement from the nearest
modern-sector plant and, therefore, the local small-scale cement plant would
"pay-for-itself" after producing only 10,000 tons. Furthermore, once the
water conservancy project was completed, the local area had a local source
of cement for other farm construction projects.

The water conservancy projects we were shown almost everywhere we
went in China's countryside are a vital prerequisite to China's attempt to
secure high and stable yields in agriculture. Thus, the benefits of these rural,
small-scale cement plants are quite high.[6] On the cost side, under the
this cost, 200,000 yuan of the water conservancy project funds were used to
realistic assumption that the central government and modern sector would
find it difficult to mobilize local funds, poor quality raw materials, and
agricultural labor which are used in these plants, it is difficult to think of a
more productive use for these resources. Thus, there can be little doubt that
the benefits far outweigh the costs.

A detailed description of the technology adopted and an analysis of
how effectively it is used in these rural, small-scale cement plants is the
subject of a later chapter of this report, and only a brief summary of our
most important impressions and conclusions regarding this subject are
presented here. (For a summary of the economic and technical information
we were able to obtain for the cement plants visited, see Table IV-4.) Despite
the great emphasis given to indigenous solution of technological problems
and the role of local innovation in producing the equipment required in the
rural, small-scale industries and our observing examples of this in several
plants we visited in other industries, the technology utilized in the rural,
small-scale cement plants is both widely known and has been widely used

railways or waterways, has been a significant factor in the Chinese emphasis of local manufacture in relatively small plants." Sigurdson, *op. cit.*, p. 427. According to Sigurdson's
estimates, even if a large-scale, modern cement plant were built in the center of a nine-county
area, its cost of production would need to be more than 12.70 yuan lower per ton than rural,
small-scale cement plants located in each county to offset transport costs if trucks were used
for transportation and more than 21.70 yuan lower per ton if horsecarts were used. Sigurdson
believes it unlikely that the cost differences between the rural, small-scale plants and the
large-scale, modern plants are this large.

6. The provision of cement for local farm construction and irrigation projects, formerly
prohibited by the high transport costs involved in obtaining cement from the urban, large-scale,
modern sector, is only one benefit of the output of these plants. Another, and equally
important benefit, is the substitution of the locally produced cement for the cement that was
supplied by the urban, large-scale, modern sector, i.e., cement actually allocated to the rural
sector despite the relatively high transport costs. This substitution made available a larger
share of the higher quality cement produced in the urban, large-scale, modern sector for use
in the nonrural sector of the economy.

Table IV-4

ECONOMIC AND TECHNICAL INFORMATION FOR CEMENT PLANTS VISITED

	Tachai Cement Plant	Hui County Cement Plant	Nan-hai County Cement Plant
Location	Eastern Shansi, South of the Yang River	Northern Honan, north of Hsin-hsiang	Central Kwangtung, west of Canton
Origin	Started operation, 1968	Started operation, 1964[1]	Began construction, 1958 Started operation, 1960
Development	Output 1968 3,500 tons 1969 7,000 tons 1970 10,300 tons 1971 12,000 tons 1972 14,000 tons 1974 20,000 tons	Output 1974, Planned 40,000 tons Actual 50,000 tons Output 1975, (Jan.-May), 40,000 tons	Output 1960 7,500 tons 1963 32,000 tons 1969 64,000 tons 1974 103,000 tons 1975 120,000 tons Target 1975 Actual 1975 (Jan.-June) 58,000 tons
Product	Mark 400. Packaged in 50 kg. bags.[2] Selling Price: 38 yuan per ton Distribution: 80% for farmland capital construction, 20% urban construction	90% shipped in bulk. 90% for farmland capital construction	Pearl River (possolan) cement Mark 400 Packaged in 50 kg. bags Shipped mostly by boat
Inputs	Anthracite coal, limestone, clay, iron ore	Bituminous coke, limestone, clay, iron ore	Coal, limestone, clay, iron powder
Investment	350,000 yuan	n.a.	5 million yuan (cumulative) 3 million yuan provided by province 2 million yuan provided by region and county
Equipment	1 Crusher grinding mill 1 Vertical shaft kiln[3]	8 grinding mills 6 underground egg kilns	5 grinding mills 2 vertical shaft kilns
Labor Force	144 workers 3 shifts	500 workers (15% women)	549 workers 3 shifts

1. Started with 27 workers and investment of 1,700 yuan. Produced 4 tons a day.
2. Some output shipped in bulk.
3. Plant was in process of constructing a second vertical shaft kiln.

for producing cement throughout the world.[7] Furthermore, much of the equipment itself is provided by the modern sector. The reason for the adoption of this standard, well-known technology is quite simple. A single homogeneous product is being produced, and the process of production consists of two basic steps—the preparation of the fuel in crushers and ball mills and the burning of the fuel in the kiln. This equipment can be made in China and is supplied by both large-scale machinery factories in the modern sector or produced at the local level. For example, we visited a commune machine shop which was machining and assembling a small ball mill to be used in a rural, small-scale cement plant the commune was building.

Moreover, the technology adopted in these rural, small-scale cement plants is quite normal for plants producing at this scale. It represents a very mechanized process of production, and these plants are well equipped to produce cement by means of this technology. A major feature of this technology is that the machines do the producing, and labor has little to do with it; i.e., once filled to capacity, these machines must be operated at that pace which produces the correct size feed (the ball mills) and obtains a uniform and thorough burning of the feed (the kiln). The inputs are put into these machines, and cement comes out at the end of this process. Any attempt to insert too much or too little of the input or to operate the machines too fast or too slow only ruins the final product.

As can be seen in Table IV-4, the county cement plants we visited varied greatly in size, when size is measured by output or employment. The smallest plant had an annual output of 20,000 tons (1974), and the largest an output of 100,000 tons. The third plant had an output of 50,000 tons. The quality of the output, of course, depends on the quality of the inputs used. Because these plants are utilizing local sources of limestone, clay, coke, and iron ore of relatively poor quality, the quality of the cement being produced is not terribly high (the question of cement quality is discussed further in Chapter

7. The three different types of technology used (running from small-scale, primitive to large-scale, more modern) in the plants we visited were: (a) ground level kilns, i.e., egg shaped kilns at Hui County Cement Plant, with an output of 4 tons per day, (b) stationary vertical shaft kilns, i.e., those at Hui County Cement Plant (1.5 x 7.0 m.), with an output of 3 tons per hour, and those at Nan-hai County Cement Plant (2.5 x 9.1 m.), with an output of 6 tons per hour, and (c) mechanized shaft kilns, i.e., those at Hui County Cement Plant (2.5 x 10 m.) with an output of 8 tons per hour. These examples, of course, are taken from the limited number of plants we visited and probably are not illustrative of the typical differences in productivity between these three types of technology. According to Sigurdson, commune level cement plants with an intermittent production of 200–5000 tons per year use small stationary vertical kilns, county level cement plants with an intermittent production of less than 15,000 tons per year use ground level kilns, region and county level plants with continuous production of 10,000 to 50,000 tons a year use large stationary vertical shaft kilns, and national and provincial level cement plants with continuous production of over 150,000 tons a year use mechanized kilns. Sigurdson, *op. cit.,* p. 424.

VII). Nonetheless, we judged the quality of the cement being produced as quite adequate for most rural water conservancy and farm construction. At one plant we visited, slag from a local iron and steel plant was being added to the cement being produced, increasing the volume of the produce by some 30–40% of the volume of final product. Although the addition of some slag or slag and clinker does reduce the strength of the cement, the reduction in quality is very slight compared to the increase in volume, with the final product being adequate for its intended use in rural construction. In the smallest plant we visited, 90% of the output was shipped in bulk and about 80% of the output went to rural areas, 20% to urban areas. In another county visited, some of the output of the local rural, small-scale cement plant was used in a nearby rural, small-scale cement products plant to make telephone poles and preformed slabs and bars, which had been formed on taut-drawn (prestressed) steel rods (although these were really not pulled very taut in the plant we visited) to increase the tensile strength of the cement.

Although we were able to obtain financial cost data at only two rural, small-scale cement plants, that information indicates the capital costs of the smallest plants was not terribly high (relative to the high return on rural construction projects), and thus provided for a fairly rapid return of the county's investment. The capital construction costs were approximately 17.5 yuan per ton of annual output, and the rate of profit was 8 yuan per ton.[8] As a result, for the plant where we were given financial and cost data, it took a little over two years to turn over the county's investment. This plant, however, was running at close to full actual capacity with three shifts, and the lower levels of output in previous years indicates a considerable lag before full capacity utilization was achieved.[9]

8. Data from the Tachai Cement Plant. Profit was 21% of selling price and 27% of costs. The "designed" capacity of this plant was 7000 tons, resulting in an investment cost of 50 yuan per ton of "designed" capacity. An industrial handbook compiled by the Peking Industrial Construction Planning Bureau, Ministry of Construction and Engineering (1963) gives the investment cost per ton of "designed" annual production as 37.5 yuan for a cement plant of 32,000 tons capacity, 19.5 yuan per ton for a plant of 492,000 tons capacity, and 17.6 yuan per ton for a plant of 709,000 tons capacity. See Sigurdson, op. cit., p. 426. A United Nations study estimates the "minimal fixed investment costs per ton of capacity appropriate to the developing countries—using an exchange rate of 1.9 yuan per U.S. dollar—to be: 85.5–95 yuan per ton in plants with a capacity of 50,000 tons, 66.5–76 yuan per ton with a capacity of 100,000 tons, 57–66.5 yuan per ton with a capacity of 200,000 tons, and 47.5–57 yuan per ton with a capacity of 400,000 tons." "Pre-investment Data for The Cement Industry," in Studies in Economics of Industry, prepared by the Research and Evaluation Division of the Centre for Industrial Development, Department of Economic and Social Affairs, United Nations, April, 1963, p. 5 (Sales No. 63IIB3).

9. Based on the data for actual and "designed" capacity we were given, it would appear quite probable that "designed" capacity figures are calculated on a per shift basis or are simply very biased underestimates of potential outputs.

The cumulative investment in the largest plant we visited, was approximately 50 yuan per ton of actual annual output, about three times the investment per actual ton produced in the smallest plant.[10] It was quite obvious, however, that the largest plant was much more capital intensive, i.e., mechanized, than the small plant. Furthermore, the province had provided over 3 million yuan worth of equipment in the largest plant, so that the actual investment cost to the county was only 20 yuan per ton of annual output; about the same investment cost to the county as in the smaller plant.

Given the technology being used in these rural, small-scale cement plants, which involves a very high capital–labor ratio with almost no possible substitution of labor for capital, only the material handling part of the production process and the production of equipment by the plant itself can be made labor intensive. Our observations confirmed that this had been done and that the labor used per ton of output, as a result, was unusually high for the technology being used. Total employment ranged from about 150 to about 500 in the county-run plants that we visited, with average productivity (output divided by total staff) ranging from 100 to 182 tons of cement per worker, per year.[11]

Contrary to expectations, the lowest productivity was in the medium-sized plant. The smallest plant, with a level of output one-fifth that in the largest plant, had achieved a level of productivity only 25% below that in the largest plant, which was much more mechanized. In other words, the medium-sized plant employed almost four times the labor employed in the smallest plant, but obtained only two and one-half times the output; or employed about the same amount of labor as the biggest plant, but produced only half the output. The probable explanation for this result is that the smallest and largest plant appeared to be operating at close to full capacity, whereas the medium-sized plant was not.

This substitution of labor for capital in material handling, in internal production of equipment and, where possible, in the production process

10. Because the investment data for this largest plant specifically referred to the cumulative investment for 1958–1974, the comparisons made in the paragraph do not contradict necessarily the existence of declining investment costs per ton of "designed" capacity as scale increases. See Note 5.

11. According to the industrial handbook referred to in Note 5, productivity per worker in cement plants with a "designed" capacity of 32,000 tons per year is 89 tons per worker. The United Nations study referred to in Note 5 also estimates the labor requirements per thousand tons of cement production for new plants in underdeveloped countries: 1.4–1.7 worker per thousand tons of output in plants with a capacity of 50,000 tons and 1.1–1.4 for a plant with a capacity of 100,000 tons, "Pre-investment Data for the Cement Industry," op. cit., p. 9. The observed values for the Chinese plants we visited ranged from 5.5–10 workers per 1000 tons of output. Data presented in the United Nations study indicates cement plants in India (1956) required 5.4 workers per 1000 tons of output. The average capacity of the Indian plant from which this data is obtained, however, undoubtedly was much larger than those in China. "Pre-investment Data for the Cement Industry," op. cit., p. 6.

itself was rational, because labor employed in these rural, small-scale cement plants is very productive compared to its alternative uses in the rural areas. On the average, workers on county-run industries are paid approximately 45 yuan a month, and in the largest cement plant we visited, the average wage was 57 yuan. In the plants we visited, therefore, wages would account for less than 15% of the cost of the output per worker; a little high but quite comparable to the cost structure of cement production in other countries. Furthermore, the profit per worker in the smallest plant we visited was more than double the average wage. These money costs, of course, do not reflect real costs, but there should be little doubt that these money costs (i.e., the wage) were greater than the real costs (the shadow price) of labor in the rural sector. Furthermore, the money price of output in the cement industry understates its real value (shadow price) in agriculture as evidenced by the fact that demand for cement generally appeared to exceed the available supply. Thus, the real net benefits of these plants exceeded profits by an unknown but substantial margin.

The shadow wage of workers is below the money wage in the cement industry, of course, because the alternative for most workers is lower-productivity employment in agriculture. Workers employed in the rural, small-scale industries come from the pool of regular agricultural workers, and the method of selection is designed to obtain them from units with surplus labor and units that are willing to give them up. Communes and brigades in a county are advised of the industry's needs by the county's labor bureau, after which they nominate candidates for the jobs available. Thus, the reduction in the brigade work force may not have much of an impact on their output, and it does reduce the numbers who have a claim on that output.

In any event, although somewhat labor-intensive—given the technology utilized—total employment in these county-run, small-scale cement plants was very small compared with the total labor force of the average county. Furthermore, the Chinese explicitly stated they are attempting to increase the degree of mechanization in the rural, small-scale cement plants we visited so as to increase labor productivity, the latter being viewed as the best means for increasing output rather than relying on increases in the level of employment.

Although there is, in general, a rational basis for the creation of a small-scale cement industry in China, there are certain specific aspects of this sector which may not be considered as efficient. For example, we have already stated these plants utilize a widely-known and used technology for producing cement, it is an appropriate technology for the scale of production in these plants, and they are relatively well equipped to produce with this technology. Nonetheless, given their ability to produce rotary horizontal kilns, the continued use of the stationary vertical shaft kiln represents a serious potential source of inefficiency for the future. This technology has no economies of scale beyond a rather low level of output, and quality control is poor, even when these kilns are operated well. This is why they were replaced by the rotary horizontal kiln in the United States, almost 50 years ago.

A more serious problem in these rural, small-scale cement plants would appear to be in the area of X-efficiency; the problem of operating these plants at full capacity. Two of the three plants we visited were undoubtedly operating at or close to full capacity. The record of their levels of output in previous years, however, indicates the existence of a significant "learning curve" with about a five-year lag in acquiring this degree of X-efficiency, the greatest gains occurring near the end of that five-year period. In the largest cement plant visited, we were told that the output per kiln per hour had been increased by about 25%, and the coal consumption per ton of clinker produced had been reduced 33⅓% in the five-year period, 1964–69; the output per kiln per hour doubling in the five years after 1969. Furthermore, this plant also had one ball mill which was still operating at less than 60% of capacity, perhaps due to the grinding media being used. This time lag in achieving full capacity output, of course, can be expected when developing new small-scale industries in the countryside. The medium-size cement plant we visited had just been renovated in 1974, and this probably explains why it produced only half the output of the larger plant even though both plants had approximately the same size labor force.

If these plants can solve these problems of X-efficiency through "learning by doing" in the short run as the two plants we visited apparently had been able to do—at least to the point where they were operating close to full capacity—the problem of long-run efficiency would appear to be merely a matter of the continuous duplication of existing plants. The size of these plants would remain small relative to say those in the United States, because the size of the area in which their output is used is limited by relatively high transport costs for such a bulky and heavy product.

Surprisingly, duplication of this sort does not appear to be the Chinese objective. The people in the cement plants we visited made it very clear to us that they viewed their objective as increasing the productivity of labor and the scale of output in their plant by continuous mechanization, which was being accomplished by adding new equipment or improving old equipment, and we were shown many examples where this had in fact been done.

This objective makes clear why these small cement plants had a large labor force for their level of cement production. A significant share of that labor force was not producing cement, but was producing equipment to further mechanize the cement-making process. Unable to completely equip these plants from the modern large-scale sector, these plants instead were provided with a good stock of all-purpose machine tools and allocated a significant share of the total labor force they employed to produce the additional equipment they needed "through their own efforts." The commonly repeated phrase, "we built it ourselves," did not usually refer to the crushers and ball mills, the most essential pieces of mechanized equipment in the production of cement in these rural, small-scale cement plants, but to the large number and steadily growing pieces of "ancillary" equipment designed to increase the capital intensity and output capacity of these plants. This feature of China's rural, small-scale cement industry provides it with a very large potential for increasing dynamic efficiency, i.e., increasing levels of output over time from the existing capital stock and labor force now employed in these plants.

RURAL, SMALL-SCALE CHEMICAL FERTILIZER PLANTS

The thinking underlying China's massive expansion of rural, small-scale fertilizer plants was laid out for us in a series of lectures and briefings in Peking. We were told that China's economic planning takes agriculture as the foundation and aims at developing the economy primarily with domestic resources. In practice, self-sufficiency in grain is an important national objective. As one of our hosts put it, without self-sufficiency in grain, China's political independence is not guaranteed. Similar thinking leads the Chinese to adopt provincial and local self-sufficiency in grain supply as major economic goals.

Chemical fertilizer appears to be an important example of our hosts' observation that China is not yet able to equip large numbers of modern, large-scale plants. Big plants form the backbone of the industry, but we were told that they cannot meet China's total fertilizer requirements. This leaves China to choose among two alternatives: allowing fertilizer production to be limited to existing large plants and waiting to expand output until additional large plants can be built or imported, or embarking on a major program of building small and medium-sized fertilizer plants.

The latter alternative, which our hosts described as "fighting with available weapons," has been adopted. Since 1965, an average of over 100 new fertilizer plants has been established annually, compared with only 10 plants per year during 1958-64. There are now 1100 small nitrogenous fertilizer plants; all provinces and about half of China's roughly 2100 counties produce chemical fertilizers.

Small and medium plants now account for over 50% of China's output of nitrogenous fertilizers. Since the share of small plants in total fertilizer output was only 12% in 1965, it is evident that these enterprises have made a major contribution to the 330% rise in fertilizer output reported by Chou En-lai for the years 1964-74.[12] With grain yield expected to rise by three

12. 12% figure from SCMP 4812 (1971), p. 77. Fertilizer figure from *Peking Review* 4 (1975), p. 22.

and possibly more kilograms per kilogram of added fertilizer application, small fertilizer plants also have made important contributions to the 25% increase in grain output recorded during the same period.[13]

THE PLANTS

Basic data for the three chemical fertilizer plants visited by our group are summarized in Table IV-5. These plants appear to represent the larger, more modern portion of China's small fertilizer industry. All three are substantially larger than the "typical" unit mentioned in Peking, which cost 2.5 million yuan to construct and produces 3000 tons of ammonia per year. The Hui county plant was one of 17 fertilizer producers in that county, but accounted for at least one eighth of the 69,000 tons, which the county turned out in 1973 (more if the 69,000 tons referred to fertilizer rather than ammonia production).

These plants seem to be built according to standard designs originating at the national level (this was definitely the case at the Hsi-yang plant). The organization, pace, and timing of the production process seems almost entirely determined by the chemical requirements of the product. We were told that capital requirements per ton of product are similar for large and small plants. Capital–labor ratios are high. The figures shown for two enterprises in Tavle IV-5 are higher than national averages for large-scale chemical plants during the mid-1950s.[14]

Substitution of labor for capital seems to be confined to construction rather than operation of the plants. Both the Lin and Hui County plants had lowered building costs by mobilizing local labor to provide granite, brick, lime, cement, etc. from local materials to replace stainless steel, reinforced concrete, and other industrial products.

Once the plant begins to operate, however, there appears to be little opportunity to substitute labor for machinery. Bagging is performed manually in some plants, but as this exposes the workers to fumes and dust, automatic bagging will be introduced in the near future. Lump, brown, powdered, and sulpherous coal, inferior local materials which have reportedly been successfully introduced as substitutes for anthracite and bituminous coal at many small plants, were not used at any of the three plants.

Even though the plants are relatively small in terms of production capacity, their technology is far from simple, and equipment requirements

13. Li Ch'eng-jui stated that 1 ton of fertilizers can add 3 tons to grain output. T'ang Chung-nan, a fertilizer specialist from the Ministry of Petrochemical Industries stated that although the yield response to ammonia bicarbonate (a leading product of small fertilizer plants) at various levels of application is a complex subject, each additional kilogram of this product, if properly applied, could raise grain yield by 3–5 kg. in north China.

14. Average capital per production worker in state and joint state-private chemical plans was 11,114 yuan in 1955 (Nai-ruenn Chen, *Chinese Economic Statistics* (Chicago, 1967), p. 260 from *JMJP* 7/5/57.

Table IV-5

FERTILIZER PLANT DATA

	Hsi-yang County Chemical Fertilizer Factory	Lin County Chemical Fertilizer Factory Unit 1	Lin County Chemical Fertilizer Factory Unit 2	Hui County Chemical Fertilizer Factory
Construction began	April 1967	Winter 1968 Construction took twice as long as for Unit 2	July 1973	1969
Production began	December 1968		January 1974[a]	September 1970
Source of main equipment	Shanghai	Honan	Shanghai	No data; plant built accessories and replacement
Construction cost (yuan)	7.5 million	2.8 million (50–60% for machinery)	3.2 million	No data
Construction cost per annual ton	375 yuan[b]	150 yuan[c]		No data
Employment	450	520	50	536
Average wage (yuan/month)	40 +			No data
1974 gross output (yuan)	2.7 million	No data		No data
Designed capacity (synthetic ammonia)	5,000 t.	3,000 t.	3,000 t.	5,000 t.
Recent output	10,000 t. ammonia converted to 20,000 t. ammonium nitrate	1974 plan 4,000 t. actual 7,000 t. 1975 plan strive for 10,000 t. converted 80% to ammonium bicarb. 20% to ammonium liquor		1970 reached design capacity 1971 6,600 t. 1972 8,048 t. 1973 8,282 t. 1974 10,510 t. 1975 6,979 (Jan.–May)

	No data	Local	Loan from local bank in which peasants have deposits
Source of finance			
Main raw material	Local anthracite	Local coal, anthracite and bituminous	Local anthracite
Fixed capital[d] per worker (yuan)	16,667	11,538	No data
Gross output value per worker (yuan)	6,000		

[a] Construction was completed in seven months.
[b] Based on 20,000 tons of ammonium nitrate.
[c] Based on 40,000 tons of ammonia bicarbonate.
[d] Fixed capital assumed equal to construction cost.

EXPLANATORY NOTE:
The Lin County plant consisted of two separate production units. Construction cost per annual ton, Employment, Average wage, Designed capacity, Recent output, and Fixed capital are for both units combined.

are far beyond the capacity of most local producers. At least two of the four plants in the three units visited received their basic equipment from Shanghai, as is the case with hundreds of other fertilizer plants. Given the emphasis on self-reliance, this considerable dependence on far-away Shanghai suppliers suggests that production of equipment even for small fertilizer plants is highly complex and perhaps subject to important scale economies.[15]

The impression of technological complexity was reinforced by our tour of the Hsin-hsiang Region Chemical Equipment and Accessory Plant, which employs 330 workers and manufactures compressors and other accessories for small fertilizer plants. Relative to its size, this enterprise owned far more imported machinery, including several large, new and very sophisticated items, than any other plant we visited. The necessity of deploying machinery from Korea, Japan, Italy, and the Soviet Union as well as equipment from several of China's leading producers (Peking, Tientsin, Wu-han, Ch'ang-chun, Kwei-lin) to produce spare parts for small and medium fertilizer plants emphasizes the significance of our hosts' remarks concerning China's inability to equip large numbers of big plants, and also may explain China's decision to purchase large quantities of American and Japanese fertilizer equipment.

All of the plants report current production well above designated capacity, and the officials at the Lin and Hui county plants reported large reductions in unit consumption of power, raw materials and/or fuel. This suggests that engineering and management techniques in this industry are in a state of flux, with strong efforts being made to raise productivity and reduce costs. Innovations and suggestions are spread by means of a communication network in which all three plants were closely involved.

Representatives of the Hsi-yang plant regularly attend such meetings at the provincial and national level. One technician at the Lin County plant had studied for five months in Shanghai. Outside technicians are invited to teach local workers, and workers are sometimes sent outside to study. The Hui County plant has extended technical assistance to many other units: engraved banners and mirrors sent by other plants as tokens of appreciation and displayed in the plant's meeting room came from Peking, Tientsin, Yunnan, Anhwei, Shantung, Shansi, Chekiang, and Shensi as well as other counties in Honan province.

EFFICIENCY

Table IV-6 presents information on costs and prices of fertilizers produced during 1956–57 by large plants together with information collected

---

15. Between 1970 and 1972, a group of over 400 Shanghai factories supplied 300 sets of equipment for synthetic ammonia plants throughout China (FBIS, August 24, 1973, p. C7).

Table IV-6

FERTILIZER COSTS AND PRICES
(YUAN PER TON)

	Large Plants 1956-57	Small Plants 1975
Ammonium nitrate production cost	125 (625)	200 (1000)
Price to producer	—	260-265 (1300-1325)
Purchase price to user	310-316 (1550-1580)	300 (1500)
Producer profit per ton product	—	60-65 yuan
Annual rate of return to construction cost	—	16-17.3%
Ammonia bicarbonate production cost	—	130 (763.18)
Price to producer	—	180 (1058.52)
Producer profit per ton product	—	50
Annual rate of return to construction cost	—	33%

SOURCES: 1956-57 data from Jung-chao Liu, *China's Fertilizer Economy* (Chicago, 1971), pp. 32, 89. 1975 data for ammonium nitrate are from the Hsi-yang County plant; for ammonia bicarbonate are from the Lin County plant (as analyzed in Chapter VII of this report).

NOTE: Figures in parentheses are yuan per ton of nitrogen content.

— = data not available or large plants of this type (ammonia bicarbonate) do not exist.

during our trip. These data show that the Hsi-yang County Plant, which we visited, is able to supply nitrogenous fertilizers to farmers at prices lower than those charges for the products of large fertilizer plants 20 years ago.

These figures demonstrate the potential economic contribution of small-scale fertilizer production in China today. Fertilizer remains in short supply. Sale of extra fertilizer as a form of reward to units which satisfy state requirements for grain production (reported at Lin County's Ta-ts'ai-yuan Brigade) shows that as in the past, farming units would be willing to purchase and apply more fertilizer than can presently be supplied. Under such conditions of excess demand, any fertilizer which can be manufactured and delivered to farming units at a cost substantially below the current farm-gate price, undoubtedly makes a positive contribution to the agricultural economy as well as to accumulation and technical training.

This condition appears to be met by both the Hsi-yang and Lin County plants (lack of data make it impossible to judge the Hui County operation). Both plants earn a substantial return on fixed investment. The Hsi-yang plant turns out ammonium nitrate at two-thirds the price paid by local consumers (Tachai Brigade pays 0.15 yuan per catty or 0.15 x 2000 = 300 yuan/ton for locally manufactured ammonium nitrate), and the current price is marginally lower than in 1956–57.

These results show that even if, as we were told, production costs are higher at small plants than at large ones, and despite the continued existence of technical problems, small fertilizer plants of the sort which we encountered make a definite positive contribution to China's economy. This conclusion is certainly valid for any plants which manufacture useful fertilizer for less than the present retail price of *1500 yuan per ton* of nitrogen equivalent (reported at Tachai Brigade, see Table IV-6). Even if costs exceed this level,

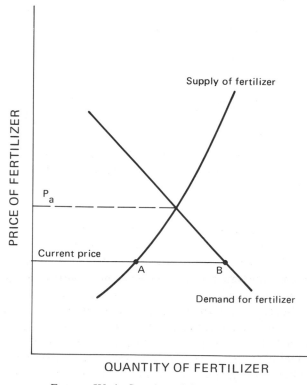

QUANTITY OF FERTILIZER

FIGURE IV-4. Supply and demand for fertilizer.

production is justifiable if costs can be held below the market-clearing price level (labeled P_u in Figure IV 1). Although this price, one sufficiently high to eliminate unsatisfied demand (amounting to AB at current prices) for available fertilizer supplies (which are only slightly affected by price changes), is not known, it is certainly higher than the present prices, which reflect the government's vigorous efforts to improve agriculture's terms of trade with the urban and industrial sectors of China's economy.

IRON AND STEEL INDUSTRY

China produces 25–30 million tons of steel annually, corresponding to Japanese output levels of the early 1960s. Steel and steel products are manufactured by a wide range of enterprises ranging in size from multi-million ton integrated operations at An-shan, Wu-han, and Pao-t'ou, to rural plants which turn out several hundred tons of products annually.

The rationale for simultaneous existence of large, medium, and small producers—a phenomenon which has been noted in the leading nations[16]—is not difficult to understand. The output of large steel producers, which is limited by China's capacity to manufacture or import large blast furnaces, rolling mills, and to develop large-scale sources of iron ore and other raw materials, is mainly absorbed by the production and construction activities of urban industry.

Rural areas are urged to expand agricultural mechanization and construction, but the steel needed for these tasks may not be easy to obtain. If provinces and localities can develop their own steel-making facilities and supply part of their steel requirements at reasonable cost, the whole economy will gain. Rural areas will benefit from expanded steel supplies, and the larger steel-makers will be better able to devote their energies to improvements in assortment and product quality urgently needed by technically sophisticated segments of the machinery and other industries. Small plants can provide other advantages as well, including opportunities to exploit local resource deposits, relaxation of pressure on overburdened long-distance transport facilities, and labor training.

Chinese economists used these arguments to support proposals for expanding small-scale rural ironworks in 1957. This policy was implemented in 1958, and soon developed into a massive national campaign to build "backyard" iron and steel plants. Most of these very small projects were uneconomic and most were closed down during the early 1960s. The policy of developing rural, small-scale iron and steel production facilities was given renewed emphasis in the 1960s, and local metallurgy is again expanding.

16. A Cockerill, *The Steel Industry: International Comparisons of Industrial Structure and Performance* (Cambridge, 1974), Chapter 6.

Mr. Ch'ieh K'o-ming of the Ministry of Metallurgy informed us that state economic plans now include the output of small plants, mainly run by counties and districts, producing from a few hundred to 50,000 tons annually, mainly for local use. Today's small units are more mechanized and better able to carry out good quality metallurgy than the 1958 generation of enterprises. Cold-air blasts have been replaced with hot blasts of up to 900°C.; mechanized crushing of ore and coke is now common; casting machines have replaced hand operations, and furnace bodies are made of steel rather than brick.

THE PLANTS[17]

Economic data for the three steel plants which we visited appear in Table IV-7. Comparison of these enterprises, particularly the Shou-tu and Wu-hsi plants—both of which manufacture steel ingots and rolled products—illustrates the widely varying technical conditions existing within China's steel industry.

There are enormous differences between labor productivity at the large Shou-tu plant and the smaller plants, which are severely understated by the figures in Lines 7C, 8A, and 8B of Table IV-7, since the rate of value added is much higher for a fully integrated plant like Capital than for one which melts scrap and rolls semi-processed shapes (Wu-hsi), or which shapes pre-rolled sections (Shanghai). A computation based on value added rather than gross value would substantially increase the productivity advantage of the Shou-tu steelworks.

Another indication of major interplant variation in technology can be seen from the nature of the labor force at the Capital and Wu-hsi plants (this topic was not discussed at the Shanghai plant). At Capital (a national plant), great stress was placed on extensive and lengthy on-the-job training. Workers were mostly junior high school graduates (some have spent a few years in rural villages after graduation), who must serve a three-year apprenticeship before becoming regular workers. In Wu-hsi (a county plant), on the other hand, our hosts emphasized the ease with which newcomers mastered their work. Most workers are army veterans, ex-peasants, or returned educated youth (i.e., those who have spent time working in rural areas), and they enter

17. The three plants in the iron and steel industry we visited included the Capital Iron and Steel Works in Peking (a national plant), Wu-hsi County Iron and Steel Works (a county plant which produced steel rods), and the Shanghai Shaped Steel Tubing Plant (a municipal plant). Only one of these plants is classified as a rural, small-scale industry, and that plant did not produce pig iron. Thus, the plants we visited in the iron and steel industry do not allow for a valid assessment of rural, small-scale iron and steel plants in China.

Using the information gathered during our visit, however, the remaining discussion in this section of the Chapter is a comparative analysis of the three particular plants we visited which does yield some useful tentative conclusions concerning the economics of the iron and steel sector as a whole in China today.

Table IV-7

IRON AND STEEL PLANT DATA

	Capital Iron and Steel	Wu-hsi	Shanghai
1. Employment	20,000[a]	805	814
2. Physical output (tons)			
A. Pig iron	sufficient for its ingot output	0	0
B. Ingot	1,000,000	110,000	0
C. Rolled products	1,000,000	10,000	9,000
3. Average price of rolled products (yuan/ton)	perhaps 600	approx. 500	1,167
4. Gross output (sales) value in 1974 yuan	500,000,000[b]	9,000,000	15,000,000
5. Average monthly wage (yuan)	60	47	60
6. Wage bill (yuan)	14,400,000	454,020	586,080
7. Labor costs			
a. Wage bill/gross output	.029	.05	.039
b. Wage bill/production expenses	.048[c]	—	—
c. Wage cost/ton of rolled product (yuan)	14.4	45.4	65.12
8. Productivity			
a. Gross output/man-year (yuan)	25,000	11,180	18,427
b. Tons of rolled products/ man-year	50	12.4	11.0
9. Net profit rate	30–50%	—	—

[a]Excludes another 20,000 in mining and construction.
[b]Based on products sold outside the enterprise.
[c]Based on profit equal to 40% of gross output value.

EXPLANATORY NOTE:
    As mentioned in Note 17 to Chapter IV, it is important to note the Capital plant is a national plant, the Wu-hsi plant is a county plant, and the Shanghai is a municipal plant.

productive work as soon as they arrive at the plant. With the help of fraternal plants and old workers, they learn the technology in a short period, and many have become capable managers and technicians. There are only about 40–50 apprentices (5% of the work force).

One element of uniformity among all three plants was the small share of labor costs in the overall cost structure of this industry. Even if wages are related to production expenses (Line 7B), rather than to output value (which includes profits), the share of wages is very low by international standards.[18]

18. Data for 1963-1964 show that wages and salaries accounted for the following percentages of gross output value in the steel industry: EEC countries, 17.7%; U.K., 18.5%; U.S.A., 21.8%; Japan, 13.6% (Cockerill, p. 28).

Inflating wage costs to allow for fringe benefits and amortization on factory-supplied housing would not alter this observation.

This suggests that in this industry at least, Chinese managers can gain relatively little cost reduction from exploring possible means of reducing the number of workers. The cost of possible excess labor is low in relation to total expenses and must be balanced against the training and experience gained by (possibly) nonproductive workers. This is particularly clear in the case of the Wu-hsi plant in which the outlay on electricity in the melt shop alone (70 yuan per ton of ingot times 10,000 tons or 700,000 yuan) exceeds the plant's entire wage bill by 54%!

Under these circumstances, it is not surprising to find that some ancillary operations at Capital were carried out with labor-intensive methods. This was especially evident in the transport sector. Within the plant compound, which covers an area of five square kilometers, we observed a wide variety of transport techniques ranging from hand-, animal-, and bicycle-drawn carts to railways, fork-lift trucks, large and small motor vehicles, and power shovels.

A high degree of labor intensity also is evident in some aspects of the Wu-hsi plant's operations. There seemed to be about 16 attendants at the electric furnace, perhaps as many as were operating the vastly larger 1200 cubic meter blast furnace, which we inspected at Capital. There also were areas of considerable mechanization at Wu-hsi. The melting furnace was charged with an overhead crane manufactured on the spot, and in the rolling mill, rods were cut, moved to and from the rolling machine and stacked mechanically. We did not ask whether these improvements were undertaken primarily to improve product quality, to reduce heavy labor, to conserve agricultural manpower, or for other reasons.

As with chemical fertilizer, there appears to be an extensive network of communication within the steel industry, which encourages exchange of technical data and suggestions. Some workers at Wu-hsi had been sent elsewhere for technical training. The Shanghai plant seemed especially active in this field, reporting that its personnel made frequent tours to other plants in and outside Shanghai, mainly to study customer requirements.

Efficiency

Each of the three plants makes a substantial positive contribution to the economy. The function of the large Capital plant is twofold: production of a large volume of basic industrial materials, plus its contribution to accumulation and hence increased investment. On the basis of our rather sketchy observations, the firm's technical level appears adequate by international standards. The blast furnaces now use only 500 kg. of coke per ton of pig iron, a substantial improvement over 1958 figures of 690–750 kg., which foreign observers praised as "excellent performance," approaching "the best Soviet practice of the time."[19] Although problems in the soaking pits resulted in down time of 35% in the rolling mill, such difficulties are not uncommon in other countries. Our overall impression was of well-organized, business-like productive activity throughout the compound.

The Shanghai Steel Tubing Plant—a municipal plant—represents the type of small job shop which is needed to provide flexibility in any economy.[20] The plant appears to specialize in producing small batches of products, which would be difficult for a large, specialized mill to duplicate unless it could produce long output runs, in which case limited demand, transport costs, and communication problems might partially or totally offset possible economies of scale.

The Shanghai plant provides an example of the stimulus to China's innovative capabilities resulting from the withdrawal of Soviet technical assistance in 1960, and shows how defense-linked innovations can spill over into the civilian sector. Production of import substitutes has been a challenging task for this rather poorly-equipped enterprise: flexible bellows-shaped tubes were trial-produced only after 5½ months of experimentation, corrugated fin-tubes only after 30 unsuccessful attempts, and ridged cylindrical tubes required 180 experiments before a single sample was turned out.

Successful completion of this sequence of innovative tasks has left this unit with a regular system of product development, which will serve as a valuable asset in the future. Workers and managers understand that manufacture of new products requires time and effort, and often involves costly delays and initial failure. Workers have learned to scour local libraries for useful technical information for domestic and foreign publications. Mass campaigns and worker suggestions play an important role in the innovative process; at the same time, there are two or three members of the plant's revolutionary committee who are responsible for product development.

The Wu-hsi plant—a county plant, i.e., the only rural, small-scale iron and steel plant in our sample—had been converted from manufacturing tools into steel production in response to rising local demand—providing steel for local uses, which are not sufficiently urgent to receive close attention from planning authorities at the national or provincial level. Despite its present inability to carry out rough rolling on its 250 mm. rolling mill and the obviously wasteful cross-hauling and reheating operations resulting from this shortcoming, which will be eliminated when a new 500 mm. rolling mill is completed, the Wu-hsi plant appears able to supply local users with steel products at a price no higher than that charged for products of the Capital

19. M. Gardner Clark, *The Development of China's Steel Industry and Soviet Technical Aid* (Ithaca, 1973), p. 18.

20. Cockerill, p. 110, notes the continued existence of "small units (frequently using electric arc furnaces) serving specialist or localized markets" in each of the advanced industrial states covered by his study.

Works. As in the case of small fertilizer plants, the finding that small steel producers can manufacture useful products at costs apparently below price levels of the 1950s makes it difficult to doubt the economic rationality of building such plants.[21]

Not all counties in China, however, may be able to develop steel plants. Even though Wu-hsi County is blessed with a considerable agricultural surplus and a variety of machinery plants, initial cooperation from the more advanced industries of Wu-hsi City has been essential to getting the county steelworks on its feet.

Plants of this sort may disappear from China's economic landscape in the long run. Areas like Wu-hsi may be served by large steel-makers in nearby Shanghai. Alternatively, existing small plants may be merged into larger units, just as handicraft shops have developed into factories in the past.

For the time being, however, small plants like the one at Wu-hsi can help to develop the economy. Construction and transport needs do not seem to strain local facilities, nor does output (11.1 kg. per capita in Wu-hsi County) appear large in relation to the national average of about 30 kg. per capita. Except for electricity and part of the equipment, the resources consumed at the Wu-hsi plant: local scrap, labor, coal and auxiliary materials, are of negligible value to higher levels. At Wu-hsi, as long as the value of the products exceeds the opportunity cost of labor, power and fuel to the local economy (and this seems difficult to doubt), the impact on the local economy will be positive even without considering the educational and political benefits involved.

These benefits are not small. Operating even a small plant in a continuous-flow industry poses problems of scheduling, quality control, resource mobilization etc., whose full or partial solution facilitates the development of similar competence in other sectors. In the political sphere, small-scale development allows Wu-hsi to fulfill its ambition of local industrialization (abolishing the former situation of an "iron-less county") without requiring the center and province to either raise taxes or reduce their own investment activities.

Furthermore, the contribution of the steel plant to the development of machine manufacture and construction, and through them to agriculture and other industries reinforces the "don't wait for massive outside support" philosophy expounded by both our Peking hosts and factory informants. (In fact, outside support is probably least likely to come to those who show no inclination for self-help.)

21. Published sources indicate that the average price of steel products was about 1000 yuan/ton during the mid-1950s.

RURAL, SMALL-SCALE HYDROELECTRIC POWER STATIONS

Rural, small-scale, hydroelectric power stations differ in many respects from the other kinds of rural, small-scale industries analyzed above; differences as to the determination of what is a rural, small-scale industry, source of financing, the extent of higher-level control over their operation, and distribution of output. Only in this sector were we given a size definition for determining whether a particular station was considered small-scale or not, i.e., it did not depend on who "owned" and "operated" the station. Small-scale hydroelectric power stations are those stations with a generating capacity of less than 6000 kw.[22]

The probable reason for the special status of rural, small-scale hydroelectric power stations among the rural, small-scale industries is the restriction of their location to specific areas in China, i.e., where the volume and rate of flow of water is sufficient to pay for the investment required, and the need for the state to harness and control all these potential sources to meet the tremendous needs for electricity in the rural areas, regardless of the local units' ability to finance these projects. Thus, although included among those projects in the rural areas which relied on local financing and control before the Cultural Revolution, the results of this effort undoubtedly proved to be very inefficient and unsuccessful and did not go very far in meeting the local demands for electricity. These pre-Cultural Revolution, small-scale, hydroelectric power stations often relied on the seasonal flow of water, and their average generating capacity was less than 100 kw.[23]

With the completion of many rural, large water conservation projects, and the rapid increase in the demand for electric power due to the spread of rural, small-scale industries in these rural areas, a much more rational approach to the utilization of the available water power for generation of electricity was adopted. During the Cultural Revolution more local, small-scale, hydroelectric power stations were constructed than had been built in the previous ten years. To facilitate this rapid increase, there was a much larger participation of the state in financing and equipping these rural, small-scale hydroelectric power stations than was true of the other rural, small-scale industries. In other words, because of the urgent, nationwide need and limited local ability to develop this sector where such development

22. Although defined as hydroelectric power stations of less than 6000 kw. capacity, stations this small obviously also were run, like other rural, small-scale industries, by counties, communes, and brigades. At the time of our visit, we were told there were 50,000 rural, small-scale hydroelectric power stations in China, an eightfold increase over the number in 1965.

23. Another important change since the Cultural Revolution is in the use of the electricity generated by these rural, small-scale hydroelectric power stations from providing rural households and sideline activities with electric power to providing the needs of the rural, small-scale industries.

was possible so as to meet these needs (i.e., not necessarily those of the local area), much less emphasis was placed on the need for local financing and production of the necessary equipment. Nonetheless, we were told that although the state originally had to supply these stations with their equipment—i.e., the generators, the necessary controls, and control panels—some provinces, districts, and counties are *now* able to produce their own equipment. In the same vein, we were told that self-financing by the counties and communes themselves was increasing.

This difference in the state's role in the financing and provision of equipment for these rural, small-scale, hydroelectric power stations also is reflected in the control over their operation and distribution of output. Because they are usually an integral part of the country's water conservation projects, drainage and irrigation management, and river navigation, these rural, small-scale, hydroelectric power stations are directly under a higher level bureau, which controls the various uses of water in the local area. Furthermore, these stations are integrated with the state's electric power network, being paid a "processing" fee for the power they generate. In other words, these rural, small-scale, hydroelectric stations supplement the electric power available in the state's electric power network and earn income for the local unit which operates these stations. They do not, however, supply electric power directly to users in that same unit. We were told the local unit had to obtain and pay for its supply of electric power from the state's electric power network just like any other user. Those local units that operate rural, small-scale hydroelectric power stations, of course, may well have a greater bargaining power in obtaining electric power for their own use than those units which do not supply electric power to the state network.

Although hydroelectric power is estimated to account for less than 1% of China's energy supply,[24] with the rapid expansion of rural, small-scale industries and the mechanization of agriculture, the contribution of these rural, small-scale, hydroelectric power stations can be significant in specific areas. For example, in Lin County these power stations supplied 50% of the total consumption of electricity in the county, whereas in Hsun-te County, a single county-run, hydroelectric power station alone supplies more than 50% of that county's needs.

Because we did not have a technical expert on hydroelectric power in our delegation, it is difficult for us to reach any conclusion concerning the efficiency of these rural, small-scale, hydroelectric power stations, but a brief summary of the information obtained from the four stations we visited is presented below.

The largest hydroelectric power station we visited was a multipurpose

---

24. *People's Republic of China: Handbook of Economic Indicators, op. cit.,* p. 15. Although less than 1% of China's total energy supply, hydroelectric power accounts for about one-fifth of China's production of electricity.

dam on a tributary of the Hsi River in Hsun-te County to the southwest of Canton. Built and operated by the county, and somewhat of an engineering curiosity, this dam was constructed in stages in 1971-74 at the entrance to the tributary, so as to control and utilize both the seasonal differences in water level and the 1.4 meter tidal differences on the main river. This dam makes the tributary navigable for 500-600 ton vessels, cutting the distance between Canton and Wu-chou by 21 kilometers; reduces the water level in the surrounding valley by 0.3 meters and eliminates waterlogging on 250,000 mu of land; and generates 12 million kwh. of electricity a year with its 22 generators. These generators have a total capacity of 5000 kw., which means that the actual electricity generated is less than 15% of total capacity. Obviously, this low capacity utilization rate is due, in part, to the fact that the generators can only be operated when the seasonal and tidal conditions make this possible.

The other rural, small-scale, hydroelectric power stations we visited were all located in Lin County, the county famous for the Red Flag Canal. Utilizing the gravity flow of water from the Canal and a large reservoir some distance away, this county has 65 rural, small-scale power stations with a total capacity of 10,400 kw.; the largest, a county-operated power station of 3200 kw. The three power stations we visited were a county station (1500 kw. capacity), a commune station (250 kw. capacity), and a brigade station (40 kw. capacity). We were told the smallest power station in the county had a generating capacity of only 10 kw. All of these power stations are tied into the state's electric power network, receiving 3.5 fen per kwh. The supply of water to these plants is controlled by the Red Flag Canal Water Management Bureau, which directly operates the county-owned power stations. The profits of the county-owned power stations are turned over to the Bureau.

The capital construction costs of the power stations we visited in Lin County were approximately 500 yuan per kw. of generating capacity; 425 yuan for the brigade power station, and 584 yuan for the county power station. The county power station generated over 9 million kw. hours of electricity, i.e., an annual gross income of approximately 350,000 yuan, which means it had chieved a capacity utilization rate of 40%. This station had a work force of 43 employees and, therefore, the gross income per worker was approximately 8000 yuan. After allowing for wages, maintenance, and other costs, the rate of return on investment in this county-operated power station was probably in the neighborhood of 20%.[25] In the brigade-operated power stations, the workers in these stations are paid by

25. This is a crude estimate at best, based on the assumption that wage costs (43 employees at an average monthly wage of 45 yuan) are approximately 25,000 yuan and maintenance and other costs (5% of total investment) are approximately 75,000 yuan. Thus, net income would amount to 250,000 yuan (350 minus 100,000 yuan) and the rate of return would be approximately 17% (250,000 yuan divided by 1,460,000 yuan).

the brigade in work points; the brigade being paid .035 yuan per kwh. for the output of the station by the state. For the brigade-operated power station we visited, if the station operated at 20% capacity, the gross income to the brigade per worker (per day) would be approximately 4 yuan.

CONCLUSION

Despite periodic setbacks, China has achieved a significant record of economic development over the past twenty-five years, especially in the urban industrial sector. Agricultural development, however, continues to be a major, perhaps the major, obstacle to continued success. During the four weeks we were in China's rural areas, we saw many examples of the current multifaceted attack, which has been launched to eliminate this obstacle; such as increases in the multicropping index, the reclamation, leveling, and improvement of cultivated farm land, the construction of large-scale projects to capture, store, and distribute water, increased mechanization and electrification of production processes, the increased use of fertilizer, experiments with new varieties, the interplanting of crops, and the change in the cropping pattern to higher yield crops. A vital element in this rapid increase in the rate of investment and technological change, or transformation of Chinese agriculture production, is the development of a rural, small-scale industrial sector to produce the cement, fertilizer, electric power, agricultural machinery, and other products that this transformation requires.

These agricultural inputs are presently being produced in China's large-scale, modern, urban industrial sector, but their supply—although increasing rapidly—is woefully inadequate for the overwhelming and rapidly growing demand of China's large and underdeveloped agricultural sector. To rely solely on increases in output capacity in the modern industrial sector obtained by investment allocations from the budgets of central, provincial, and municipal governments would considerably delay the implementation of the current programs of agricultural development. Furthermore, even when available, the distribution of the output of the modern industrial sector to the widespread agricultural units of production is severely limited and costly due to the inadequate modern transportation network in China. Social and political objectives, such as the desire to limit the growth of population in China's major industrial-urban centers and to promote the more equitable economic development of the many economic regions in China, also argue against following the Soviet pattern of concentration on the development of industrial base via modern, large-scale industries, with agriculture benefiting by means of a delayed, trickling down of the resulting industrial production.[26]

26. This point—developing industry first before engaging in the mechanization and development of agriculture—is claimed to be a major argument held by Liu Shao-ch'i and a fundamental reason for Mao's disagreement with Liu's policies.

Thus, whatever political or social benefits may be achieved, where local resources permit, the creation of these rural, small-scale industries is an obviously rational policy in economic terms alone. The areas we visited had these resources and the development of rural, small-scale industries undoubtedly has made a significant contribution to their achievement of relatively high and stable yields.

The discussion in this chapter has been devoted to an economic analysis of China's rural, small-scale plants within each of several different types of industries. This discussion makes clear the many dissimilarities among the plants we visited, even within each type of industry. Nonetheless, this conclusion is an attempt to summarize our overall evaluation of these rural, small-scale industries as a whole.

Claiming that the creation and development of rural, small-scale industry in China is a rational policy, refers only to rationality in the broad sense of means and ends; rural, small-scale industries are a feasible and positive means of furthering the end of agricultural development in China. In a more restrictive sense, however, rational policies are those which also meet the test of efficiency—making the greatest possible contribution to the desired end with the resources available, given the policy chosen—and optimally—making the greatest contribution to the desired end with the resources available, given alternative policies which could be adopted for that purpose.

A determination of the efficiency of China's rural, small-scale industrial policy can be most readily made by looking at several important, but different, dimensions of an enterprise's activity. The technical aspect of allocative efficiency depends on the choice and utilization of the most efficient technology available for producing the desired product, on the scale desired, with the resources available. The factor-mix aspect of allocative efficiency depends on employing the most efficient combination and amounts of raw materials, labor, and capital for the technology being utilized. X-efficiency depends on the management and coordination of the plants' production activities in the most successful manner, given the technology and inputs being utilized. Finally, dynamic efficiency depends on the realization of potential increases in factor productivity over time.

As for the technical aspect of efficiency, the technology utilized can be described, in the terms presented in the introduction to this Chapter, as intermediate-modern. This technology was used widely in an earlier period in modern industrialized countries and is well-suited for the designed scale of production in these plants, i.e., to supply the needs of the local area. A more modern technology is available, but would only be economically justified at significantly higher levels of output. Furthermore, the technology required is more capital intensive than a more primitive, but less productive, technology, but is well within the local area's, especially the county's, capacity to provide the financial resources necessary for the investment.

Equally important, the necessary equipment involved in this intermediate technology also is well within the supply capacity of the growing modern, urban industrial sector in China. Very few pieces of imported equipment were seen in these rural, small-scale industries, and a significant share was provided by factories in the same province. This intermediate technology, of course, also required less labor per unit of output than a more primitive technology, a desirable choice at the present time in China due to the rapidly increasing demand for labor in the rural economy generated by the program of agricultural transformation currently underway in the areas we visited. Thus, given the resources available and desired scale of operations for producing these products, the Chinese have chosen what would appear to be the most efficient technology available.

Given the technology being utilized, the factor-mix aspect of efficiency in the rural, small-scale industrial plants, *at first sight anyway,* is somewhat less optimal than the choice of technology. In other words, the plants we visited appeared to be less capital intensive and more labor intensive, i.e., used less capital and more labor than appropriate for the realization of the *designed* maximum level of output for the technology chosen. As indicated in an earlier section of this chapter, this result is probably an attempt to adapt that technology to better fit the resources available in the local area. Although the local area has sufficient financial resources for investment, and the modern sector has the productive capacity to supply the *basic* elements of the equipment required by the intermediate modern technology utilized, these sources apparently are not sufficient to supply the complete complex of machinery and equipment required for the entire production process. Thus, transportation and material handling, fabrication and packaging, and foundary operations, often did not rely on mechanized intermediate modern technology, but rather on labor intensive primitive technology. Quite simply, given the choices of technology available, the choice of the modern-intermediate technology was an efficient one, but to utilize that technology in rural China, an adjustment in the factor-mix was required due to the relative availability of these resources in China.

Nonetheless, the labor employed in these rural, small-scale industrial plants still exceeds the level required to operate these plants efficiently *in the short run.* The reason for this, as mentioned in earlier discussions in this chapter, is one of the most unique features of these plants; a significant portion of that labor force is not directly engaged in the production process. Rather, each of these plants has assigned a share of the work force, often as much as a fourth, to maintenance and construction work. Thus, some of the labor force is engaged in producing new equipment and machinery, either to improve or replace existing equipment or to mechanize those processes which are presently relying on primitive, labor-intensive technology. These maintenance and construction shops, well equipped with basic machine tools, are hard at work increasing the capital intensity of these plants so as to realize the greater productivity of the intermediate modern technology already adopted for major production processes in the plant. Strangely enough, therefore, these plants appear to be relatively labor intensive in the short run, merely due to their attempt to increase the capital–labor ratio and achieve the potential labor productivity made possible by intermediate technology adopted; a need dictated by the scarcity of necessary capital, which can be supplied by the modern sector.

The allocative efficiency in regard to raw materials used in these plants is another aspect of the Chinese adaptation of the technology chosen to better fit both their resource availability and their needs in the local area. In some cases, the technology chosen would not yield high quality products produced within strict tolerances (for example, the use of stationary vertical shaft kilns in the production of cement). More important, however, the quality of the locally available raw material inputs often is relatively poor, which precludes the production of high quality products unless considerable investments were made for the purpose of removing the impurities they contain, i.e., the development of raw material refining facilities. Some efforts in this direction undoubtedly would improve the allocative efficiency of these plants. Yet, although better quality products are to be preferred to poorer quality products (by definition), the cost of improving the quality of the raw material inputs is not necessarily worthwhile because the existing quality of the output of these plants is adequate for their intended use in the rural areas. For example, poor quality cement is suitable for dams with earthwork cores; unstable chemical fertilizer is made usable by mixing it with green manure in the compost heap, and many small pieces of agricultural machinery of limited capacity can make a significant increase in the mechanization of China's agricultural production.

The above favorable evaluations of the approximate allocative efficiency of the rural, small-scale industries are necessary, but not sufficient arguments for concluding these plants were operating efficiently in all respects. Quite the contrary, for our general impression of the plants we visited was that, on the average, they were not operating very efficiently and the most important reason why this was so was their relatively low level of X-efficiency. The explanation for this impression may well be due to the different style of work habits compared to those in the industrialized countries, which we were more familiar with; the presence of job-lot production rather than continuous serial production, the more frequent change of workers' job assignments, change of product being produced, the prevalence of workers working in groups rather than individually on specialized tasks, finding portions of the production process often being closed down during our visit while workers were assigned elsewhere, the generally slower pace of work, and the observable neglect of regularized maintenance and up-keep in these plants. This was less true, of course, in the cement and chemical fertilizer plants we visited, where the technology being utilized dictated a continuous production process. Our general impression also undoubtedly is influenced by the large number of agricultural machinery plants included in our sample. Furthermore, the lack of continuous operation may well have been the result of unavailable inputs or component parts. Finally, this observation was not true for all the plants we visited; the labor effort in some of these plants was well organized and was being applied at a fairly rapid pace. Nonetheless, the existence of relatively poor management of the supply of inputs and distribution of output (most frequently not the task of the production unit itself) and relatively poor condition of the assignment and continuous employment of the work force within the plant would appear to be a valid conclusion.

The aggregate evidence also supports this conclusion. With no significant increase in capacity or labor force, these plants exhibit significant growth in output over time. In other words, the problems of X-efficiency are reduced over time as management and the labor force gains experience and the time-lag of their learning by doing appears to be in the neighborhood of five years, which suggests the problem may be one of gaining experience, "learning-by-doing," rather than an inherent failure of management. This problem of the learning curve, of course, is a major problem for any underdeveloped country, especially one launching a program of industrialization in rural areas. In addition, the tremendous value of the industrial training being given the rural labor force, and the ability to achieve the potential output levels of these plants in approximately five years is impressive.

The prospects for dynamic efficiency in these rural, small-scale industrial plants also would appear to be favorable. With the stock of basic machine tools, the accessibility of technological and design information, and the construction and repair labor force available in these plants, the Chinese have a built-in means not only for the increased mechanization and improvement of the existing plant's capacity, but also for the creation of new capacity utilizing a more modern technology. We saw many examples of this occurring during our visit.

If the above arguments and impressions are correct, we can only conclude that the overall efficiency of these rural, small-scale plants is relatively high, expecially when considered in the light of China's level of development and the resources available to this sector of the economy. Yet, two decisive questions must be answered before China's program of rural, small-scale industrialization can be judged as the most promising, i.e., optimal, approach to achieve agricultural development in China.

First, even though the plants we visited are judged to be a relatively efficient use of the resources available for providing products which have made a significant contribution to the transformation of agricultural production in these areas, can the experience of these model areas we visited be duplicated throughout the rural areas of China? Our observations, after all, were limited to relatively high and stable yield agricultural areas, which had access to sources of the water, raw materials, and labor required by these plants, had the financial resources for the investment required, and were adequately supplied by the state with the basic machinery and equipment necessary to utilize the technology adopted. Our conclusions as to the efficiency of these rural, small-scale industries would be considerably weaker if we were to include areas of China much less well endowed with these necessary preconditions. Furthermore, one would question if the demand for the basic machinery and equipment found in these plants could be satisfied by the modern sector if they were to be duplicated in every rural county in China. Thus, it is doubtful if the complex of small-scale industrial plants being developed in the model areas we visited could be or are equally successful throughout the entire Chinese agricultural scene.

In light of the probable inability of the Chinese to duplicate the successes obtained in the areas we visited throughout all of Chinese agriculture, wouldn't it be possible to utilize the resources being used in a much better way to achieve that goal? For example, isn't it possible that the mobilization of the resources being used for the development of these rural, small-scale industries could achieve greater long-run results by being devoted to the development of large-scale factories utilizing modern technology, with greater total factor productivity, producing better quality products, and in the development of a transportation network which could distribute these products more widely throughout the rural areas? A crucial consideration in answering this question is the mobility and substitutability of the resources being used. How easily could the central government mobilize and transfer the financial investment now being made by the local units to the central government's budget for investment in the modern urban industrial sector? And, how easy would it be to provide industrial training for the rural labor force and mobilize and transfer them to the urban industrial areas, also providing the necessary housing and social overhead capital? With large-scale modern technology in the modern sector, would the poor quality inputs now being used in the rural, small-scale industries be very useful as inputs in the modern sector? And, if raw material refining and processing facilities were to be built to make them useful, how easily could they be collected and shipped to the modern sector? Furthermore, modern technology would require imports of machinery and equipment, whereas the rural, small-scale industries utilize not only machinery and equipment now produced in China, but that which increasingly is produced by the rural, small-scale factories themselves. These imports, of course, would require exports, and the Chinese are presently experiencing a serious import surplus due to large-scale imports of both agricultural products and machinery and equipment for the current level of investment in the modern sector.

Even if we were to conclude that this alternative approach were feasible and more profitable in terms of providing more and better quality inputs for the agricultural sector within a finite time horizon of a decade or so, the calculation of these comparative benefits of alternative policies cannot ignore some of the more fundamental objectives of China's economic development policy. Among the more important of these objectives are the limiting of the pace of urbanization traditionally associated with industrial development; the limiting of the need to depend on foreign technology and supplies of machinery and equipment; the desire to reduce the social and economic status differences between the urban and rural, industrial and agricultural sectors; the desire for greater popular participation and initiative in the development process; and the desire to spread technical capabilities throughout the rural population. In short, one could easily argue that the development of rural, small-scale industries is an important variable in the objective function of China's leaders and, therefore, the development of these industries is the only way to optimally allocate these resources to achieve this end.

But this is too easy an answer to the question being asked. Obviously, the Chinese would be better off if they had a modern sector capable of producing all the inputs needed to transform China's agricultural production to a higher level, and a transportation network fully capable of distributing these inputs throughout China. The Chinese recognize this and argue that this is where the development of the rural, small-scale industries is hoped to ultimately end up. In other words, the most efficient of these plants are to expand and be equipped, often with equipment they will be able to produce themselves, so they will eventually become large-scale modern plants. As they grow, so will the area for the distribution of their output. The prerequisite for this growth, of course, will be similar increases in local transportation facilities, quality of inputs, and supply coordination; but these same problems would exist if China were to develop these industries from the top-down instead of the bottom-up.

China, of course, is not developing these industries from the bottom-up alone; these industries are being developed at both levels—the rural, small-scale industrial sector and the urban, modern sector. Our delegation visited model rural areas, observing examples of rural, small-scale industries. Another delegation could visit these same industries in the urban, modern sector. On the basis of the particular plants we observed during our visit, however, we would conclude the attempt to develop rural, small-scale industries in China is not only a rational policy, consistent with the resources available and the objectives being sought, but also was being implemented relatively efficiently for a country at China's level of economic development. Optimality is much more difficult to assess, but considering the feasible alternative uses of these resources for increasing productivity in agriculture and the explicitly stressed objectives of China's leaders, the optimality of the policy of developing rural, small-scale industries may not be proven, but certainly cannot be rejected.

Chapter V

AGRICULTURAL MECHANIZATION AND MACHINERY PRODUCTION

Since the Great Leap Forward, China's development policies have focused on bridging the gap between the agricultural and the industrial sectors.[1] Mechanization is considered as an essential element of agricultural development which is well reflected in Chairman Mao's statement, "The fundamental way out of agriculture lies in mechanization." During the years that followed, a massive Chinese mechanization program has evolved, of which our delegation had a brief but close look.

The Chinese are actively engaged in adapting and transfering mechanization technologies from all over the world. What is perhaps unique in this program at this stage of development is the extensive small-scale agricultural machinery industry that has been established in the rural areas to support their mechanization strategy. Our delegation, unfortunately, did not have the opportunity to visit some of the research institutions that have played a significant part in this agricultural mechanization process and in the development of the rural-based farm equipment industry. Consequently, our comments on mechanization are primarily based on the agricultural machines that we observed being produced in the manufacturing plants and

1. Carl Riskin, "Small Industry and the Chinese Model of Development." *The China Quarterly*, April-June, 1971, pp. 245-273.

used in the progressive agricultural areas. These comments must therefore remain rather impressionistic in nature.

It was apparent to us that in terms of agricultural development priorities, mechanization of field operations is superseded only by the introduction of improved seed-fertilizer technology and by irrigation and land development activities. High-yielding dwarf varieties of wheat and rice have been widely introduced in most parts of the country. We were impressed with the progress made in irrigation, water control and land development, without which increased crop production would not have been possible. Their farm mechanization program has been highly effective in raising both land and labor productivity. We were repeatedly told that the country is committed to complete mechanization by 1980. Optimistic as it may sound, it makes clear the high priority China has placed on the mechanization of its agriculture.

Displacement of labor through agricultural mechanization is a delicate issue which is of major concern to policy makers in most developing countries. Consequently national policies in many developing countries tend to provide lukewarm support to the mechanization of agriculture. China has a low level of per-capita arable land and shares the same basic problems of high population density and subsistence agriculture with other developing countries. Yet, surprisingly, we did not hear a single comment indicating any fears of unemployment through agricultural mechanization. On the contrary, we consistently found that the Chinese look at mechanization as an effective tool to improve labor productivity and to release labor for more productive employment.

China has made effective use of her idle and underemployed rural manpower in the construction of irrigation and land development projects and in rural industries. The utilization of surplus farm and non-farm labor has received special attention from the Chinese planners. In traveling to the Great Wall, we saw large numbers of students and city workers from Peking harvesting wheat in the countryside, which exemplified China's efforts in mobilizing the non-farm workers during periods of peak labor demand. We felt that the judicious utilization of surplus labor and the positive outlook toward mechanization have been the two important factors in introducing agricultural mechanization in China.

In agricultural mechanization their priorities seem to be: (a) land development and irrigation, (b) food and fodder processing, (c) transportation, (d) threshing, (e) land preparation, (f) paddy transplanting, and (g) harvesting. Farm mechanization is being progressively introduced in most parts of the country with the more power-consuming and labor-intensive operations being mechanized first. Manual labor and draft animals, however, continue to be of considerable importance at this stage and are still widely used. In the more progressive areas, such as Kiangsu Province, however, increased attention is now being directed to greater land consolidation to permit full-scale farm mechanization.

While their long-range aims are to mechanize agriculture with larger farm equipment, present emphasis is on the production of a wide variety of machines ranging from simple manual and animal-drawn implements to fairly sophisticated large tractors and combines. The variety of locally produced tractors and agricultural machines is surprisingly broad in China. While the designs appeared similar to those of other industrialized countries, they have been well adapted for heavier-duty service.

Local production of tractors and farm machines is among the five important industrial activities which have been selected for major attention in recent years. These five industries are iron and steel, power, cement, fertilizer, and farm machinery. We were told at a briefing in Peking that the production of tractors has increased by 520% in China from 1964 to 1974, with a recent average annual growth of 20%, and the number of power tillers has increased 30 times since the Cultural Revolution. (These figures are somewhat substantiated by the information found in U.S. government publications, which indicate a production of 138,000 standard 15-h.p. units in 1973 against 19,300 15-h.p. units in 1964. It further gives credibility to the Chinese claim that since 1965 agricultural machinery manufacturing plants have increased by four times and the number of workers has increased by six times. Also see Table V-3.) The rate of annual increase in power tiller and diesel engine production has recently been 40% and 30%, respectively.

Apparently, China has been quite successful in transfering and adapting a wide variety of mechanization technologies from all over the world. Understandably it has placed relatively less emphasis in its early stage of development on finding indigenous solutions to some of its specific mechanization problems. We felt the diversity in the indigenous designs that originated from Japan during its early mechanization stage was far greater than what we see in China today. This shortcoming, however, is now being rectified because almost all agricultural engineering research institutions are currently working on the development of new machines to solve their local mechanization problems.

China's farm machinery manufacturing industry is currently passing through a rather dynamic period in which the products and the production processes are being rapidly changed and upgraded. Production of less complex machines, requiring lower capital investments, is decentralized to the county, commune, and brigade levels. There is a steady trend of increasing sophistication in the manufacturing operation at the lower organizational levels; thus the commune and brigade workshops are progressively tackling more challenging production problems. Self-reliance in manufacturing has helped to develop local technical capabilities among the rural people. The Chinese experiment on the development of rural farm machinery industries

Table V-1

UNIT PRICES OF SELECTED AGRICULTURAL
MACHINERY IN CHINA(1975)[a]

Item	Price in yuan
A. Prime power	
Gasoline engine, 76 h.p., 4000 rpm	2,500
Diesel engine, 55 h.p.	3,200
Four-wheel tractor, with 55-h.p. diesel engine	10,000
Crawler tractor, with 20-h.p. diesel engine	4,000
Crawler tractor, with 10-h.p. diesel engine	3,600
Power tiller, with 12-h.p. diesel engine	2,000
Diesel engine, 3.5 h.p., aircooled, 2000 rpm, 40 kwgt.	550
B. Farm machinery	
Wheat seeder, bullock-drawn, 2-row, wooden	35
Transplanter, manually drawn	60
Transplanter, power-driven, 14-row, without engine	1,000
Irrigation equipment—motor and pump, price per h.p.	210[b]

[a]Data collected from briefings.
[b]From U.S. Government publications.

is thus a continuing process and should be viewed more on the basis of its achievements rather than on the current level of mechanization technology.

MECHANIZATION

Basically the ownership of land and capital is divided among three organizational levels, namely, commune, brigade, and the production team, although some variations exist in practice. A production team, which may consist of 20–30 households, retains only the simpler agricultural equipment and hand tools used in the farming operations. The brigade and the commune provide the larger, more costly equipment (Table V-1). A brigade may control 10–15 production teams and farm an area of about 100–150 ha. The pressure for both land and labor productivity provides sufficient incentives to make use of every inch of available land. Since land is not individually owned, adjustments in field sizes easily can be made. China's efforts toward land consolidation were exemplified at the Tachai Brigade where fields have been enlarged recently up to 1.5-ha. size by consolidating smaller terraced fields to facilitate movement of larger machines.

We saw ample evidence of increasing arable land through reclamation and improvement projects in every area that we visited. In Shansi province, we saw badly eroded mountainous areas, with yellowish wind-deposited loess soils, being reclaimed for good arable land. Impressive progress was made at Hsi-yang County and at the famous Tachai Brigade in reclaiming land through terracing of mountains and filling of gullies and riverbeds (Photo V-1). In the nearby Hui County and Hsin-hsiang areas, north of the Yellow River, we came across many land development, irrigation, and water control projects, which have helped to transform sandy and marshy riverbeds into productive agricultural land. In Lin County, North Honan province, we saw the 70-km. long Red Flag Trunk Canal and its 1500-km. long distribution network. Water from the Chang River is brought from neighboring Shansi province over rugged mountainous terrain to irrigate 40,000 ha. of fertile agricultural land. The canal was built by 40,000 workers and took almost 10 years to complete.

Modern seed-fertilizer technology, improved irrigation, and land consolidation have helped the introduction of agricultural mechanization in the dryland farming areas of Peking municipality and Shansi and Honan Provinces. The climate and the agricultural production practices in these areas do not seem to present any major technical bottlenecks to mechanization; hence, mechanization is progressing rather well. For example, we learned at the Red Star Commune near Peking that the commune, with 10,800 ha. cropping area, is rapidly mechanizing its cultivation and currently

PHOTO V-1. Terraced fields at the Tachai Brigade.

has 125 four-wheel tractors and 140 threshers. The commune leaders expect each of their 129 brigades to have two to three tractors and two threshers within the next three to four years.

Rice is an important crop in the wetland areas of Shanghai municipality and Kiangsu Province, where two annual crops of wetland rice and one of winter wheat are raised. The relatively short rainy season of only one month, from mid-June to mid-July, does not present any problem in the use of modern farm machines for land preparation and threshing. These operations are almost fully mechanized through the use of four-wheel tractors, small power tillers, and stationary power threshers.

In the southern province of Kwangtung, two crops of rice and one other crop, such as sweet potato, are annually grown. This is an area of heavy rainfall spread over a long period. Rice production practices here are quite similar to those in southeast Asia and agricultural mechanization has not made as much progress as in the other parts of China that we visited. The first crop is harvested, and the second is planted during the long rainy season. The wet field and crop conditions during the rainy season make it difficult to mechanize rice production; mechanization of such wetland paddy areas is not only a problem in China, but in almost all tropical Asian rice-growing countries. We felt that greater emphasis should be placed on the development of lightweight tractors, power tillers, traction-assisting wheels, and portable power threshers to mechanize rice production in the southern part of the country.

Almost all areas that we visited had mechanically powered irrigation systems; we hardly came across any manual or animal-powered equipment for pumping water. Most communes had large pumping installations with appropriate water distribution systems. A large number of small portable pumping sets are also used for lifting water from canals, wells, and rivers in most places that we visited. In Kiangsu Province and in Shanghai municipality, we visited two brigades in which all land had been consolidated into large, well-laid rectangular fields with excellent water control systems in which networks of underground irrigation channels alternated with open drainage canals. We also saw an underground water distribution network with large sprinklers for grain production and drip irrigation systems for fruit orchards in the dryland areas of Shansi and Honan Provinces.

We were surprised at the widespread use of electric motors to power irrigation pumps, threshers, and other similar stationary agricultural machines. Long temporary extension cables are used to provide even remote fields with electric power for operating such machines. Electric power is popular because it is available at a subsidized rate for agricultural use (Table V-2). In comparison, diesel engines are generally not popular for powering stationary machines, although we saw some engines being used with irrigation pumps in Honan and Hopei Provinces.

Table V-2

PRICES OF FUEL AND ELECTRICITY IN CHINA, 1975[a]

Item	Purpose	Price in yuan (yuan)
Fuel		
Diesel, kg.	General	0.40
Diesel, kg.	Agricultural	0.27
Gasoline, l.	General	1.42
Electricity, kwh.	Household	0.07
	Industrial	0.06
	Agricultural	0.03

[a]Data collected from briefings during visit.

Most land development and reclamation work is done manually with shovels, baskets, hand-pulled carts, and other simple tools. This permits maximum use of locally available manpower and saves large capital outlay for heavy construction equipment. The magnitude and quality of some of the capital construction projects that have been undertaken with manual labor is impressive in China. In Shansi Province, we saw soil being transported manually over a 4-km. distance in small carts by thousands of men. This soil was being used to build a large dam and to cover the riverbed downstream with 1 m. topsoil. Interestingly, two large bulldozers were used on this project for spreading and compacting soil—an operation that was mechanized because it could not be satisfactorily done by manual methods. Locally built power cable winches were used to pull dirt-laden handcarts up the sides of the dam where the slope was too steep for human power. Apparently selective mechanization is practiced to supplement labor only when manual methods are difficult or not possible. The simultaneous use of hand shovels, picks, baskets, and large bulldozers on the same project, however, represented two rather extreme levels of construction technology. We felt that there was scope for intermediate level power equipment to improve labor productivity on capital construction projects.

Most communes have centralized food and fodder processing plants to handle a substantial part of the commune's production. The Red Star Commune annually processes 15 million kg. of wheat, rice, and feed. We saw a flour mill with an output capacity of 4000 tons per year in this commune. It was being operated on a three-shift basis during the busy season. All processing equipment used in this mill was locally produced in China and was of fairly modern design. The mill was designed for bulk handling and continuous-flow operation. Most brigades in this commune have smaller flour mills; about 42% of the total grain produced in the commune was processed at the brigade plants. We saw a brigade flour mill at Ch'i-li-ying Commune in Honan Province, which was milling 10,000 kg. of flour per day. This mill had fairly modern equipment and was equipped for continuous-flow operation.

We were told that mechanization of food and fodder processing has been emphasized in China to release the woman labor that had been traditionally used for these operations. Interestingly, the same reason was given at a textile mill in Lin County for the setting up of a special yarn spinning section for home weaving. Previously women used to spend two to four times as much time in spinning yarn as in weaving cloth in their homes. The spinning operation was mechanized by the mill, and weaving was still being done by women in their spare time. Their efforts to release women from traditional chores seem to have been rather effective, for today women are an important part of the labor force in China and are actively engaged in agricultural, industrial, and capital construction projects.

We were surprised by the diversity of the modes of transportation in the rural areas: baskets, manual and animal-drawn carts, power tillers, and tractor-trailer combinations. In the northern areas near Peking and Shansi, we saw relatively more animal-drawn carts than in the Kiangsu, Shanghai, and Kwangtung areas. The latter regions are well served with good canal networks and boats are widely used. The surprisingly high use of power tillers and four-wheel tractors for transport accounts for the high degree of annual tractor and power tiller usage in China. We were told that it is easier for the communes and brigades to justify the acquisition of tractors and power tillers than trucks, for these can be effectively used throughout the year for both agricultural and haulage operations. Consequently, trucks are not as widely used for short-haul farm transport; however, trucks are widely used on main intercity roads. Although a wide range of trucks are locally manufactured, we also saw many Japanese and East European trucks. But we rarely saw imported tractors or power tillers, which probably reflects the greater emphasis placed on achieving self-sufficiency in the local production of tractors and farm equipment.

We also observed that large quantities of organic fertilizer are applied in most parts of China, anywhere from 3–12 metric tons per ha. This organic fertilizer is almost entirely collected, composted, and distributed by human labor. We did not see any signs of mechanization of the labor-consuming operations related to organic fertilizer.

The variety of tractors, power tillers, and other agricultural equipment seemed unusually broad, probably because, in the early stages, China imported almost all kinds of tractors and farm equipment from all over the world and successfully adapted many of these machines to local conditions.

China produces both large and small crawler tractors. We saw locally

Photo V-2. Ten horsepower crawler tractor being trial-produced for hilly areas.

produced crawler tractors of more than 70 h.p. in land development operations, and saw two such machines being used for harrowing in Shansi and Honan Provinces. We were told that small 10-h.p. and 20-h.p. crawler tractors are better suited for hilly areas. A farm machinery plant in Hsi-yang County has produced a 10-h.p. crawler tractor (Photo V-2) on a trial production basis. This tractor was equipped with dual three-point linkages for mounting two one-way plows for operations in small terraced hilly fields. Its 10-h.p. vertical diesel engine was produced by a provincial plant at T'ai-yuan in Shansi Province.

China is producing larger four-wheel tractors of 12-, 20-, 27-, 28-, 35-, 40-, 45-, 50-, 54-, 55-, and 75-h.p. sizes. The tractors and their engines are produced at national and provincial level plants in many parts of the country. We were told that the tractor plant at Lo-yang, Honan Province, is one of the largest in China; we came across many tractors produced there during our travels. Data on the total number of plants manufacturing agricultural tractors was difficult to obtain but we concluded from the different machines that we saw and the estimates in Table V-3 that China has a large number of tractor manufacturing units spread across the country. The table, however, indicates that the power input through irrigation equipment is far greater than that obtained from tractors and power tillers in China.

Table V-3

PRODUCTION OF AGRICULTURAL TRACTORS AND IRRIGATION EQUIPMENT IN CHINA, 1975[a]

Year	Standard tractors		Garden tractors		Irrigation equipment	
	Inventory	Production	Inventory	Production	Inventory	Production
	(Thousand 15-h.p. units)[b]		(Thousand 15-h.p. units)[b]		(1000 h.p.)	
1959	59.0	9.4	NA	NA	2,535.0	1,255.0
1964	123.0	19.3	0.15	0.15	7,300.0	860.0
1969	n.a.	40.0	11.62	3.20	n.a.	n.a.
1973	354.0[c]	138.0	79.25	28.00	30,000.0	5,984.0

[a]U.S. Government publications

[b]Tractor sizes are converted into standard units of 15 drawbar horsepower as follows:

$$\text{No. of 15-h.p. units} = \frac{\text{Tractor brake horsepower}}{15} \times 0.65 = \frac{\text{Tractor drawbar horsepower}}{15}$$

[c]1972

Most smaller four-wheel riding tractors of less than 20 h.p. are produced by plants at the county and commune levels. Designs vary considerably We saw small riding tractors with both horizontal and vertical engines and with belt-drive or in-line transmissions. These tractors are widely used for transport, particularly in the north.

We found a somewhat limited variety in the designs of power tillers. In general, the Chinese power tillers are from 8–12 h.p. in size. We saw three different designs: two were in the northern areas, with single-cylinder horizontal diesel engines and V-belt drives to the transmission, and one was in Kwangtung Province, with a vertical diesel engine and an in-line shaft drive to the transmission. Almost all Chinese power tillers are equipped with a seat attachment for the operator, which is convenient for hauling trailers. We were told at some brigades that power tillers are used exclusively for transport and larger tractors for agricultural operations. However, power tillers are widely used for agricultural operations in the northern wetland paddy areas and for vegetable production near major cities. We did not see lightweight power tillers of less than 8 h.p., but we were told that such machines were imported from Japan in the early days and were found unsuitable for local conditions. Interest in lightweight power tillers is, however, reviving, for some manufacturing units indicated that they expect to produce lighter tillers in the future.

Most agricultural tractors, combines, and other agricultural machines are powered by diesel engines. The price of diesel fuel is subsidized for agricultural use at about 30% lower than for other uses, providing a strong incentive for using diesel engines wherever cheaper electric power is not conveniently available. This is probably another reason for the widespread use of diesel-powered tractors rather than gasoline-powered small trucks for farm transport.

We were told in the northern areas of China that 60–100% of the land was plowed by mechanized methods. We did not, however, observe such a high degree of mechanization in land preparation. While we did see a few large crawler and four-wheel tractors and some power tillers being used for land preparation, we saw widespread use of animals for this operation in Shansi and the Honan Provinces. This discrepancy may possibly be due to differences in the definition of the term "mechanized plowing"—as the Chinese may be classifying the use of improved animal-drawn implements among mechanized operations.

In Lin County the second crop is planted under minimum tillage practices with no land preparation. Simple one- to three-row animal-drawn seeders are widely used for planting. Most communes and brigades in the northern areas of China that we visited had a fair number of work animals. In Kiangsu Province and Shanghai municipality, however, land preparation is almost completely mechanized with power tillers and four-wheel tractors;

we saw no work animals at the communes and brigades. In the southern province of Kwangtung, animals are popularly used for wetland preparation. We were informed that only 20% of the land in this area is prepared with tractors.

Poor tractor mobility in wet paddy fields is also a problem in southern China. A four-wheel drive version of a 30-h.p. tractor manufactured by the Shanghai (Bumper Harvest) Tractor Factory has recently been offered for use in wetland paddies. Four-wheel drive improves tractor mobility; however, such a solution is costly. In Kwangtung Province, we saw four-wheel tractors being operated in paddy fields with rear steel cage wheels and saw one such tractor, bogged down, being pulled out by another. Steel tractor wheels have been used for rice cultivation in Southeast Asia; however, these have now been replaced with traction-assisting cage wheel attachments on standard tractor tires. An extendible lug wheel attachment has been recently gaining popularity in Southeast Asia.[2] It permits adjustable traction capability to suit different field conditions and provides means to extract a bogged tractor under its own power. Some of these developments can be effectively utilized in China. We feel that more research and experimental efforts are needed to solve the tractor mobility problems for wetland paddy cultivation in southern China.

Mechanization of direct seeding in dryland areas has progressed well and equipment is locally produced for tractor- and animal-drawn seeders. We were told that 90% of the wheat in Peking municipality was sown by mechanized equipment, and nearly 80% of the seeding equipment is built at the commune plants. The practice of transplanting wheat and corn after harvesting rice has recently been introduced into northern China and is gaining in popularity.

Direct seeding for wetland paddy is not practiced in China, because they feel that this reduces yields. Mechanization of paddy transplanting has received considerable attention over the last two decades. Manually operated six-row tweezer-type planters (Photo V-3) have been popular in China for years. One man can transplant 1/30 ha. per day with these machines, which are fairly low-priced, about 60 yuan. These manual transplanters are gradually being replaced with a mechanically powered riding type transplanter that was developed about five years ago in China (Photo V-4). This machine does not require specially grown seedling like the Japanese transplanters do, but can transplant seedlings conventionally grown in field nurseries. These machines are available in 10-, 12-, 14-, and 16-row sizes. Three men can transplant 2 ha. per day with a 12-row machine.

These transplanters have two rows of seedling-prongs mounted with a rotary arrangement to pull seedlings out of hoppers and drop them on the

2. Agricultural Engineering Dept., 1971. Semiannual Report No. 13, International Rice Research Institute (Los Banos, Philippines).

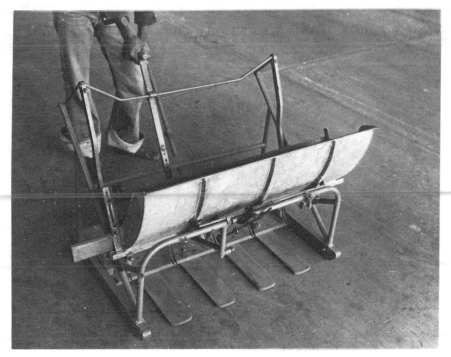

PHOTO V-3. Manually operated Chinese type transplanter.

puddled soil. We saw the production of 14- and 16-row transplanters of this type at a commune plant in Wu-hsi, Kiangsu Province. These 14- to 16-row machines are powered by 3-h.p. and 4-h.p. single-cylinder aircooled gasoline or diesel engines. Three operators ride the machine; one to drive and two to keep the individual-row seedling hoppers replenished from larger central hoppers. Current Chinese efforts to mechanize paddy transplanting are primarily directed toward popularizing this particular machine.

Almost all types of plant protection equipment are locally produced in China; manually operated backpack sprayers are still the most popular. We saw power-operated high-pressure sprayers being used from narrow levees in paddy fields in Kiangsu Province. Because of the narrow field levees, a crew of five men—two to carry the sprayer on a pole, two to carry the chemical containers, and one to handle the sprayer nozzle—were needed to operate this machine. The development of lightweight power sprayer units in which the engine pump and tanks are integrally mounted may help to reduce manpower requirements for such applications.

We saw a few small cutterbar-type harvester-windrowers being used to harvest wheat near Peking. Much of the efforts to mechanize the harvesting of dryland crops seem geared toward the introduction of large combines into the arid and semi-arid areas of northern China. All types of conventional

Photo V-4. Recently developed riding type power-operated paddy transplanter.

combine harvesters—trailed, tractor-mounted, and self-propelled machines—are being locally manufactured in China. We were told at the Red Star Commune in Peking that it had nine large combines, some of which were specially designed for rice harvesting. Unfortunately, we saw only one combine, a tractor-mounted version (Photo V-5) at a commune farm machinery shop in Wu-hsi County.. This locally manufactured machine was similar to a West European design in which the harvesting header is mounted at the front; a side-mounted conveyor delivers the harvested crop to the threshing mechanism at the rear.

Harvesting of paddy is still a manual operation and the development of small rice harvesters and combines is just beginning to receive increased attention from central and provincial agricultural machinery research institutes. We saw two side-delivery, cutterbar-type rice harvesters (Photo V-6), each about 4 ft. wide, at a commune in Kiangsu Province and were told that these are now in the trial production stage. We also learned that field tests are being conducted in Kwangtung Province on a two-row combine attachment for small power tillers which is quite different in principle from the head-stripping-type Japanese combine harvesters.

The threshing of wheat and rice has been substantially mechanized, mostly with electrically powered threshers, in the Peking, Shansi, Honan,

Photo V–5. Locally built tractor-mounted rice combine.

Kiangsu, and Shanghai areas. The grain is dried in the sun immediately after threshing. Harvested crops are transported from the fields to the threshing floors by a variety of methods ranging from manually carried bundles to animal- and tractor-drawn trailers. Interestingly, there is considerable variation in the designs of the simple throw-in type wheat threshers used in North China, ranging from simple units consisting of only a power-driven threshing cylinder to fairly complex machines with straw walkers and air-screen cleaners. The latter designs are now gaining in popularity; we saw the production of two such machines at a commune plant in Peking and at a county plant in Hsi-yang.

The wide diversity in simple throw-in designs for threshers is probably due to the many independent efforts to develop machines to suit local conditions. We saw threshers with cylindrical and conical drums; with spike tooth, raspbar, beater, and wire-loop type threshing drums; with axial-flow and through-flow material movement; and with a variety of grain-cleaning mechanisms. Except for a few larger conventional type threshers, the simpler Chinese threshers were somewhat of non-professional designs. Most of the threshers have been developed at brigade level by mechanics and farmers

PHOTO V-6. Side-delivery paddy harvester in Kiangsu province.

with considerable practical experience, but, understandably, not too much professional expertise in machinery design and development.

We felt that considerable improvements are needed in the locally designed throw-in-type threshers, particularly in the grain separation and cleaning mechanisms. Most simpler threshers did not adequately separate and clean the grain; consequently, considerable labor (Photo V-7) is required for grain separation and cleaning. Efforts also are needed to evaluate the many types of simple threshers and to standardize the more efficient throw-in type machines in China.

In the Kiangsu and Shanghai area, on the other hand, we found little variety in thresher designs. Paddy and wheat are threshed on the threshing floors with simple hold-on type threshers (Photo V-8) that consist basically of a 6- to 8-ft. long power-operated wire-loop or spiketooth type threshing drum. Four to six men manually hold paddy or wheat bundles against the rotating drum to strip the grain from the panicles. Grain is then manually separated from straw and cleaned. We did not see any throw-in type of threshers being used for paddy in China, which may be due to the fact that paddy straw is preserved for paper-making, roofing, and other industrial purposes. Hold-on type threshers do not damage the straw because it does

PHOTO V-7. Wheat threshing with small power threshers in Lin County. (Note large crew that is needed to recover grain from threshed straw.)

not enter the machine. These machines are quite simple but require relatively more labor than the throw-in type and may be preferable for labor-surplus areas.

In the southern province of Kwangtung, paddy is threshed in the field with small lightweight foot-pedal operated threshers (Photo V-9). The larger power-driven paddy threshers, as used in Kiangsu and Shanghai areas, are not successful in Kwangtung Province because of the difficulties of transporting such machines in wet paddy fields. The development of lightweight power-operated paddy threshers is an urgent necessity for Kwangtung Province where the rainy season is fairly long and field conditions at harvest time are not suitable for conventionally powered harvesting-threshing machines.

Manually operated wooden winnowers (Photo V-10) are used to clean grain in many parts of China. Grain is also winnowed on the threshing floors by manually throwing it into the air with shovels. In Lin County, we saw an interesting machine (Photo V-11), in which a rubber belt mechanically throws dirty grain into the air, simulating the traditional method of cleaning.

Photo V–8. Simple hold-on type power threshers in Shanghai.

The use of special grain-cleaning equipment after threshing is an interim solution because of the poor cleaning performance of the available threshers. It will probably disappear as better threshers are made available.

China has paid considerable attention to the development of its power-generating capacity. Of particular interest are the efforts to tap hydroelectric power in combination with the schemes for water conservation, drainage, irrigation, and river navigation. China has more than 50,000 small hydro power stations; we were told that the number of small stations (less than 6000 kw.) has increased nine times since the Cultural Revolution. The state, province, or district design offices provide the equipment and plans for building power stations; the local brigades and communes construct the stations. We saw a series of small hydroelectric stations on a canal with a 1 m³ per sec. flow in Lin County. This canal had one 250-kw. plant (Photo V-12) with a 15-m. headfall and twenty-six 40-kw. brigade-run power stations (Photo V-13) spread at intervals of 5-m. headfall. These power stations were all hooked to the state electric grid. Lin County has a total of 65 hydro power stations with a total capacity of 10,400 kw., which provided electricity to 80% of the farmhouses. Electrical power is used to process

Photo V-9. Lightweight pedal threshers popular in southern China.

80% of their farm produce. Similarly, in Kwangtung Province we saw a dam in a river estuary that was used to raise the water level to improve navigation.

Twenty-two turbo hydroelectric generators were installed in the dam to utilize the variations in water level due to tidal currents for generating electricity. This project produces 12 million kwh. of electricity annually, which is sufficient to meet half of the county's electrical requirements for agricultural production.

A good measure of the mechanization level of a country is the horse-power utilized per hectare in field operations through the use of manual, animal, and mechanical power. Giles[3] estimates that a minimum power input of 0.5 h.p. per ha. is necessary to produce average crop yields of about 2.5 tons per ha. Based on a similar analysis, estimated power used in China for field operations was 0.4 h.p. per ha. in 1973. While this power input is much higher than in other developing countries, experience with the other developed countries indicates that further increase in food production in

3. G. W. Giles, 1975. "Reorientation of Agricultural Mechanization in Developing Countries." *Agricultural Mechanization in Asia.* Vol. VI, No. 2.

PHOTO V-10. Manually operated winnower for grain cleaning.

China would require substantially higher inputs of mechanical power in agriculture.

Giles did not include the power used in irrigation in his study. The power input for irrigation in China is 30×10^6 h.p. or 0.23 h.p. per ha. (Table V-3). The total farm power input in China thus, inclusive of irrigation, is estimated to be 0.63 h.p. per ha. in 1973, which compares favorably with some of the more progressive countries in the developing world.

RESEARCH, DEVELOPMENT, AND TECHNOLOGY TRANSFER

The Institute of Agricultural Machinery at Peking, which comes under the No. 1 Machinery Ministry, is the central organization responsible for agricultural machinery research and development at the national level. Most provinces also have agricultural machinery institutes that work on local problems. The central institute at Peking does R&D work in cooperation with other organizations on problems that may be commonly present in many parts of China. It is also engaged in other research and development work

PHOTO V-11. Simple mechanical thrower for separating grain from chaff in natural air.

that cannot be conveniently handled at the provincial level. Some of the provincial tractor and farm machinery plants have their own R&D departments that develop machines in their specific areas of interest. The central institute plans and coordinates the projects that it supports at the provincial level; the provincial institutes, however, operate rather independently and are responsible only to the provincial authorities. The central institute organizes periodic conferences, discussions and exchange meetings on professional matters. This institute is solely responsible for the formulation of agricultural machinery standards in the country.

Unfortunately, we were not able to visit any of the research institutes, although we did meet some of the staff of the central machinery institute

PHOTO V–12. A 250-kw. hydroelectric station in Lin County.

in Peking and the provincial institute at Kwangtung Province. We were told that the Agricultural Machinery Research Institute at Peking has a staff of about 600, out of which 70% are engineering and technical personnel. The institute staff members spend considerable time in the field, either on research projects or on-farm jobs. As a rule, all technical staff must spend at least three months per year, and the administrative staff at least one month, working in the field. Most of the Institute's research and development projects are scattered across the country; consequently, a large part of the staff stays on field locations away from Peking. No clear distinction is made between research and development projects at the Institute, although we gathered that more emphasis is placed on the development of new and improved machines. Research is done only when necessary in the execution of machinery development projects.

Our impression was that agricultural machinery research institutes are concerned mostly with the development of simpler machines such as threshers, transplanters, harvesters, and combines. More complex equipment, such as internal combustion engines and four-wheel tractors and power tillers, are developed by the engine and tractor manufacturing units. Farm

PHOTO V-13. Power generation room of a 40-kw. brigade-run hydroelectric station.

machinery research institutes, however, play an important role in the evaluation, transfer and dissemination of machinery designs and provide technical assistance to manufacturing plants. The institute follows these steps in the development of new machines:

(a) survey of local machinery needs and farming conditions
(b) research and experimental studies, if needed
(c) design, fabrication, and evaluation of prototype machines
(d) establishment of a project committee, with representatives from the institute, potential manufacturers and end-users
(e) approval of the project committee for continuation of the project
(f) preparation of detailed engineering drawings and their release for trial production to county or city manufacturing plants
(g) testing and evaluation of trial-produced machines
(h) approval of any design changes and performance results of the trial-production machine by the project committee
(i) release of design for regular production

   Interestingly, the research institutes follow a machinery development strategy quite similar to that followed worldwide by established machinery manufacturers. Machines are developed only in response to specific needs, which are established by surveys that could be compared with market research and product planning in private industry. This is an effective approach, compared with the one followed by public research organizations in most developing countries, in which projects are often initiated without establishing their need.

The Provincial Farm Machinery Institute in Kwangtung Province has a staff of 150–160 people, of which about 60 are professionals. This institute is slightly larger than average provincial institutes. The institute is organized in six sections consisting of: (1) land preparation-cultivation and transplanting, (2) harvesting-threshing and processing, (3) engine improvements and modifications, (4) technology development (new products, methods), (5) technology innovation-manufacturing extension, and (6) information and reference. They have a design and prototype shop. Their main concern is to mechanize the cultivation of rice, bananas, and sugarcane. Their current research emphasizes paddy seedling removal from nurseries, transplanting, harvesting, and threshing of paddy, and the development of 20-h.p. riding tractors. We saw widespread use of sun-drying on roads and concrete floors in Kwangtung and other parts of China, but for some reason they have placed very little emphasis on paddy drying at the Kwangtung provincial research institute.

Some of the larger national and provincial manufacturing units have their own design and development departments. The Internal Combustion Engine Plant in Peking, a textile plant in Hsin-hsiang, and a machine tool plant in Shanghai, which we visited, were doing their own design and development work. As mentioned earlier, R&D at these industrial units is concerned with the design and development of more sophisticated machines, such as internal combustion engines, large tractors, and heavy machine tools, among other types. Shanghai has an institute for internal combustion engines, which sometimes provides engine designs to manufacturing units. We saw only one county plant in Wu-hsi producing a single-cylinder aircooled gasoline engine, which was designed by this institute.

We were told that in the early stages of mechanization in China, the development and manufacture of agricultural machines was rather centralized. This often resulted in the overproduction of inappropriate machines. Subsequently, a decentralized R&D and machinery manufacturing policy was instituted that has minimized some of the earlier problems. The research and development activities and machinery production are more relevant to the local needs. Considerable emphasis is now placed on thorough field testing and evaluation of new machines. To safeguard against subsequent field problems, machines are generally produced for one or two years on a trial basis before commencing regular production.

In response to our queries on who designs new machines, we were invariably told that a three-in-one approach is followed in the development process. It was evident in the discussions that the design engineers work rather closely with the production engineers and potential end-users to ensure that the machine meets the utilization as well as the manufacturing criteria. The team approach is preferred and encouraged over individual efforts. We came across no cases in which an individual was credited for the design of a machine.

The designs of the larger four-wheel tractors and other agricultural machines in China are patterned after machines from other industrialized countries. China has undoubtedly learned from the mechanization experience of other countries and has successfully adapted and improved conventional machines to suit local conditions. We find that most Chinese machines have been well adapted for the functional and low-volume production aspects. Extensive use of cast iron and aluminum castings is made to facilitate production by small foundries in the rural areas. Relatively less attention is paid to styling, industrial design, and fancy sheet metal work to improve machine appearance. Most mobile agricultural machines use slow-speed diesel engines that need less maintenance and result in trouble-free operation. Low-powered aircooled gasoline engines are seldom used in agricultural machines except for some paddy transplanters and harvesters where light weight is necessary to improve field mobility in wet fields.

Higher authorities often assign responsibilities to larger manufacturing units for developing new machines to suit specific needs. Since inventions and new machinery designs are not considered as proprietary items in China, engineering drawings and other technical information are readily exchanged with other manufacturing units. Because of this free flow of machinery designs and production knowhow, one finds that the same machine is often produced by different manufacturing units in many parts of the country. For example, the engines produced at the Internal Combustion Engine Plant at Peking are also produced by five other plants in the country. Similarly, a new lightweight diesel engine design, which is planned for production at the Peking plant in 1976, has already been released to another manufacturing unit. In the same manner, the 10-h.p. crawler tractor for hilly areas, being produced in Hsi-yang County, was developed with the help of the Lo-yang No. 1 Research Center of the state-run tractor plant. This 10-h.p. tractor also is being trial-produced in small batches in a few other states.

Apparently, there is no single pattern for transfering machinery design. The manufacturing units seem to have considerable flexibility in either obtaining new designs from outside sources or conducting their own design and development work. For example, a commune-operated agricultural machinery plant in Wu-hsi indicated that it does not work at all with the national or provincial research institutes, but gets the new designs from the more advanced machinery manufacturing units whenever it is in need of a new design.

Quite often, the central, state, and municipal governments also act as channels for the transfer of machinery designs from one manufacturing plant to another. We were told at the Red Star Commune that they pass any new development in machinery to the authorities of the Peking municipality, which holds regular exchange meetings to disperse information on new machinery developments and helps in exchanging information among interested parties. The 12-h.p. power tiller that was being trial-produced in Lin County was based on a design that the state had provided from the larger state-run power tiller plant at Cheng-chou, the state capital. The state-run Cheng-chou plant also trained the engineers from the county plant and provided complete production knowhow. Technical personnel are freely exchanged between manufacturing units and on-the-job training and personal contacts are the most popular methods of technology transfer. The more successful communes, brigades, and industrial shops serve as demonstration models and have regular streams of visitors from all over China. This technique is effectively used to demonstrate and teach modern agricultural and industrial methods. For example, the famous Ta-chai Brigade receives thousands of visitors every day. We were told that their record for the maximum number of visitors on a single day stands at 30,000. We felt that there is much less dependence on written communication for transfering industrial technology in China than in most other industrialized countries. Production workers are normally trained through an apprenticeship process; we saw many apprentices working beside experienced machine operators in almost every plant. The apprentices receive one or two years of on-the-job training. Some of the larger factories operate industrial colleges in which selected employees obtain two years of combined engineering studies along with practical shop experience. The Internal Combustion Engine Plant in Peking, the machine tool plant in Shanghai, and the textile plant in Cheng-chou all operate industrial colleges to train workers in their respective engineering fields.

MANUFACTURE OF AGRICULTURAL MACHINERY

The Chinese Government is committed to a policy of decentralization of small-scale industries to the rural areas; farm machinery production is one of the country's important small-scale industries. Broadly speaking, the manufacture of tractors and agricultural machines is organized at three levels: (1) national and provincial, (2) county and city, and (3) commune and brigade. The complexity of the machine and the production process dictate the level at which a machine is produced in China.

Interestingly, farm equipment manufacturing has served as a foundation for many of the large industrial plants that we visited. Some of the early farm machinery plants have now transformed into giant industries that produce other industrial machines and products, such as gasoline and diesel engines, machine tools, and textile equipment among others. The smaller plants initially produce a wider variety of products. As new markets develop for some products, new specialized plants are set up. In Hsi-yang, a steel plant, an electric motor plant, and a small crawler tractor plant have all developed from a parent plant producing agricultural machinery. Similarly, we were told that the Peking Internal Combustion Engine Plant started as a farm machinery plant in 1949, producing horse-drawn ploughs, reapers, and cultivators. This plant was converted to engine production in 1964 and multiplied into 11 other plants during the period 1964–1974.

To facilitate production of some of the machines at the local level, the more complex machine elements, such as carburetors, fuel injection equipment, electrical and hydraulic components, have been standardized, and these are produced at selected centralized plants in the country. Generally, the more complex agricultural machines, such as larger four-wheel tractors of over 20-h.p. size and the larger four- and six-cylinder diesel and gasoline engines, are produced by national or provincial factories. Machines of medium complexity such as small one- or two-cylinder diesel and gasoline engines, smaller four-wheel riding tractors of less than 20 h.p., and power tillers, are produced at county- or city-managed plants. The least complex machines, such as irrigation pumps, threshers, transplanters, feed grinders, tractor implements and trailers, are produced at commune or, in some cases, at brigade level plants.

Production of internal combustion engines of more than 40-h.p. size has been well stabilized at the national or provincial level. We saw the nationally managed Internal Combustion Engine Plant at Peking, which produces 30,000 diesel and gasoline engines annually in 45-h.p. to 75-h.p. sizes. We also saw a provincial tractor plant in Shanghai (Photo V-14), which was producing 6500 four-wheel tractors annually in 27- and 35-h.p. sizes.

Production of smaller four-wheel tractors and engines of less than 20 h.p. is being decentralized to the county and commune level plants. We were impressed by the rapidity with which this decentralization is taking place. The county- and commune-level farm machinery plants that we visited had only recently started production on a trial basis and were planning to start regular production sometime in 1976. These plants were producing 12-h.p., four-wheel riding tractors at Hsin-hsiang, 12-h.p. power tillers in Lin County, 10-h.p. crawler tractors in Hsi-yang, Shansi Province, 18-h.p. diesel engines at Chia-ting County, 18-row paddy transplanters at

PHOTO V-14. The "Bumper Harvest" tractor made at a provincial tractor plant in Shanghai.

Wu-hsi, Kiangsu Province, and single-cylinder aircooled gasoline engines at Ma-lu Commune, Shanghai municipality. All of these plants were previously producing simpler agricultural machines, such as threshers, pumps, and feed processing equipment. The production of the simpler machines was either terminated due to saturation of local demand or was transferred to lower-level plants. We also learned that Kwangtung and Honan Provinces originally had one power tiller factory each in the capital cities, Canton and Cheng-chou, but small power tiller plants have recently been set up in most counties.

In China, most manufacturing units are provided an annual production target by the higher authorities. The county and city plants are included in the provincial planning schemes, and their production targets are approved by the provincial authorities. Most plants that we visited claimed to produce in excess of their production quotas. Availability of additional raw material to produce beyond the set quota seems not to be too serious a problem. Due to the emphasis on self-sufficiency, most county, commune, and brigade level manufacturing units distribute their products in their own areas. Rarely did we come across small-scale manufacturing units supplying their products beyond their own geographic region. We saw a small electrical transformer manufacturing plant operated by a commune in Shanghai municipality, which supplied its products outside the commune, but most of the other county and lower-level machinery plants produced only for their own consumption. Markets for the county and lower-level plants are, therefore, quite small and production is usually in small volumes.

The limited size of the local market and decentralized production necessitates a highly flexible manufacturing operation with minimum investments in jigs, fixtures, and special production equipment. The factories often switch to the production of new machines as soon as local demand for a machine has been fully met. We came across many cases where production of threshers and other agricultural machines was discontinued because of local market saturation. Our opinion was that the limited size of the local markets has, to some extent, constrained the development of mechanization technology and improvements in the designs of agricultural machines and their production quality, particularly of the simpler farm machines produced at the lower-level plants. While the decentralized production approach may not look very efficient from Western standards, it has, nevertheless, served well in meeting local needs in China, which would have been difficult otherwise. We felt, however, that the decentralization of machinery production seems too rapid at times and has perhaps resulted in considerable discontinuous production.

The national and provincial level plants are quite well equipped with modern mass production machines. We were impressed with the production equipment at the Internal Combustion Engine Plant at Peking. Most of the engine components were machined on specialized automatic and semi-automatic production machines. They had designed their own multispindle boring machines for machining engine blocks and cylinder heads. Their foundry was highly mechanized with the sand conditioning, mould and core production (Photo V-15), and metal pouring done mechanically with rather advanced machines. This plant had two assembly lines, one for gasoline engines and one for diesel engines.

Similarly, at the power tiller manufacturing plant (Photo V-16) in Wu-hsi County, Kiangsu Province, we were impressed by the use of modern specialized production equipment. The three faces of the transmission casings were being simultaneously machined on automatic machines. The plant was equipped with a wide variety of semi-automated and automated machine tools. The plant had high-speed gear shavers and hobbers, as well as electric spark erosion machines for the production of power tiller transmission gears. The heat treatment section had atmospheric and salt bath furnaces and induction hardening machines. In a nearby county-managed electric motor plant, we saw electric spark erosion machines being used to make punching dies for rotor stampings from hardened tool steel.

PHOTO V-15. Filling of large moulds with a mechanical sand ejector at a machine tool plant in Shanghai.

In our visits to county and commune level plants, we were impressed by the judicious mixing of rather modern methods of mass production and simple methods of manual production. For example, it was not uncommon to see large pneumatic power hammers being used along with manual forging operations (Photo V-17). Most county and lower-level plants do not use special production equipment, but depend on standard machine tools. Production of farm machines at the county and commune level plants is quite labor-intensive and offers considerable potential for improvement in labor productivity. For example, we were told that at a commune farm machinery plant in Peking, they had 171 workers and had produced 140 threshers and 50 transplanters last year. Figures available in the Philippines on production of similar types of threshers and other machines with highly labor-intensive methods indicate a requirement of less than half as much labor to produce as many machines. The small size of the local market and the wide variety in the product mix is responsible, to a certain extent, for this low labor productivity. It seems that the emphasis on self-sufficiency in production is more important to China at this moment, and that they are

Photo V-16. The "Tung-fang-12" power tillers being manufactured at a plant in Wu-hsi County, Kiangsu Province.

willing to sacrifice some production efficiency in their early stage of industrialization.

Almost all county and commune level plants have small foundries. The foundry is an important part in most manufacturing units, for castings are liberally used in the production of machines. Most foundry operations of sand conditioning, mould preparation, and metal pouring are done manually at the county and lower-level plants. In only a few larger county plants did we see the use of overhead traveling cranes for transporting molten metal and the use of portable vibrators for tamping sand in the mould boxes.

The use of sheet metal, both stamped and formed, is not popular in the production of agricultural machinery. Perhaps this may be because of the high cost of sheet metal or the shortage of the metal sheets. Fabrication of sheet metal parts requires large investments in stamping presses and dies and is often justified only for larger-volume production. Because of smaller production volumes at the local plants, sheet metal is sparingly used in the production of machine components. In our opinion, sheet metal fabrication was the least developed section in most farm machinery manufacturing plants that we saw. At the Shanghai (Bumper Harvest) Tractor Factory, the

Photo V-17. Mixing of traditional and modern production equipment at a farm machinery plant in Shansi province.

rear tractor sheet metal fenders were hand-fabricated and were full of hammer marks, although they were quite strong. Since sheet metal components are often used to enhance machine appearance, little attention is paid in China to improving the quality of sheet metal components in most agricultural machines.

On the other hand, considerable emphasis has been placed on the development of machining capabilities and most small plants are well equipped with lathes, milling machines, shapers, and other standard machine tools. We were repeatedly told of the many self-made machines that were fabricated by the manufacturing units, and we saw some in operation. The self-made machine approach is still being followed at many plants although these machines are no longer the cobbled-up versions that we had envisioned. Most of the plants produce rather modern machine tools for their own use, which are often comparable to factory-built machine tools. Designs of the machine tools are obtained from the larger machine tool plants and national research institutes. It was our impression, however, that the self-made machine tools approach is beginning to decline as more factory-built machines become available and as production efficiency dictates more specialized machines.

SERVICE AND MAINTENANCE OF FARM MACHINES

Almost 95% of the communes in China have farm machinery workshops. The commune workshops have three main functions: (a) reconditioning of tractors, trucks, and other large equipment; (b) training of technicians, mechanics, and tractor drivers; and (c) production of locally needed simple farm equipment. The brigade workshops are usually smaller and are equipped primarily for servicing and minor repair of the brigade-owned farm equipment. It is not uncommon, however, to see some manufacturing activity at the brigade workshops, particularly of simple farm equipment such as manual and animal-drawn implements.

The Red Star Commune in Peking has a large agricultural machinery facility that is equipped to handle major overhauls of trucks and tractors. The facilities included well-equipped shops for metal working and machining, engine rebuilding, radiator repairing, electrical repair and rewinding, carpentry, and painting. This facility also has a manufacturing section in which fairly large wheat threshers of conventional design are produced (Photo V-18). These wheat threshers are powered by 22-h.p. electric motors and have threshing outputs of 3 tons per h. We were told that the thresher design was obtained from another manufacturing plant in North China. The threshers are distributed only within the commune, and they had produced 140 such machines in 1974. This machinery repair and manufacturing facility has a total of 231 workers with approximately 60 persons working exclusively on repair of machines. The total revenue of their machinery repair and manufacturing facility for 1974 was 574,000 yuan, with approximately half coming from repair and servicing operations. The Red Star Commune has 127 large tractors, 358 walking tractors, 109 trucks, and 411 small machines, such as pumps and generators. The commune workshop handles all major overhaul and repair of these machines.

We saw a few machinery repair shops at the production brigade level. Most of these shops have a few trained mechanics, machine operators, and one or two electricians. These small repair and machine shop facilities have a few lathes and other standard machine shop equipment. In some cases the brigade shops have small foundries and are producing simple threshers, animal-drawn plows, seeders, and other similar equipment. Many commune and some brigade work shops have mobile teams to provide field service during the busy harvesting and threshing season. During slack periods, these teams conduct machinery surveys, collect information on the different machines operating in their areas, study their service and parts needs, and prepare for the next season.

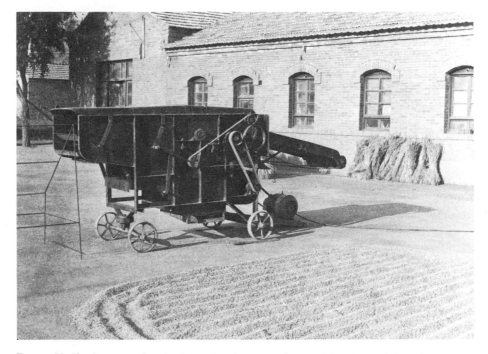

Photo V-18. A conventional wheat thresher manufactured by the Red Star Commune near Peking.

The larger manufacturing units at the national and provincial level, which produce tractors and other large agricultural machines, guarantee their products against manufacturing defects. The diesel and gasoline engines produced by the Internal Combustion Engine Plant at Peking are guaranteed for 100,000 km. of use in minibuses. We were told that fewer than 1% of the engines are returned to the factory for reworking under their warranty scheme. In addition to their regular production the plant annually produces approximately 10–15% additional fast-moving spare parts for diesel engines and 8–10% for gasoline engines. Availability of spare parts in the rural areas is not too serious a problem since many farm machines are produced at the local level and communication is fairly well developed in the rural areas. We were told that most brigade headquarters have telephones, and that obtaining parts from the provincial and national plants is not difficult.

At the Shanghai (Bumper Harvest) Tractor Factory, we learned that their tractors require major overhauls every two to three years after approximately 4000 to 5000 hours of service. From our observations and discussions in China, we believe that the annual tractor and power tiller usage is about 2000 to 2500 hours, which is almost four times that of Japan and about 2.5 times that of the U.S. This high degree of tractor and power tiller usage is possible because machines are often used around the clock with three operators during the busy harvest and planting seasons, and are also regularly used for transport throughout the year.

Agricultural tractors and machines in China seem to be subjected only to a critical level of maintenance involving periodic fuel and lubrication checks. We saw two power tillers being used in Cheng-chou for hauling loads on trailers. They had only one V-belt instead of the three standard belts provided by the manufacturer. Both power tillers had spare V-belts wrapped around the steering handles for emergency use. We also saw quite a number of power tillers in Shanghai municipality in which axle bearings were being replaced on the road. These tractors were being used with trailers for transporting heavy loads, which probably created excessive loading of the main axle bearings.

Apparently, little attention is paid to periodic cleaning of tractors and farm machines; throughout our visit we saw no machines in use which had been recently cleaned. This observation perhaps reflects the continuous heavy-duty use to which the Chinese machines are subjected throughout the year. This apparent lack of maintenance, however, is adequately offset by the heavier-duty designs and sturdiness of the Chinese tractors and other agricultural machines. The use of low-speed diesel engines in small tractors, power tillers, and other farm machines also minimizes service requirements.

Throughout our travel, we never saw yards full of scrapped agricultural machines that one often comes across in other developing countries. Most communes and brigades seem to make good use of their older machines. Ready availability of parts and service facilities in the rural areas keeps the older machines in good working order. Another possible reason for this observation may be the fact that China places great emphasis on the recycling of scrap materials. In Wu-hsi, we saw a county-run steel mill that was producing round steel bars and angle irons from scrap iron collected from the county.

Tractor operators, servicemen, and other technicians are mostly trained through the apprenticeship process at the commune and brigade level shops. In most farm machinery workshops, we saw young apprentices working along with trained operators repairing and operating all kinds of machines.

Well-illustrated maintenance and service manuals on all types of agricultural machines and farm equipment are published by the government press. These publications are quite inexpensive and are available through the bookstores found in almost every small town. Simple handbooks and other written materials are produced on a wide variety of agro-technical subjects that have potential application in the rural areas. For example, in the bookstores we saw Chinese books on all aspects of agricultural production and related subjects such as: seed, fertilizer, and insecticide application; agricultural mechanization; food and fodder processing; hydroelectric plants; design and construction of dams, canals, and reservoirs; and manufacture of cement and fertilizer among others. These are written in a do-it-yourself style and are widely used in brigades and communes in the rural areas. These books are in great demand; we saw people lined up to purchase newer issues at bookstores throughout the country.

CONCLUSION

China has undoubtedly made impressive progress in mechanizing its agriculture and in decentralizing the production of tractors and other agricultural machines. Available mechanization technologies from many parts of the world have been successfully transferred and adapted to suit local farming and manufacturing conditions. In addition, the country has been effectively balancing the demand and supply of labor in the rural areas among three sectors, namely, farming, rural industries, and farm capital construction. The demand for labor in capital construction projects is easier to control, and consequently, this sector has played an important role in absorbing the seasonal surpluses of labor in China.

The progress achieved in irrigation and land development in the dryland areas has assisted the mechanization of agriculture; one sees no major technical bottlenecks to the mechanization of this agroclimatic zone of China. In the wetland paddy cultivation areas, however, some technical problems will require greater research and development efforts. Considerable progress has been achieved in recent years in the development of power-operated paddy transplanters; the new Chinese transplanters have potential for application in almost all developing countries. But not as much progress has been made in the development of machines to solve some of the other problems indigenous to Chinese agriculture. This area needs further attention.

In agricultural mechanization, China is decidedly moving toward the use of larger tractors and other farm equipment. With greater land consolidation, the larger machines will undoubtedly gain substantial popularity in the dryland areas of China. The power tillers, small threshers, and other low-powered machines, however, will continue to be quite popular in the wetland paddy areas. Production of large tractors and other complex agricultural machines is well established and is of fairly high quality at the national and provincial level. The production of machines of medium complexity, such as 10- to 20-h.p. riding tractors, power tillers, and small diesel engines, is being expanded and rapidly decentralized to the city, county and, in some cases, the commune level plants. We believe that in the interest of greater production efficiency, and technological development, the production of such machines will probably stabilize at the county and city levels. In the long run, the commune-level plants will mostly specialize in machine rebuilding and the production of simpler farm machines and implements.

It appears that in the immediate future, the small-scale industries will continue to grow at the county and commune levels at a more rapid pace than in the larger metropolitan areas. The agricultural and related industrial achievements that we saw during our trip no doubt indicate that China will have a highly mechanized agriculture in the not-too-distant future.

Chapter VI

SMALL-SCALE CHEMICAL FERTILIZER TECHNOLOGY

A fertilizer is a material, naturally occurring or synthetically produced, that provides one or more of the plant nutrients, nitrogen, phosphorous, or potassium to living plants. It also may contain other elements such as sulfur, manganese, boron, copper, zinc, and molybdenum, which are often necessary to achieve optimum plant growth. These elements normally required only in minor amounts are referred to as micronutrients, while nitrogen, phosphorous, and potassium are called primary plant nutrients. The complex mechanisms through which plants make use of the primary nutrients and micronutrients are not thoroughly understood, but numerous researchers have proven experimentally that countries striving to improve crop yields will need fertilizers.

Visits were made to the chemical fertilizer factories in Hsi-yang County, Shansi Province; Lin County, and Hui County, Honan Province. Ammonia, ammonium bicarbonate, and ammonium nitrate products were being produced in Hsi-yang and Hui Counties, while in Lin County only ammonia and ammonium bicarbonate products were being made. Most of the discussion in this section for nitrogen production technology is based on briefings and visits to these factories. Phosphate technology was obtained primarily from Chinese literature, as visits to phosphate factories were not included in the itinerary.

SPECIFIC FERTILIZER TERMINOLOGY

In order to better describe a fertilizer product certain specific terms have been developed over the years that must be understood; some of the terms as used apply only to fertilizer and have been adopted through convention. Some of the more common terms and definitions are:

1. *Chemical analysis*: This denotes the concentration of the nutrients in the material that are needed by plants such as nitrogen, N; phosphorous pentoxide, P_2O_5, and potassium oxide, K_2O. Note that two of the elements, phosphorous and potassium, are expressed in terms of the oxides. Some countries are now adopting a method of expressing the analysis on a weight percent basis as simply nitrogen (N), phosphorous (P), and potassium (K). The analysis is usually expressed in weight percent and denotes the weight of the element divided by the molecular weight times 100. For example, the chemical formula for ammonia is NH_3, which has a molecular weight of 17 (14 for N, plus 3×1 for H), and the N content or analysis is equal to $14 \div 17 \times 100 = 82.4\%$. Therefore, for every 100 pounds of pure ammonia, there would be 82.4 pounds of nitrogen. It is slightly more complicated for the oxide forms since the number of elements may be greater in the oxide form than in the product formula. In this case, phosphoric acid of conventional strength is written as H_3PO_4 (orthophosphoric acid), which requires two moles of the acid to give one mole of P_2O_5. The H_3PO_4 molecular weight must be multiplied by two. The molecular weight of H_3PO_4 is $98 (3H \times 1 + 1P \times 31 + 4 \times 16)$; the molecular weight of phosphorous pentoxide (P_2O_5) is 142. The P_2O_5 content on a pure acid basis is $142 \div 196 \times 100 = 72.4\%$; H_3PO_4 is not shipped in pure form but in aqueous solution, which reduces the P_2O_5 concentration to 54% P_2O_5. It also is usually contaminated by impurities, which tend to lower its analysis. An acid of 54% P_2O_5 concentration is usually referred to as ordinary or ortho wet-process phosphoric acid. This is the acid traded in international markets and is the base for phosphate statistics in supply-demand data; ammonia is the base taken in statistical data on nitrogen in most countries.

2. *Grade of fertilizer*: This denotes the plant nutrient content of a fertilizer expressed in weight percent and is given in the order of N, P_2O_5, and K_2O, except in the case cited above where N, P, and K are given. For example, a 14-14-14 grade indicates 14% N, 14% P_2O_5, and 14% K_2O. This indicates that all three major nutrients are present. A material containing only nitrogen, such as urea, would be expressed as 46-0-0 indicating 46% N, 0% P_2O_5, and 0% K_2O. If micronutrients are present the weight percent and element are given last in the grade. With urea again containing 0.2% zinc, the grade would be 45-0-0, 0.2 Zn, etc. Micronutrients are usually present only in small quantities.

Several other terms used in this chapter are defined when used for the convenience of the reader.

SMALL-SCALE INDUSTRY DEFINITION

One of the many objectives of the delegation assigned for this study was to determine the technology used in fertilizer production in the small-scale industries scattered throughout the country. Representatives of the Ministry of Petrochemical Industries summarized the status and plans for the small-scale nitrogenous fertilizer industry during a briefing in Peking. During the tour the delegation was able to view the factories and discuss details of the operation. Although attempts were made to gain knowledge of the phosphate fertilizer industry, this report deals primarily with the nitrogenous fertilizer industry and more specifically with the small-scale plants. Therefore, the main product is ammonia and associated by-product, which can be converted into other fertilizer materials.

Table VI-1 gives a description of fertilizer materials frequently used in China along with the chemical analysis and method of manufacture. One of the most striking differences in the fertilizer industry in China is the production and use of ammonium bicarbonate as fertilizer, which is one of the prime products of small-scale industry. This appears to be the only country, developed or developing, using this material in substantial quantities as fertilizer. Most other countries use ammonia as ammonia, ammonium sulfate, ammonium nitrate, or urea. According to the Ministry, ammonium bicarbonate can be produced by a simpler process, requires less investment, and plants can be in production quickly. Ammonium bicarbonate is made by the reaction of ammonia with carbon dioxide usually carried out in a simple reactor. The procedure is described in the technology section.

During the period 1958–1965, or eight years before the Cultural Revolution, only about 90 plants for the production of ammonia had been established. From 1966–1974 about 1100 of the small-scale, coal-based ammonia plants were built with an average of 100 new plants per year now being added. The design capacity based on ammonia ranges from 3000 m.t. per year up to 20,000 m.t. per year in the modern small-scale plant, and some of the newer plants produce ammonium nitrate in addition to the solid ammonium bicarbonate. Ammonium nitrate plants represent a greater degree of complexity since nitric acid is an intermediate during the production of ammonium nitrate. These factory complexes are certainly more expensive than those which only make ammonium bicarbonate. At present 29 provinces are reported to have ammonia production capacity. In 1974 the small plants accounted for about 45% or more of the total nitrogen produced in the country; the remaining nitrogen production is from larger scale plants using feedstocks, such as shale oil, natural gas, and refinery off-gas.

Although actual figures for the country cannot be given, a considerable amount of the ammonia produced in small-scale plants is converted into

Table VI-1

FERTILIZERS FREQUENTLY USED IN CHINA

Name	Grade (Wt.%[a]) N-P_2O_5-K_2O[b]	Method of Manufacture
1. Ammonia	82:0:0	Reaction of nitrogen with hydrogen
2. Liquor ammonia (aqua ammonia)	16–25:0:0	Ammonia dissolved in water
3. Ammonium bicarbonate	17.5:0:0	Reaction of ammonia with carbon dioxide, CO_2
4. Ammonium nitrate	32–35:0:0	Reaction of nitric acid with ammonia
5. Ammonium sulfate	20–21:0:0	Reaction of sulfuric acid with ammonia
6. Urea	46:0:0	Reaction of ammonia with carbon dioxide, CO_2
7. Calcium super phosphate	0:20:0	Reaction of phosphate rock with sulfuric acid
8. Basic slag	0:12–18:0	Byproduct of steel production
9. Calcium magnesium phosphate	0:14–18:0	Burned phosphate ore
10. Ammonium phosphate	11.2:50–60:0	Reaction of ammonia with phosphoric acid
11. Potassium sulfate	0:0:52.8	Reaction of potassium chloride with sulfuric acid

[a]Ranges of nutrient content given which may vary depending on product purity.
[b]First number denotes range of nitrogen content on a percent-by-weight basis; second number denotes range of P_2O_5; third number denotes range of K_2O content.

liquor ammonia (aqua ammonia). Ammonia gas is bubbled into water while cooling to form ammonium hydroxide (NH_4OH) with a concentration of 16-25% nitrogen. The concentration is kept low so that the final solution exhibits no gauge pressure, although it has a vapor pressure, and can be transported in non-pressure containers. The containers must be kept closed, however, to avoid losses of ammonia due to volatilization. This method is simpler and less expensive since pressure equipment for transportation, storage, and handling is not needed. In many countries such as the United States, anhydrous ammonia containing no water is used directly as fertilizer. Since ammonia is a gas at ordinary temperature it must be kept under pressure to maintain liquid form. China does not yet have the pressure equipment on a large scale to handle the volatile anhydrous liquid ammonia. No indication was given in the counties, communes, or brigades visited that they are attempting to produce equipment to allow the direct use of liquid ammonia at the farm level for agriculture. Small applicators for liquor ammonia were observed at several locations. Application methods for solid and liquid fertilizers are discussed in a later section.

China has the technology to construct and operate urea plants of certain capacities. This is an important fertilizer material in the country. However, no plants of the small-scale industry type were observed during the visit and therefore the technology is only briefly described in this report. Likewise, the production of ammonium sulfate was not observed. What little information could be gained on the production methods for phosphate fertilizers in China also are given in a later section.

RAW MATERIALS

The basic building block of all nitrogen fertilizers is ammonia. It is one of the truly fundamental raw materials for modern civilization, and its importance to agricultural production cannot be overemphasized. A very high percentage of that produced in the world (about 85%) is used directly or indirectly as a fertilizer although it also finds uses in the manufacture of such materials as soda ash, nitric acid, nylon, plastics, lacquers, dyes, rubber, and numerous other products.

Ammonia is produced in the synthesis step by combining nitrogen and hydrogen in the proper proportions at specified conditions of temperature and pressure and in the presence of a catalyst. Nitrogen for the process is taken from the air and organic materials, such as coal, natural gas (methane), naphtha, oil, or even water can provide the source of hydrogen. In fact almost any material containing hydrogen is a potential raw material. The production of ammonia by the combination of nitrogen and hydrogen is a relatively simple process; complications occur in obtaining the gases for the synthesis reaction. The gases must be produced, cleaned, mixed, etc., which makes ammonia production a rather complicated process.

China has coal in large amounts and well distributed throughout the country except for the south, and it can be used as a raw material for ammonia production. Coal reserves in China compare favorably with those of the United States and the USSR. It is claimed that coal has been found in every province in China, although the size as well as the type of deposits vary considerably. Coals range from lignite to anthracite, with bituminous types being predominant. In the small plants visited, coal was used both for feedstock and fuel. It is known that China has substantial quantities of natural gas which is an even better feedstock than coal, but plants of this type were not visited. Anthracite or semi-anthracite grade of coal was being used, and lumps were used for feedstock, while the powdered coal was used for fuel. The Ministry of Petrochemical Industries reported that high-sulfur coals and lower grade coals were being used. A method was said to have

Table VI-2

TYPICAL ANALYSIS (ULTIMATE) AND HEATING VALUE OF VARIOUS COALS[a]

Rank	Ultimate Analysis, %					Heating Value Btu/Pound
	C	H	N	O	S	
Anthracite-semi	85.4	3.28	1.12	3.59	0.80	14,100
Bituminous	81.73	4.74	1.50	6.54	0.7	14,600
Sub-bituminous	59.8	5.6	1.3	21.0	1.1	10,600
Lignite	36.3	7.0	0.7	45.8	0.49	6,300

[a]Analyses corresponding to American Society for Testing Materials ranking; ranges of values between samples may occur in each rank.

been developed for producing "artificial coal," whereby powdered coals not suitable for feedstock due to small particle size were converted to lumps by briquetting. No details of the briquetting procedure were given. As gases must be reacted with the coal, lumps are needed to assure good contact of gas and coal and to have free passage of product gas through the bed. The use of high-sulfur coal requires more elaborate and more expensive methods to remove the sulfur; sulfur is detrimental to the process and must be removed. The availability of high-grade anthracite coal in many locations is a great advantage for small-scale plants and thus provides an opportunity for locating the factory very near the use area. It is interesting to compare the Chinese approach with that in the United States. In China, basic production units producing final products are located near the use area, whereas in the United States, large complexes provide raw materials and intermediates, which are transported to the use area and further processed by such methods as bulk blending or granulation to create final products. China is moving toward the large complex in nitrogen production, and thus will have to improve the transportation system to serve these factories.

Table VI-2 gives a typical composition and heating value of various coals; it should be recognized that specific values will vary somewhat for the same type of coal. These are shown only to give an indication of the variety of raw materials the Chinese said they had used for the production of ammonia. The analyses were not given to us during our visit.

The quantity of carbon in a coal indicates its relative suitability for use in ammonia production; i.e. the higher the carbon content the better suited is that coal, because less will have to be handled in the reactors. The lower the sulfur content the better, because sulfur is an impurity which interferes with the ammonia synthesis reaction; sulfur or sulfur gases must be removed

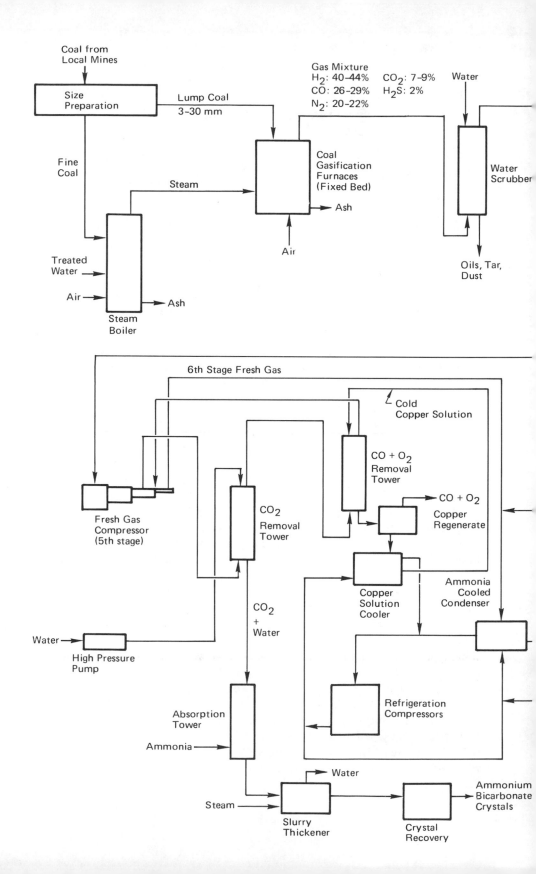

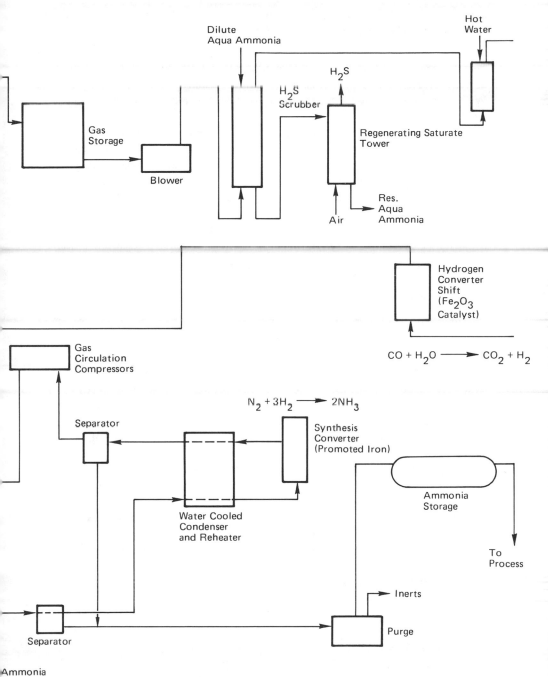

FIGURE VI-1. Small-scale ammonia and ammonium bicarbonate based on coal.

before nitrogen and hydrogen are reacted to form ammonia, because sulfur and sulfur compounds will poison the catalyst, thus lowering its reactivity. With these precautions, all of the above materials can be used for ammonia production.

The mining of coal was not actually observed by the delegation, although during travel, numerous small mines were noted near the roadside. Coal, both lump and powdered, was observed being transported for various uses by trucks, also equipped with trailing rubber-tired wagons, trailers pulled by medium-size and hand tractors, and in two-wheel carts pulled by animals or by hand. One fertilizer plant visited was receiving coal by rail. Very little data could be obtained on the transport cost of coal to the factories. Nevertheless, a rough estimate of the cost of coal delivered to the factory is possible and was presented in Chapter IV.

GAS GENERATION USING COAL

The following section is a brief description of the technology being used in the small-scale plants visited in which coal was the feedstock-fuel. The plant described is capable of producing up to 10,000 m.t. per year ammonia. In China, certain parts of plant operations are referred to in terms of work-shops. For example, a part of the plant for gas generation most likely will be called a gas generating workshop. Figure VI-1 is a flow sheet showing ammonia production in the small-scale plant.

In this part of the plant the initial reaction toward the ammonia syn-thesis process begins. This operation is needed to furnish both hydrogen and nitrogen for the final synthesis step. Lump coal is charged to the top of each generator (area of $3m^2$, round), and for the size of plant described here, three generators are used. The only gas generators observed are of the fixed-bed type, which must be discharged manually. Reference is made in the Chinese literature to a rotary type, which automatically discharges dust and residue. In some of the discussion, the equipment was referred to as furnaces. Air is blown into each generator, which causes heat to be generated by combustion of some of the coal by the following reaction:

$$C + O_2 \rightarrow CO_2$$

This part of the operation is referred to as the "blow." The carbon reacts with oxygen from air forming carbon dioxide; the carbon dioxide is removed from the gasses and used in other processes to produce ammonium bicar-bonate or urea; it is a byproduct of ammonia synthesis. After the bed is heated during the "blow" operation, this is followed by a "run" operation according to the following reaction:

$$C + H_2O \text{ (steam)} \rightarrow CO + H_2$$

This reaction is endothermic or requires heat, and thus the bed is cooled. In this step, hydrogen gas and carbon monoxide are generated; hydrogen is one of the final gases needed for ammonia synthesis. In the above reaction sequence, nitrogen gas, which is the other gas needed, is supplied by air. Thus the two raw materials for the final ammonia reaction between hydrogen and nitrogen are made and mixed in the proper proportions along with other gases which are removed prior to synthesis. In the plants, the "blow-run" operation was being done automatically, with means provided for manual operation in case of automatic failure. The cycle was on a timed sequence of three minutes with the "blow" operation for one-third of the time and "run" operation for two-thirds of the time. Thus, air was admitted for 1 minute to heat the bed, followed by steam for 2 minutes, which cooled the bed. This cycle was repeated giving a gas mixture consisting of carbon monoxide (CO), carbon dioxide CO_2), hydrogen (H_2), nitrogen (N_2), methane (CH_4), oxygen (O_2), hydrogen sulfide (H_2S), and argon (Ar). The gas was transported by Roots blowers to storage; storage tanks were built of steel, and some were made of stone and concrete. The stone tank was said to give a considerable saving since all materials were locally available. The temperature was not measured in the generator. Steam is produced in steam boilers using the finely-divided coal not of sufficient size for use in the generators. No catalyst is needed for the above reactions.

Following storage, the gas is treated to remove hydrogen sulfide and dust. Water is used for gas washing for dust and dilute ammonium hydroxide is used to remove hydrogen sulfide; the ammonium hydroxide is regenerated.

CARBON MONOXIDE CONVERSION

Gas after cleaning for dust and hydrogen sulfide removal is mixed with an excess of steam and passed over a bed of catalyst consisting of iron oxide (Fe_2O_3). In this reaction, called the shift reaction, carbon monoxide reacts with steam according to the following:

$$CO + H_2O \text{ (steam)} \rightarrow CO_2 + H_2$$

In this manner additional hydrogen gas is formed and converts most of the carbon monoxide to carbon dioxide; no data were given on the conversion efficiency, but probably this was no higher than 90%. Therefore, some carbon monoxide remains, which must be removed along with the carbon dioxide and other impurities prior to synthesis. The temperature of the conversion reaction is 500°C. After conversion, the gas is cooled before beginning additional gas purification operations. At this point, the gases have the correct mole ratio of hydrogen to nitrogen of 3:1 for synthesis, but still contain carbon dioxide and carbon monoxide, which must be removed.

GAS COMPRESSION AND PURIFICATION

After conversion of most of the carbon monoxide to hydrogen, the gases are subjected to a sequence of compression and purification steps. The gas is compressed in six stages, with intercoolers between stages, until a pressure of 100 kg./cm.^{2} is reached in the fifth stage. Water is pumped into an absorption tower where the carbon dioxide is dissolved. No data were given as to where energy is recovered from the let-down of the water-carbon dioxide solution. It is assumed that no system exists for this. Carbon dioxide recovered in this step is used for production of ammonium bicarbonate.

Removal of the carbon monoxide, oxygen, residual carbon dioxide, and other gases is carried out by further scrubbing after water scrubbing with a cold solution of ammoniacal copper formate. Gas is contacted in a scrubbing tower with the cold solution to absorb carbon monoxide and oxygen. The copper liquor is oxidized in the scrubbing tower during removal of carbon monoxide and is called spent solution. After scrubbing, the spent solution goes to a reflux scrubber where ammonia is absorbed. From the reflux scrubber the liquor goes to a reduction vessel where it is heated under pressure and reduced back to the cuprous form by the dissolved carbon monoxide. Carbon monoxide and carbon dioxide are released from the solution. After regeneration the copper solution is again cooled by ammonia refrigeration to be recycled. At this point the final gases, hydrogen, and nitrogen, are in a condition for the synthesis reaction.

AMMONIA SYNTHESIS

After compression to 320 kg./cm.^{2} the purified synthesis gas is mixed with circulated gas. The combined volume of new and recirculated gas pass through an ammonia-cooled condenser; the gases and condensed ammonia are passed through a separator where liquid ammonia is removed. Liquid ammonia is pumped to storage. Pressure type storage is used in the small-scale plants. After separation of ammonia, the gases are heated by off-gas from the converter in an exchanger and enter the ammonia synthesis converter where they pass through the catalyst bed. The catalyst was not known by plant personnel, but was designated A6. It is assumed to be reduced iron oxide, because a nitrogen blanket is required during periods of shutdown. The converter operates at 500°C. and, as given before, 320 kg./cm.^{2}. The reaction of hydrogen and nitrogen to form ammonia is an equilibrium reaction according to the following:

$$N_2 + 3H_2 \rightleftarrows 2NH_3$$

The actual quantity of ammonia formed per pass through the converter depends upon the pressure, temperature, and reactivity of the catalyst. At a given temperature, the conversion is increased by pressure, and at a given pressure, the conversion decreases with an increase in temperature. The catalyst speeds up the reaction rate in order to achieve an economical level of space velocity; this is the number of cubic feet or volume of gas that pass over one cubic foot or volume of catalyst space per hour. At the above conditions only about 15–20% conversion is obtained per pass; thus a considerable quantity of gas must be recirculated. As the reaction of hydrogen and nitrogen to ammonia is highly exothermic, heat must be removed from the converter to maintain the desired temperature. The ammonia converter is 0.5 m. dia. x 6 m. high. Gas and ammonia from the converter pass through a water-cooled condenser and then to a separator where ammonia is removed. This ammonia also goes to storage. Unreacted gases go to the section of the recirculation compressors.

AMMONIA STORAGE

Steel tanks of a horizontal, cylindrical type were used for ammonia storage; the storage volume was 30 m.^{3} for the small-scale plants. Ammonia in vapor or gaseous form is used in other products. No liquid anhydrous ammonia is used for direct application. Ammonia is used for the production of liquor ammonia, ammonium bicarbonate, or ammonium nitrate.

It was striking to note the similarity in the small-scale ammonia plants in China with a plant previously operated by the Tennessee Valley Authority in the United States. In the fall of 1942 the plant began production of ammonia using coke and operated on that feedstock until 1951 when it was converted to natural gas. The TVA plant was much larger, having a design capacity of about 44,000 m.t./yr. of ammonia. Coke is a somewhat cleaner feedstock compared with coal and was selected primarily for that reason by TVA. Technical steps involved including gas preparation, cleaning, compression, removal of impurities, and synthesis were very similar in both plants. The original coke-based plant converted to natural gas at TVA has now been replaced with a more modern technology plant, which also uses natural gas.

TECHNOLOGY OF PRODUCTS MADE FROM AMMONIA

Only three fertilizer products containing straight nitrogen were observed being made and their use made mention of during the visit. These were ammonium bicarbonate, ammonia liquor, and ammonium nitrate. Brief explanations are given for each of these materials.

1. *Ammonium bicarbonate*: This material is sometimes called ammonium hydrogen carbonate or ammonium acid carbonate and contains 17.5% nitrogen, which makes it a relatively low-analysis fertilizer. It is a

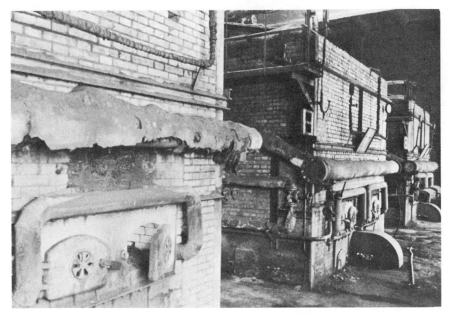

PHOTO VI-1. Gas generators where coal is reacted with air and steam to produce a gas mixture of H_2, N_2, CO_2 and H_2S.

PHOTO VI-2. An overview of compressor room; note the orderly arrangement and well-kept appearance.

PHOTO VI-3. Ammonia plant absorption towers; note the use of indigenous materials and methods in equipment.

PHOTO VI-4. Control room; much of the process is controlled manually.

PHOTO VI-5. Gas analyses are done by wet methods; sophisticated instruments are nice but not necessary.

PHOTO VI-6. View of ammonia plant; note converter in center where $N_2 + H_2$ is reacted to form NH_3.

Photo VI-7. All solid fertilizer observed in China is delivered to the farm in bagged form.

rather easy compound to prepare and is made according to the following reaction:

$$NH_3 + H_2O + CO_2 \rightarrow NH_4HCO_3$$

An aqueous solution of ammonia (NH_4OH) is contacted with gaseous carbon dioxide, and this is done in an absorption column where the ammonia solution flows downward, and the gas flows upward. As the reaction produces heat, it is necessary to cool the solution. As the solution becomes saturated, crystallization occurs. In the small plants, steam was used to dry up the solution or concentrate the solution to cause crystallization and drying; no separate drying step was carried out. The semi-dry crystals had a wet appearance and smelled strongly of ammonia. The crystals were collected in a holding hopper and bagged by hand into a 25 kg. plastic bag and tied closed. A small quantity of bagged product was stored temporarily outside, alongside the bagging building. The workers around the bagging unit were wearing a cloth covering over the nose and mouth, and a fan was blowing the ammonia fumes away from them. Neither the masks nor fan were doing an adequate job of protecting the workers. During discussions, the people stated that ammonium bicarbonate was difficult to use, as it tended to lose ammonia. Of course, this is a very simple way of converting the ammonia into a solid form which can be transported by the means

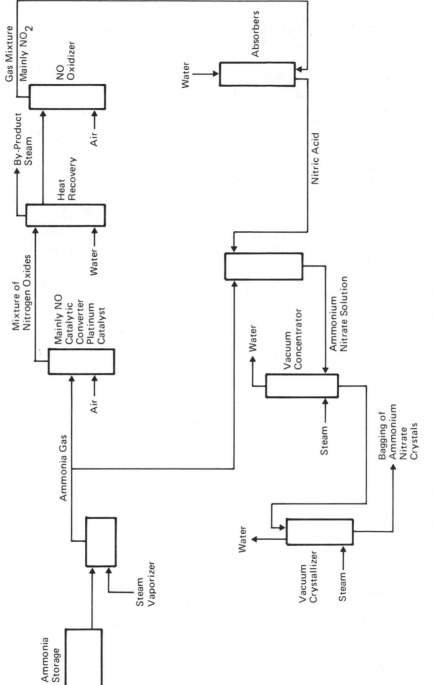

FIGURE VI-2. Small-scale production of nitric acid and ammonium nitrate from ammonia.

available. This portion of the plant could be improved to give a better working atmosphere for the workers. Carbon dioxide for the reaction is a recovered byproduct, and thus contributes no cost to the product. Figure VI-2 shows the production scheme.

2. *Liquor ammonia* (*aqua ammonia*): The production of liquor ammonia is also a very simple process. The gaseous ammonia is contacted with water according to the following reaction:

$$NH_3 + H_2O \rightarrow NH_4OH$$

During the reaction, heat is generated which must be removed. The final solution has no gauge pressure, and thus can be handled in ordinary tanks or even glass containers. It does have a partial pressure of ammonia, which means that ammonia will escape unless the containers are kept closed. Figure VI-2 also shows the production of liquor ammonia.

3. *Ammonium nitrate*: As shown in Figure VI-2, some plants were observed to be making nitric acid from part of the ammonia production and converting the nitric acid to ammonium nitrate according to the following reaction:

$$NH_3 + HNO_3 \rightarrow NH_4NO_3$$

Gaseous ammonia is reacted with air at 800°C. using a platinum catalyst to produce nitrogen oxides; the pressure is 1 kg./cm.^{2} The main product is nitric oxide (NO), but at the same time other nitrogen oxides are formed. The nitrogen oxide (NO) is further reacted with cooling air to convert it to nitrogen dioxide (NO_2); no catalyst is required for this. The nitrogen dioxide is absorbed by water in packed towers to form nitric acid. In China the acid concentration was 40%. Even at this concentration, considerable losses of nitrogen oxides were observed at the stack discharge. Modern nitric acid plants operating under pressure produce 56% nitric acid. Equations for the main reactions are as follows:

$$4NH_3 + 5O_2 \rightarrow 4NO + 6H_2O$$
$$2NO + O_2 \rightarrow 2NO_2$$
$$3NO_2 + H_2O \rightarrow 2HNO_3 + NO$$

Acid was withdrawn from storage and reacted with gaseous ammonia to produce an ammonium nitrate solution of 60% concentration. The solution is concentrated by vacuum evaporation to 80-90% ammonium nitrate using steam. Following this a vacuum crystallization (batch operation) produces solid ammonium nitrate. The product particle size is less than 1 mm. After vacuum crystallization, the vacuum is released, and a door is opened manually. Ammonium nitrate crystals fall down a chute to an open belt conveyor onto a manual bagging hopper. No further drying or conditioning was done. The crystals felt to be about 110-115°F. when being bagged and felt moist to the touch. Bags consisted of 2-ply paper with no plastic liner being used; the bags were weak and tore easily. It was a 25-kg. weight and was labeled 34% nitrogen on the bag. Some bagged product that felt to be quite hard was stored nearby. The plant people stated that before the amonium nitrate was used, it was usually ground with a stone grinder. Some of the product was used for blasting, and the remainder was used for fertilizer. Again, the production scheme for ammonium nitrate could be changed to greatly improve the product quality. They said that a prilling tower is being considered for one of the plants visited. China has experience in the operation of a pan-type granulator or pelletizer used in the preparation of feed particles for the vertical shaft kilns in the cement plants. A similar principle could be used to prepare a high quality granular ammonium nitrate. A melt consisting of 98–99.5% ammonium nitrate (a melt made by heating with steam) could be sprayed over the moving bed in the pan. When the melt is being sprayed, the rotating particles increase to the desired size and are separated and cooled for packaging. The small particles are returned to the pan to serve as nuclei for the production of additional product-size particles. Equipment includes the pan granulator, cooler, screens, oversize crushing mill, elevators, and screens, all of which the Chinese can readily fabricate. Product made in this manner would cost no more than that to be made in a prilling tower and should have superior physical characteristics.

Ammonium bicarbonate cannot be melted without decomposition and cannot be processed as previously mentioned for ammonium nitrate. However, it could be compacted, such as in briquetting machines, to give various particle shapes. Also, ammonium bicarbonate could be pressed between pressure rolls into a sheet and then broken into uniform sizes by screening. For the small production units, even tabletting could be considered.

4. *Urea*: China is known to have some small plants operating that produce urea. This material is made by a pressure reaction of ammonia with carbon dioxide at elevated temperatures. Since no plants were visited which made this product, no data can be given. Some discussion is presented on this material under future trends.

It is known that China is greatly increasing its nitrogen production capacity through installation of modern ammonia-urea plants. Although not dealt with during the visit, it seems appropriate to briefly consider the impact. We could not learn specifically what ratio of nitrogen, phosphate, and potash is used in the country, but it is probably of the order of 1:0.5:0.5 in terms of $N:P_2O_5:K_2O$ weight ratio. Therefore, when nitrogen availability significantly increases, say by 1978, the quantities of phosphate and potassium must likewise be increased to maintain the proper ratio. It would seem that a considerable potential exists to supply the increased demand of these nutrients, and probably a considerable amount must come from imports. If new nitrogen capacity by 1978 equals 3.5 million tons, then phosphate and potash capacities should be 1.75 million tons each to maintain the above ratio. Once again our delegation was not able to ascertain the consumption ratio on a country basis.

TECHNOLOGY OF PHOSPHATE PRODUCTION

Although in numerous discussions the use of phosphate fertilizers was mentioned, little data could be obtained on the materials and the technology of production, and no plants were visited which produced phosphate-type fertilizers.

Apparently, compared with the small-scale nitrogenous fertilizer industry, a small-scale phosphate fertilizer industry has not evolved in a comparable way or at least to the degree that the nitrogen industry has. There are known scattered deposits of phosphate ore in the country, but in all of our discussions, the material being used was said to be allocated by the state. This also could include imported ores as well as domestically-mined ores. Depending upon impurities in the ore, the P_2O_5 content can vary over a wide range. The ore may or may not be suitable for direct use as a fertilizer, depending on its chemical composition and agricultural conditions. Generally, some chemical reaction must be carried out with the ore to improve its P_2O_5 availability; this is a method of expressing the ability of the growing plant to utilize the phosphate component. The reaction changes the chemical composition of the phosphate ore and puts it in a form that can be used by the plant either through an improvement in water solubility or citrate solubility.

In Chinese literature, the use of powdered or fine-ground phosphate rock for direct application is described. They recommend that sedimentary rock be ground and mixed with manure and lime for direct application to acid soils in the following rates: 50 kg. (100 jin[1]) of manure, 2 kg. (4 jin) of phosphate rock, and 2.5 kg. (5 jin) of lime. It is recommended that the mixture be applied one week before seeding at the rate of 375 to 750 kg./ ha. (50 to 100 jin/mu.[2]).

There was occasional reference to plants that produce "burned" phosphates; these products were referred to as calcium magnesium phosphate containing 14–18% P_2O_5. It is assumed that they are made by heating the ore in the presence of a magnesium source to a relatively high temperature whereby magnesium is incorporated in the product. This would be expected to improve the availability. The measurement of availability is an empirical method based on the solubility of a certain amount of

1. 1 jin. = 1/2 kg. = 1.1 lbs.
2. 1 mu. = 1/6 a. = 0.167 a. = .067 ha.

product in an ammonium citrate solution. Generally, the higher the solubility, the higher the availability to growing plants. References are given in Chinese literature to the reaction of magnesium silicate with phosphate rock and with the use of coal. A flow sheet is given as described by them in Figure VI-3. Magnesium silicate, phosphate rock, and coal are screened into lumps and powder. The mixture is melted, followed by quenching it in water, drying, and grinding it to produce calcium magnesium phosphate. Based on other plant visits, the Chinese have the technology and indigenous equipment to carry out the process. They have considerable experience in fabrication and operation of electric furnaces, shaft kilns, rotary driers and coolers, ball mills for grinding, and screening equipment. Much of this equipment was observed in visits to rural,, small-scale cement factories.

During a visit to the Industrial Exhibition in Shanghai, samples of NPK compound granular fertilizer were being shown. However, the hosts were unable to give any details except that it was only being trial produced.

TRANSPORT OF FERTILIZERS

Information on how the fertilizers were transported from the factory to the farm was obtained through personal observation.

Since the plants are located in relatively close proximity to the use area, two rather unsophisticated methods could be used in transport. A 12-h.p. "walking" tractor is used with a two-wheel metal trailer for a large part of the bagged fertilizer. This was said to convey up to 1 m.t. Another method was a two-wheel (heavy-duty, bicycle-type wheel) hand cart with a wooden bed; sideboards were made of wood or wire mesh. These were drawn by donkeys or humans. If a donkey was used, it was attached by a loose rope, and the human guided and also pulled it by two beams on each side. In many cases, two to three men and women were pulling the hand carts using shoulder straps or ropes with one person guiding the cart. In a few cases larger tractors and four-wheel, rubber-tired wagons and trucks also were observed. Cost data on fertilizer transport could not be obtained. At any rate, the production plant was not responsible for delivering the product.

For liquor ammonia some black bags appearing to be made of rubber transported by two-wheel hand carts were used. Some old oil drums also could have been used for liquor ammonia. Concrete tanks also have been seen by others where small boats are available.

SUMMARY

In assessing the role of small-scale fertilizer plants in China and the level of technology, several factors must be kept in mind. One important factor is the availability and wide dispersion of coal in the country. Through

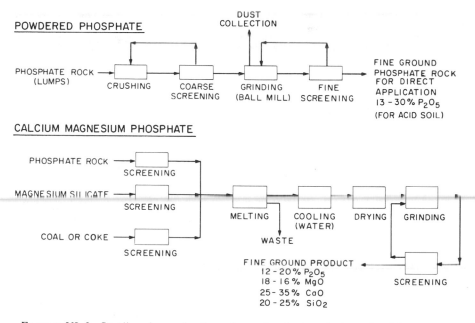

FIGURE VI-3. Small-scale production of powdered phosphate and calcium magnesium phosphate.

some unknown mechanism the technology for using coal for ammonia production became available to the Chinese. They never claimed to have developed the fundamental knowledge during any of the visits. Certain statements were made indicating that they had made improvements and adapted methods better suited to Chinese conditions. Had other feedstocks such as natural gas or oil been as available as coal, they probably would have been used. These plants follow very closely the theme of self-reliance and taking the initiative in their own hands as the feedstock-fuel requires no foreign exchange, plus essentially all of the equipment can be fabricated indigenously, and most of the metal is available in-country. The process does not require special alloys, which probably are not available, except by importation. The reactor vessels are of small size as well as the compressors, which can be fabricated in local and regional shops. Another very significant factor is the location of the plant very near the fertilizer-use area. Transportation is a problem, and the small factory allows the local population to improvise in methods of fertilizer transport. In large complexes, the factory will be required to invest in transportation and distribution facilities, and product will move a much longer distance from production to the point of use. Small locally oriented factories allow the use of relatively low analysis materials to be used economically. As the marketing area becomes larger, there is usually a need to increase the analysis so that the delivered cost per unit of plant nutrient can be kept relatively low.

It was surprising to learn of the number of small-scale nitrogen fertilizer factories utilizing the relatively complex technology required for ammonia production. The technology is similar to that used in other countries before natural gas was available. In fact, the Tennessee Valley Authority of the United States began operation of an ammonia plant in 1942 using coke to produce about 44,000 tons per year. Many of the processing steps in this plant were similar to those observed in China.

In general, the small plants in China were well designed and appeared to be well managed. Unfortunately, time did not permit a detailed inspection of the equipment or process details. The impression gained was that the quality of workmanship in design and layout was good, and this has been standardized to the extent possible, allowing for maximum use of non-metals in some steps based on local options (in scrubbing towers, etc.). Individual workshops were neat and orderly. In most instances safety, such as no smoking signs and the use of safety apparel for the workers, was stressed. Exposed work areas were marked for worker protection. There appeared to be a coordinated scheme for carrying out maintenance, and management appeared to be preventative maintenance-oriented. They often stated that they were working to reduce pollution from the fertilizer factories. These small plants have a high level of manual labor input, and they seemed to be striving for labor-saving methods, but automatic control of most steps was not yet achieved. However, it is likely that these plants will remain oriented to manual labor for the next several years, and attention to automation and labor-saving devices will be directed to the large complexes, whether producing fertilizer or other materials.

One area that would justify further attention would be to improve the quality of the solid products leaving the factory. Although the Chinese literature refers to modern methods of fertilizer finishing such as prilling or granulation, none were observed during the visit. In visits to cement factories or medicinal laboratories, the principle of pan granulation was observed. This technique could be easily applied to solid fertilizers. Formation of ammonium bicarbonate into pellets by such methods as briquetting would improve its handling properties. Prilling of ammonium nitrate with incorporation of additives would improve this product.

It seems that the small-scale fertilizer factory is playing an important role in China and will continue to do so. This type of approach also may be applicable to other countries and situations in the developing world. The small-scale fertilizer industry is certainly establishing a cadre of personnel with training that will be appropriate and helpful in developing a large-scale fertilizer industry in China.

Chapter VII

SMALL-SCALE CEMENT
INDUSTRY TECHNOLOGY

Small-scale cement plants began to be built in China in 1958. At this time, in other parts of the world, large rotary kilns with internal heat recouperating devices and external suspension pre-heaters were being installed. The kiln is the heart of any cement-producing facility. Another key feature of cement manufacture is that the product being manufactured is a heavy and relatively low-cost item, and generally speaking must be marketed within a small radius of the factory, because the cost of transport adds significantly to the cost of the product. This is a perishable product and must be protected from contact with moisture.

China has not chosen to take the same steps in increasing its cement-producing capacity as the rest of the world. In China there have been additions of large rotary kilns near large cities where transportation is better developed, but a major capacity increase also has taken place from small "egg-shaped" and shaft kilns. The "egg-shaped" kilns are built below ground level and are lined with brick. They are very small in size. They must be charged, and the material removed manually and are what is known in chemical processing as "batch"-type operations. The shaft kiln is an old technology that has been used to heat many types of minerals and was the type of kiln used in the manufacture of the first portland cement.

Portland cement was first produced by Joseph Aspdin, a bricklayer and mason in Leeds, England, in 1824. It was different from the material used in many parts of the world as a hydraulic binder. Most of the early binders were mixtures of lime and volcanic ash from various eruptions. Mr. Aspdin used limestone and clay in proper proportions and intimately fused these materials by heat treatment to form new compounds. The name "portland" came to the process as a result of the product color, which closely resembled the color of the stone cliffs on the Isle of Portland.

Portland cement is an important product to a developing or a growing nation. It is used almost exclusively in the construction industry. It is the glue when mixed with sand, coarse aggregates, and water that hardens to a stone-like mass, which is used to build water canals, dams, sanitation systems, roads, buildings, and untold other structures. It can be molded and shaped with great ease, so as to decrease the need for hand-cut stone.

Portland cement is made from a myriad of naturally existing minerals, and in some cases, waste materials from other industries. The major chemical compounds formed are tri-calcium silicate (C_3S), di-calcium silicate (C_2S), tri-calcium aluminate (C_3A), and tetra-calcium-aluminoferrites (C_4AF). Thus, it can be seen that a combination of materials which furnish calcium, silica, alumina, and iron are the prime requirements. Such materials as limestone, marls, and oyster shells are commonly used to furnish the calcium minerals. They must be low in magnesia minerals. The other elements come from a varied list; such as, clay, shales, iron ore, and slags. These need to be low in sodium, potassium, and phosphorus minerals.

Exact information concerning cement capacity, production, number of plants, and location were not available to us. We did learn during a briefing on small-scale industries by Institute personnel in Peking that small-scale plants had increased production by a three-fold factor since 1965. In an earlier briefing we learned that China had 2800 small-scale portland cement plants located in 80% of the counties and producing 50% of China's total cement output. Published figures[1] for earlier years show local small-scale production as a share of national total output to be 14% for 1959 and 48% for 1972. The first facilities under this plan were installed in 1958. In those days small mills such as those used in the milling of rice were used to prepare the feed and finished product. Hand crushing was used. One of the early plants was built for an investment of 1000 yuan and employed ten people, who produced 25 kg./da.

One must try to understand the reasons for proceeding in such a manner, because none of the facilities have the economy of scale that would be built in the United States. By 1973, if one estimates that 15.4 million tons were produced by various small-scale processes, the average plant size must have reached 5356 metric tons per year. All of the plants on which we

---

1. Jon Sigurdson, "Technology and Employment in China," *World Development,* Vol. 2, No. 3, March 1974.

received information, however, were in excess of 25,000 m.t./yr. This means that many of the plants must still be of very small size.

In a briefing concerning cement processes given by Mr. Liu Chien-hsun and Mr. Liu Kung-ch'eng of the Chinese Silicate Society, five points as to why small-scale cement plants were being developed were given. Specifically, they use:

1. Funds from the masses
2. Local raw materials
3. Equipment made locally
4. A low technology base (indigenous methods)

And, they must serve: Agriculture

There are several ways to finance such projects. Financial help could come from the province or county level. Lower commune levels also could use their accumulation funds to erect such plants, which relieves the central state government from having to allocate funds for a large central plant and still have a difficult transport problem to the job site. Such plants could be built by local authorities as a part of a water conservation project. In fact, many were built in this manner. Seventy (70) % of production goes to agriculture and 30% to local industry. Of course, in a given year these numbers will vary according to need.

Local raw materials should be used. In fact, many areas have small deposits that would not support a larger plant. Clay seems to be abundant throughout China, and small limestone operations were already operating for the stone cutting trades. Local fuel supplies also were important. Many small and low-grade fuels were available and could be used in the shaft-type kiln operation. The low heating value fuels cannot be used in the rotary kiln process.

Much of the equipment was of the type that could be made locally. Plant designs (the earliest of which go back before 1958) were made available by the appropriate industrial ministry. Specific standard designs would have to be altered to meet the existing local conditions. In one example that we saw where expansion had taken place, it was obvious that a compromise had been made with the original lay-out. The basic design types are listed in Table VII-1.

Indigenous methods were required as a result of a low-level of technical capability. The shaft kiln would lend itself to such a situation. Quality of product has been one of the shortcomings of the shaft kiln. We learned that much progress has been made so that now Mark 400 (28-day strengths of 5688 p.s.i.—400 kg./c.m.^{2}) amd Mark 500 (28-day strengths of 7110 p.s.i.—500 kg./c.m.^{2}) can be made. We did not learn if this product is made in all plants at all times. Several Chinese publications obtained indicated that lesser quality has been used in major construction products.

Table VII-1

SMALL-SCALE CEMENT PLANT EQUIPMENT
(DESIGN BY INDUSTRIAL INSTITUTE)

| | KILN | | | | MILL | | |
Capacity	Diameter	Height	Discharge	No.	Diameter	Length	Kw
7,000	1.5	7.0 m.	Manual	2	1.2 m.	4.5 m.	80
20,000 t.	2.0 m.	8.0 m.	Semi-mech.	2	1.5 m.	5.7 m.	135
25,000 t.	2.5 m.	10.0 m.	Semi-mech.	2	2.2	6.5 m.	350
44,000 t.	2.5 m.	10.0 m.	Mechanical	3	1.83	6.1 m.	245

Technicians have been selected from the local people. Assistance has been given by some of the larger factories. Local personnel have traveled to other plants, and other plant personnel have offered on-the-spot assistance.

The shaft kiln lends itself to meeting such criteria as:

1. The use of local manpower
2. Limiting foreign exchange, because whatever was to be done would be done at home
3. Obtaining capital from local accumulations
4. Avoidance of technology not available in rural areas
5. The use of local, small deposits of raw materials which would otherwise not support larger modern plants
6. Relieve an already short supply of transportation
7. Shorter plant erection time

In fact, Jon Sigurdson[2] mentions that India is also using the shaft kiln to advantage under certain circumstances. In a personal conversation with a member of the India Portland Cement Association, this was confirmed. I'm sure that much has been learned since entering this process in 1958. Control of pelletizing moisture is a must for this operation. The pellet formed must retain its shape as it moves through the shaft kiln. Many improvements to control dust were mentioned. Several times it was mentioned that a plant was operating in a "civilized manner." This statement means that working atmospheres have been improved by major dust abatement programs. Packing and shipping is reported as being dusty, but attention is being given to this.

Fuel efficiencies for the small-scale shaft kilns were reported as follows:

Highest —1300 kcl./kg.
Low   — 750–800 kcl./kg.
Average — 950 kcl./kg.

2. Ibid.

Product quality has improved since 1958 from as low as Mark 150. In fact, it was reported that one plant makes 98% Mark 500. They use a dry mortar for making strength tests. A 15–25% water content is used which will tend to make strengths appear higher than we are accustomed to seeing. The chemical and fineness data indicate a lower than normal strength by our standards. They do plan to go to a wet mortar method similar to our ASTM procedures. Slight differences will be made in the testing procedure. This will then allow for a better quality comparison.

During our briefing by the China Silicate Society in Peking, we asked "where are the best small-scale cement plants located?" The Tachai plant in Hsi-yang County and Hui County Plant (formerly Pai-ch'uan) in Huihsien County were rated as being amont their best plants. We were able to spend a short time in each of these plants.

Tavle VII-2 is a summary of the pertinent details for the three plants we visited.

Table VII-2 tabulates many of the details of plant production and equipment. The following paragraphs will furnish further details.

1. *Tachai Cement Factory.* This plant employed conventional wet chemical methods for raw materials, clinker, and cement analysis. They were analyzing for silica, alumina, iron, calcium, and magnesia. The magnesia content was about 1.0–1.5%. Physical testing of cement was not as complete as we would conduct it, but seemed adequate. Tests were made for time of setting, tensil, and compressive strength.

This plant is considered a model plant. Tachai has sent workers to other factories to learn and teach, and some thirty plants have sent personnel to this plant for observation and training.

The limiting factor appears to be raw mix production. To produce 2.5 tph of clinker would require 3.82 tons of raw mix. A flow diagram (Figure VII-1) is included for this plant and is typical of the process being used in the small-scale cement industry in China.

2. *Hui County Cement Factory.* The product from this plant is used in local projects, such as: water conservation, pump stations, canals, reservoirs, roads, and bridges. This is typical of how this industry supports agriculture. There are six other plants located in this county.

The trip through the plant was very hurried, and many items were not developed. It was reported that 70% of the items were built and installed by plant personnel. Some 64 items fall into this category.

Manpower reduction had taken place, and the reported present compliment should have been 800 according to plant management. The new plant expansion comprising two new mills and the automatic shaft kiln was installed in 4.5 months by the plant. During this reconstruction, 100 rooms for workers also were completed.

Table VII-2

SMALL-SCALE CEMENT PLANTS VISITED IN CHINA

Plant:	Tachai	Hui County	Nan-hai
County:	Hsi-yang	Hui County	Nan-hai
Province:	Shansi	Honan	Kwangtung
Origin:	Construction 1967 Production 1968	Construction 1964 Production 1964	Construction 1958[c] Production 1960
Personnel:	144	27 Original 500 Now[a] 15% Women	549[f] 12.7% Women
Capacity:	Designed 7,000 m.t./yr. 1968—3,500 m.t./yr. 1969—7,000 m.t./yr. 1970—10,300 m.t./yr. 1971—12,000 m.t./yr. 1972—14,000 m.t./yr. 1974—20,000 m.t./yr. Plan to double capacity	1964—4 m.t./day 1974—50,000 m.t./yr. 1975—132,000 m.t./yr.[b]	1960—7,500 t.py.[e] 1962—32,000 1965—--[e] 1969—64,000 1974—103,000[e] 1975—6 mos. 58,000 1975—Goal 120,000
Use:	80% used in county capital projects and water conservation 20% in urban projects	90% used locally	All in county
Investment:	350,000 yuan	1,700 yuan Original Total—not available	5,000,000 yuan Total[g] 3,000,000 yuan Province 2,000,000 yuan County
Raw materials:	Limestone—77% Clay —20% Iron ore — 3% Fluorite — -- Coal—15% of total raw materials	Limestone—77% Clay —15% Iron ore —8% Fluorite — -- Coal—13% of total raw materials	Limestone—82% Clay —10.6% Iron ore — 2% Fluorite —0.6% Coal—5% of Total raw materials
Fuel:	Type: Anthracite Ash: 10% Cost: 3.5 yuan/t. Heating Value: n.a.	Type: Bituminous Ash: 13% Cost: n.a. Heating value: n.a.	Type: Anthracite Ash: 20% Cost: n.a. Heating value: 7000 kcl./kg.
Crushing:	250 mm. x 4 mm.	80 cm. x 60 cm. jaw 12 t./hr.	Jaw 24 in. Hammermill 12.0 mm.

	Plant 1	Plant 2	Plant 3
Milling:	Feeders — Table Type mill—Ball Circuit —Open Number —1 Size —1.27 m. x 4.5 m. Production—2.8 t/hr. Motor —80 kw.	Feeders — Vibrating Type mill—ball Circuit —Open Number —2 Size —2.5 m. x 6.5 m. Motor —380 kw.	Feeders — Table Type mill—Ball Circuit —Open Number —2 Size —1.83 m. x 6.1 m. Production—12 t/h. each Motor —245 kw.
Feed preparation:	Type —Pelletizing Type —Rotating disc Water —15%	Type —Pelletizing Type —Disc Water—15%	Type —Pelletizing Type —2.5 m. disc
Kiln:	Type—Shaft Size—1.6 m. x 7.0 m. Temperature— 1200-1400°C. Production—2.5 t./hr. Kcl./t.—4000 Refractories— Special mortar Slag Alumina brick Discharge—Manual	Type—(6) Egg Shape Type—(3) Shaft—Manual Type—(1) Shaft—Automatic Size—(3) 1.5 m. x 7.0 m. Size—(1) 2.5 m. x 10.0 m. Production—(6) 4 t./d.[c] Production—(3) 3 t./h. Production—(1) 8 t./h. Discharge—See above	Type—Shaft—Two Size—2.5 m. x 9.1 m. Production—6.0 t/h. each Kcl./t.—120 kg./t. Discharge—Automatic
Cement milling:	Type —Ball Circuit —Open Number—Two Size—1.37 m. x 4.5 m. Production—1.6 t./hr. Motor—80 kw.	Type —Ball Circuit —Open Size—(2) 1.5 m. x 5.5 m. Size—(4) 1.2 m. x 4.7 m. Motor—135 kw.	Type —Ball Circuit —Open Number—Three Size—(2) 1.83 m. x 6.1 m. Size—(1) 2.2 m. x 5.5 m. Motor—(2) 245 kw.
Products:	Portland, Mark 400 Slag cements	Portland	Pozzolanic and slag cements
Storage:	Two silos	Eight silos	
Packing:	Majority—Bag 50 kg.	10% Bag 90% Bulk truck	Bag
Price:	38/t.	n.a.	Wages: Max. 80
Cost:	30/t.	n.a.	Min. 40
Profit:	8/t.	n.a.	Avg. 57

[a] Government standard was for 800 plant personnel.
[b] Production—January through May at 400 t./d. rate; 300 days operation = 132,000 m.t./year.
[c] Not presently in use.
[d] Built in three stages—1st 1958-1960; 2nd 1964-1969; and 3rd 1970 to present.
[e] Productivity—Tons per worker; 1960—20; 1965—12?; and 1974—260.
[f] Does not include employees for stone extraction.
[g] For a plant of 100,000 t./yr. 8,000,000 yuan would be anticipated.

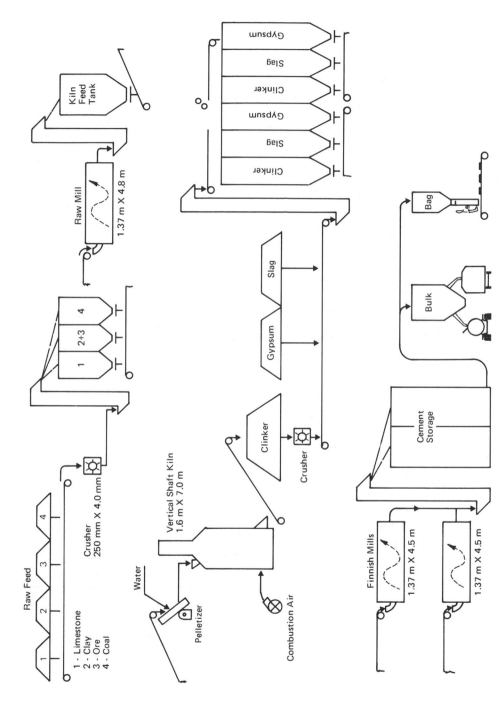

FIGURE VII-1. Flow Diagram, Tachai Plant.

It is our belief that this plant has a much greater potential capacity than is presently shown. Equipment of this type should operate a high percentage of the available time. Using 350 days, or 95.8%, operating time for one's calculations, this would total as follows:

type	tpd	days	no.	tons
6 egg-shaped kilns	4	350	6	8,400
3 shaft	72	350	3	75,600
1 shaft (automatic)	192	350	1	67,200
Total				151,200

There appears to be just enough raw grind capacity to sustain the four shaft kilns, so the actual capacity probably should be about 142,000 tons. The "egg-shaped" kilns were not being operated, and we did not see them during our hurried tour. The plant was clean, and appeared to be well maintained.

3. *Nan-hai County Cement Factory.* Construction started in 1958 and went into production in 1960. The plant is a county-run enterprise. The plant was actually built in three stages. The second phase took place from 1964–69. During this phase a call for technical innovation resulted in many changes. Two ball mills were installed; they were 1.83 m. diameter by 6.1 m. long and were powered by 245 kw. motors. Renovation to the shaft kiln resulted in a change from a crude method of pelletizing to 2.5 m. diameter disk-type machines. Feed to the kiln up to now was done manually. An automatic method of charging also was accomplished and improvements in production increased from 2.6 t./h./kiln to 3.4 t./h./kiln. Coal used decreased from 180 kg./t. to 120 kg./t.

The third phase was from 1970 to the present. "Three-in-one" groups were formed, and a further renovation of the shaft kiln was completed. The discharge, which had been manual, was changed to automatic. This was designed, manufactured, and installed by plant personnel. The production was increased from 3.4 t./h./kiln to 6.0 t./h./kiln. Daily production was increased from 110–200 to 220–230 tons. An additional ball mill 2.5 m. diameter and 5.5 m. long was installed in this phase. This allowed achievement of balance in production.

Product was ground into a series of bins and could be extracted by screw type conveyors. All product was packed in bags at a rate of five per minute. These were collected on an automatic stacker and conveyed to a warehouse by hand cart. The bags were a self-sealing type, manufactured at the plant and were 4-ply. Most of the production was shipped in boats having a capacity of 20, 30, and 300 tons. Stock from the warehouse is taken to the dock in two cars powered by a 7.5 kw. motor which can transport 20 tons per trip. Hand loading is practiced at the boat.

The plant is equipped with a good machine shop. Many pieces of equipment have been made here, including the overhead crane for the shop. Duct work for the dust collectors also were being made. A foundry is operated for use at the plant.

Future plans to improve the plant include major attention to the abatement of dust, and several small dust removal units have been designed and installed. The two major areas of concern are the clay dryers and the shaft kilns. Dust from the shaft kiln is high in potassium, so it is planned to be used as a fertilizer. They have erected the superstructure and plan to complete this project very soon. They expect this project to abate 97% of the particulate from the shaft kilns and to collect from 3.3 tons per day of dust to be used as fertilizer. Another project expected to increase production is the replacement of the present Type No. 9 blowers on the shaft kilns with a Type 200 blower. Present blowers have 80 kw. units on each kiln. This should allow for further increases in kiln production.

The Nan-hai County Cement Factory was originally built from plans supplied by the state. Preventive maintenance is practiced because they usually go down with equipment two days per month and an annual major overhaul of 15 to 20 days is routine, in which each piece of equipment is checked. Yearly profit accumulations are partially allocated to maintenance and innovation.

Gross value and price of materials were not available, but we were advised that the cost of raw materials, fuel, and electricity were down, and production was up, so that costs at the plant had to be reduced.

Safety devices were provided, and it was reported that the safety record was good. Three plants, of course, do not make up an adequate sample from which to draw overall conclusions about all 2800 existing small-scale plants. It is clear to me, nevertheless, that the small-scale Portland Cement plant utilizing shaft kilns does meet a need for China under the circumstances and criteria set forth earlier in this report, and this need may still exist for some time into the future. However, as transportation is improved, a more centrally located plant with a much higher productivity and improved quality of product should become more acceptable. For example, the largest plant we saw was producing 103,000 tons of pozzolanic and slag cements. This was being done with 549 workers, not including the quarry personnel. This calculates to 187 tons per worker versus the production of 5200 tons per worker in a very modern cement plant. With some of the new world technology, productivity will improve even further.

Quality of product must become a major concern. The two main reasons why shaft kilns are not used throughout the world are low productivity and unreliable quality. The latter will become more important as more complex structures are required. Very brief observations indicate to me that the making of Mark 400 and 500 products continuously might pose a problem.

It should be repeated that Chinese and American test methods for compressive strength do differ significantly. The Chinese use a dry mortar method which utilizes from 15–25% water. The American wet method uses from 43–45% water. The water content will drastically alter the reported strength. Generally speaking, the lower the water content, the higher the strength. One analysis of Chinese cement indicates that it is ground more coarsely than U.S. products and does indeed develop significantly lower strengths when tested comparatively.

In conclusion, small-scale Portland Cement plants have served a need for China, but in my opinion it is a short-time expedient. Productivity and quality will dictate a different procedure when transportation and materials handling problems can be solved.

Photo VII-1. Hui County cement plant.

Photo VII-2. Manufacture of a grinding mill.

Photo VII-3. Shaft kiln.

PHOTO VII-4. Coal storage.

PHOTO VII-5. Raw material storage and handling equipment.

Photo VII-6. 350 h.p. grinding mill.

Photo VII-7. 85 h.p. grinding mill.

Photo VII–8. New grinding mill head.

Photo VII-9. A concrete boat.

Chapter VIII

HOW SMALL-SCALE INDUSTRY SERVES AGRICULTURE

In Chinese plans, "Agriculture is the foundation." Other sectors may receive more financial and material resources, but unless food output keeps ahead of population, all else will eventually come to a halt. The key to raising agricultural production in China is raising yields per unit of arable land. Expansion of land under cultivation, as will become apparent from the discussion below, is not a major means of increasing output.

In the Chinese rural development model, there is a clear sequence to the process of raising yields, an ordering that in a fundamental way is the reverse side of the coin of the rural small-scale industry development sequence. In fact, as already indicated, it is rural industry's impact on farm yields that provides the main reason for that industry's existence.

Agricultural development, in the Chinese scheme, begins with water management and land improvement, the two being closely linked but not identical. With the provision of timely and adequate supplies of water, it becomes possible to introduce fertilizer-responsive plant varieties together with the fertilizer needed to achieve high yields from these varieties. Effective water management also may make it possible to increase the cropping index from one to two, or two to three, crops a year, and this increase will in turn require more fertilizer.

All of the above steps raise the demand for rural labor. Water conservancy efforts, particularly as these are carried out in China with minimal use of machinery except for pumps require large amounts of labor. Provision of chemical fertilizers does not use many man days of effort, but organic fertilizer does, and the Chinese use prodigious amounts. Finally, as yields rise, more time is required to harvest, thresh, and mill the increased output. And the appearance of greater surpluses means that someone must move these surpluses to market. If Chinese labor were truly surplus in the sense of being unemployed, of course, provision of ever greater numbers of workers would present few problems. But rural China's labor is not surplus in this sense. Although the marginal product of much of this labor is extremely low particularly in the off season, it is not zero, and therefore changes of the kind now occurring cut into labor already in use elsewhere. The answer, of course, is to mechanize those functions where labor supply is becoming a major bottleneck.

The areas our delegation visited already had progressed far along the above described path. As advanced areas, they were the models that it was hoped the rest of the nation would follow in time. A four-week visit, of course, is not sufficient to attempt to appraise how rapidly the rest of China is catching up with these models, although some insight on this question was gained.

FARMLAND CAPITAL CONSTRUCTION

Described simply, farmland capital construction in China is aimed at molding the fundamental geographic features of an area to provide a firm base, so that the correct mix of other inputs—labor, machinery, fertilizer, improved seed strains—can bring about high and stable yields. Guaranteeing a stable supply of sufficient water or drainage and leveling and squaring the land or building terraced fields are the key points in the process. Without fundamental attention to water control and land improvement, yields will remain low, and the whole mutual development sequence between agriculture and industry will suffer. All the areas we visited from the national model of Tachai to the delta regions of east and southeast China analyzed their problems in these terms, and hence began their development programs with farmland capital construction efforts.

As already indicated, in all areas the major thrust appeared to be toward improvement of land already under cultivation. Land reclamation, while not ignored, definitely occupied a secondary role. To be sure, we were shown areas where new land had been brought under cultivation. An-p'ing Commune (Shansi) had created 3000 mu (200 hectares) of farmland in a former river bed. And in Lin County (Honan) farmers were doing the same thing, first by removing many of the rocks from the river bed, using them to build a dike, and then bringing earth down from a nearby mountainside using baskets and shoulder poles. In Hui County (Honan) we visited an area where some 27,000 mu (1800 hectares) had been carved out of what formerly had been wasteland.

But from what we could gather, both nationally and in the regions we visited, there had been little if any *net* increase in the cultivated area. New land was being brought under cultivation, but old arable land was also being alienated to industrial and water conservancy uses. Nationally, for example, we were told that 11% of the total land area was being cultivated; in 1957 the published figure was 11.7%.[1] Similarly in Honan Province where we spent much of our time, total arable land at present is 7.38 million hectares whereas in the 1950s the total varied between 8.8 and 9.0 million hectares.[2] We did not collect figures on changes in the cultivated acreage in the regions we visited, but information on the area under grain crops can be derived from statistics we were given, and these data are presented in Table VIII-1. Grain acreage, of course, is not the same as total cultivated acreage, but it is unlikely an expansion of cash crop acreage accounts in the main for the indicated stagnation or decline in grain acreage.

While we did not see much expansion of acreage, we did see massive efforts to reshape the land in ways that would make high stable yields possible. Any visitor to Tachai, of which an average of 3000 plus can be expected on any given day from all over China, has to come away impressed with what has been done to this formerly barren area. Sloping, small pieces of land where crops were washed away by summer rains and perished from lack of water at other times have been converted into large, flat, irrigated fields protected from flooding.

In farmland capital construction, as elsewhere, China's dominant economic theme, self-reliance, favors projects at the county level or below. Every county, commune, and production brigade visited had taken part in, if not been responsible for agricultural construction projects.

A considerable amount of local autonomy seems to exist at any given level in determining how best to go about improving the land. Depending on the geographic conditions and what are considered to be the unit's most pressing needs, relatively more emphasis may be placed on leveling hilltops, filling in ravines and washes, and constructing terraced fields as in Tachai, or reclaiming waste land and building new fields as in Hui County, or in squaring off plots and constructing underground drainage channels as in Wu-hsi. All of this is done against a background of water control projects— reservoirs, canals, irrigation and drainage channels, pumping stations, and tube wells—that generally form the key underpinning for any unit's agricultural construction projects.

1. N. R. Chen, *Chinese Economic Statistics* (Chicago: Aldine, 1967), pp. 123 and 285.
2. *Peking Review*, August 8, 1975, p. 17 and *Provincial Agricultural Statistics* (Committee on the Economy of China, 1969), p. 40.

Table VIII-1

GRAIN ACREAGE (IN MU)

Area	1949	1953	1966	1971	1973
Hsi-yang County (grain acreage)	—	—	374,936	368,487	368,827
—Tachai Brigade					
grain acreage	—	847	706[a]	698	750
total acreage	—	—	—	—	846[b]
—An-p'ing Commune					
grain acreage	—	—	—	—	23,019[b]
total acreage	—	—	—	—	25,500[b]
Hui County					
grain acreage	918,367	—	766,129[a]	—	714,097
total acreage	—	—	—	—	950,000

[a]The Tachai figure is for 1964 and Hui County figure is for 1963.
[b]These figures are for the year 1974.
NOTE: Estimates in this table were derived by dividing total grain output for the region by yield per mu. of cultivated land.

When irrigation projects begin to involve the interests of neighboring units, however, then higher approval and some coordination with the affected units is called for. Counties we visited had water management bureaus that approved capital construction plans and served as a coordinating body for distribution of water as well as supervising county-level projects. In most cases the chain of command continues up through water management bureaus at the special administrative region and the province.

Capital construction projects at the county level and higher are also distinguished by permanent year round construction teams, whereas the smaller commune and brigade projects are largely confined to slack season activity. One commune in Wu-hsi, for example, had formulated an ambitious plan to improve its water control and land features by 1980. Although the plan would require sizeable labor inputs, the commune officials made it clear that construction work would only be done in the slack winter season and that the pace of construction would depend on the availability of labor.

A county-level project we saw in Hsi-yang County involved the construction of a reservoir of seven million cubic meters capacity, plus 50 kilometers of channels. A permanent, all-year-round work force of 2100 (equivalent to about 2.5% of the county's total labor force) was at the construction site. An additional 200 cadres per day also are participating. The work force comes from nearby production brigades who have been assigned a labor quota by the county. (NOTE: The labor quota was not pro rated on the basis of expected benefit as it was with some other projects we visited and as is known to be the case in other parts of China.) The production brigades continue to give work points to the construction workers, who also receive a supplement from the county of 2.3 catties (chin) and .40 yuan per day. This same system of state supplements was found to be the rule at a number of other year-round construction sites.

The short-term costs of these kinds of projects are not slight in manpower, material, or monetary terms. The Nan-ku-tung Reservoir in Lin County is a medium-sized reservoir with a capacity of 69 million cubic meters. (NOTE: We were told by Peking officials that a "small" reservoir is less than 10 million cubic meters, and a "large" reservoir is more than 100 million cubic meters.) Five communes took part in the construction over a more than two-year period. The communes, who contributed manpower proportionate to the benefit each expected to obtain from the reservoir, spent over 3 million work days on the project and moved over 1 million cubic meters of earth and stone. The workers received a state supplement from the county (grain plus .35 yuan per day) similar to that at the county project in Hsi-yang County mentioned previously. According to Lin County officials, the total cost of the reservoir was about 5 million yuan, with the state bearing 10.5% of the cost. It would seem obvious that projects of this magnitude are too expensive for most units below the county level to undertake on their own, and even at the county level some sort of state financial support is needed.

Other costs, such as loss of arable land to reservoirs, are more than compensated for by increased yields on what was previously marginal or low-yield land. One other potential problem is the conflicting demands for labor between the affected communes and brigades—hard pressed with their own agricultural production targets—and the state's need for inputs to large capital construction projects. At present labor is a major restraint on speeding up the pace of water control projects, and it is likely to remain a restraint as long as rational planning is followed.

Finally, the development of farmland and water management infrastructure creates a demand for large amounts of material products such as cement, bricks, iron and steel, pumps, other irrigation and drainage machinery, and hydroelectric equipment. Because most of these items can be produced locally by small-scale factories, however, the opportunity cost of these products is reduced over what would be the case if all these items had to be shipped from large urban plants.

In principle, China's north stands to gain more from farmland capital construction projects than the south, because it is the north where the shortage of water is most acute, and in the northern areas we visited the gains were indeed dramatic. As is apparent from the figures in Table VIII-2,

Table VIII-2

INNIQATCD AONCAQC

Region	Cultivated Acreage (in mu.)	Irrigated Acreage (in mu.)	(%)
Shansi: An-p'ing Commune—now	25,500	6,000	23.5
An-p'ing Commune—soon	25,500	13,000	51.0
Shih-p'ing Brigade	3,200	3–400	9–12.5
Tachai Brigade	846	592	70.0
Wuchiaping Brigade	—	—	80.0
Honan: An-yang District	12,500,000	7,000,000	56.0
—Lin County—before	890,000	12,000	1.3
Lin County—now	890,000	600,000	67.4
—Ta-ts'ai-yuan Brigade	1,560	1,560	100.0
Hui County	950,000	640,000	67.4
—Hsin-liang-ts'un Commune	42,000	42,000	100.0
Chi-li-ying Commune	93,000	83,700	90.0
Kiangsu: Wu-hsi County	800,000	800,000	100.0
—Mei-ts'un Commune	29,500	29,500	100.0
Shanghai: Ma-lu Commune	33,915	33,236	98.0
All China	1,600,000,000	—	41.0[a]

[a]This figure is for 1973. It is based on a 40% figure (for 1972) given to an American water management delegation and the officially reported increase in irrigated acreage between 1972 and 1973 (*Peking Review,* January 4, 1974, p. 10).

a majority of the cultivated land in the regions we visited was under irrigation.

But, as a visit to the Yellow River Exhibition in Cheng-chou makes clear, most of north China is not so extensively irrigated, and further progress, in the Yellow River basin at least, is going to be slow and expensive. The amount of work accomplished to date is already massive by most standards, and the curse of flooding does appear to have been eliminated through, among other things, the construction and improvement of thousands of kilometers of dikes. The irrigated acreage in the river's drainage basin, which had fallen to 12 million mu (800 thousand hectares) in 1949 had been increased to 48 million mu (3.2 million hectares) in 1972 and to over 50 million mu (33 + million hectares) in 1974. The goal, however, is to achieve one mu of irrigated land per capita in this drainage area or a total irrigated acreage of 110 million mu (7.3 million hectares). But that goal is to be attained over a period of ten to twenty years, and even then the percentage of irrigated land will be below 40% (110/300 = 36.7%).

Elsewhere in north China, particularly on the North China Plain only part of which is in the Yellow River area, irrigation has been extended by the digging of tube wells. In Hopei Province, for example, there are now 400,000 tube wells in operation, 300,000 of which have been sunk since 1966. In the northern part of the same province, control of the Hai river, which included the construction of over 1000 reservoirs of different sizes, has raised the irrigated acreage in that region to one mu per person.

The effort to irrigate China's parched northern soils, therefore, continues on many fronts. The task has not been an easy one in the past as the enormous human investment required by the Tachai fields and the Red Flag Canal so dramatically attest. And this task isn't going to get much easier anytime soon.

FERTILIZER APPLICATION

Limited amounts of chemical fertilizer and much larger quantities of organic fertilizer can be used even on fields unirrigated and inadequately served by rainfall. But where water is in sufficient supply, large increases in yields can be achieved by means of the massive application of plant nutrients. In all the areas we visited, great quantities of fertilizer were being applied with organic varieties still outstripping manufactured chemical fertilizers.

No precise figure is available for the average amount of nutrient supplied per hectare by chemical fertilizers, because the Chinese report their production in gross tonnage, not nutrient terms. In 1974 chemical fertilizer production plus imports in these terms was about 30 million tons, which converts to something over 6 million tons of nutrient, or around 60 kilograms of nutrient per hectare.[3] There are similar problems in converting the data we received for individual communes into nutrient equivalents, and hence the estimates given us are presented in both converted and unconverted form in Table VIII-3. The major conversion problem is with organic fertilizers. Tables are available in China giving the nutrient content of various kinds of manure and green fertilizer, but we were not in any one place long enough to find out precisely what the proportion of each type was in the organic weight total given us. The nutrient figures for organic fertilizer in the table, therefore, are illustrative only and may err on either the high or low side.

Whatever the precise figures are, there is no doubt that with chemical and organic fertilizers the Chinese are putting an enormous amount of nutrient back into the soil. In the areas we visited, the amount of nitrogen alone must have been at least 300 to 400 kilograms per hectare and possibly higher. Applications of this magnitude put China in a class with some of the world's highest users of fertilizers including Japan.

3. These production figures have to be reconstructed from reported percentage increases and then converted by very rough means into nutrient equivalent. The conservative conversion rate of 20% has been used; this is higher than the rate for ammonium bicarbonate (17.5%), but lower than the rate for most other chemical fertilizers (see Chapter VI).

It is beyond the scope of this chapter to determine whether or not this level of fertilizer usage was typical of the nation as a whole. If national average usage for chemical fertilizer was around 60 kilograms/hectare, then all of the regions we visited were above average, but then all areas with adequate supplies of water were probably above average.

Where China appears to differ markedly from other nations is in the proportion of nutrient that is supplied by organic fertilizers. Our delegation had no way of determining whether the amounts used in the areas we visited were unusually high for China or not. What is clear is that the amounts were enormous. In part, probably in large part, this level of organic fertilizer use was a product of commune organization. For green fertilizers in particular the ability to mobilize labor for collection purposes and the lack of barriers caused by private land ownership has undoubtedly been a help.

Thus with fertilizer as with water control construction, small-scale industries are playing an increasing role in the development of Chinese agriculture. But as in the case of water control construction, a high proportion of what is being accomplished still rests in the hands of the commune members themselves. Eventually factories small and large may provide China with most of its rural construction materials and fertilizer, but in the meantime farmers are doing much of the providing themselves.

MECHANIZATION

The complexity of mechanizing Chinese agriculture staggers both the imagination and the observer. But it is a task being pursued with enormous diligence and resources from Production Brigades to National Ministries. The purpose here is not to tell the mechanization story itself, for that refer back to Chapter V, but to place the agricultural mechanization efforts in their intermediate context between small-scale rural industry and farming.

The complexity of Chinese mechanization efforts also makes a complete description of what is happening impossible even when confined to the areas we visited. It is possible, however, to present an abstraction of our experience designed to mirror the planned interest of our itinerary, i.e., to understand the model for development of Chinese agriculture as laid out by the Chinese themselves. Understanding policy—understanding what the leadership *wants* to happen—is quite as important as understanding what *is* happening in an overall sense if there is ample evidence that the policy does work in model areas. This the Chinese demonstrated to us with considerable enthusiasm and effect. The remaining question, the speed of diffusion of the basic model, is not a question easily answered except by time and the Chinese themselves.

The basic story unfolds in the following manner. Pre-liberation China was trapped in a low-level equilibrium with agricultural productivity balanced by the resources available and incentives and organization structures

Table VIII-3

RATES OF CHEMICAL AND ORGANIC FERTILIZER APPLICATION (IN KG./HA.)
(IN KG./HA.)

Region	Crop	Type of Fertilizer	Gross Weight	Nutrient Equivalent
Peking:				
Red Star Commune	Wheat	Ammonium sulphate and bicarbonate	150	30
Red Star Commune	Corn	Ammonium sulphate and bicarbonate	300	60
Red Star Commune	Rice	Ammonium sulphate and bicarbonate	450	90
Red Star Commune	Grain	Organic	45–52,500	112–131
Shansi:				
An-p'ing Commune	Grain	Ammonium nitrate	450	153
An-p'ing Commune	Grain	Calcium superphosphate	300	60
An-p'ing Commune	Grain	Organic	60,000	150
Tachai Brigade	Grain	Ammonium nitrate and phosphates	300	88
Tachai Brigade	Grain	Organic	90,000	225
Honan:				
Lin County	Grain	Ammonium bicarbonate	750	131
Lin County	Grain	Phosphate	750	150
Lin County	Grain	Organicc	75,000	188
Hsinhsiang Area[a]	Grain	Chemical	675*	118
Hui County				
Hsin-liang-ts'un	Grain	Ammonium bicarbonate	1,500	263
Hsin-liang-ts'un	Grain	Phosphate	800	160
Hsin-liang-ts'un	Grain	Organic	150,000	375

Ch'i-li-ying Commune	Cotton and grain	Nitrogenous	450	79
Ch'i-li-ying Commune	Cotton and grain	Phosphate	525	105
Ch'i-li-ying Commune	Cotton and grain	Organic	75,000	188
Kiangsu:				
Wu-hsi County[b]	Grain	Nitrogenous	450–600	79–105
Wu-hsi County[b]	Grain	Organic	225,000	563
Mei-ts'un Commune	Rice	Nitrogenous	675–900	188–158
Mei-ts'un Commune	Rice	Organic	225,000	563
Mei-ts'un Commune	Mulberry	Nitrogenous	Little	Little
Mei-ts'un Commune	Mulberry	Organic	112,500	281
Shanghai:				
Ma-lu Commune	Grain	Ammonium Sulphate	1,200	240
Ma-lu Commune	Grain	Superphosphate	450	90
Ma-lu Commune	Grain	Organic	112,500	281
Ma-lu Commune	Grain	Nitrogenous	less than grain	—

[a] *Peking Review,* August 8, 1975, pp. 16–17.
[b] In Wu-hsi County, phosphate fertilizers are only used on poor land (300–575 kg./ha. gross weight).

CONVERSION RATES:
Ammonium bicarbonate .175
Nitrogenous .175 (Conservatively assumed to all be ammonium bicarbonate.)
Ammonium nitrate .340
Ammonium sulphate .200
Superphosphate .200
Organic

Any conversion rate used here will be a rough estimate at best since organic fertilizer is a mixture of manure, mud, grasses, etc. According to one source (*Fei-liao chih-shih* [Fertilizer Knowledge] (Shanghai: 1974), pp. 15, 19, 38, 39] the N content of hog manure is 0.6%, of cattle manure .32%, and of various green fertilizers .15 to 1.32%. For illustrative purposes we have used a rate of 0.25% in this table.

for change. While it is possible that a full-blown private economy provided with appropriate inputs would have raised agricultural output somewhat, it is quite doubtful that much progress could be made without substantial restructuring of the ownership of the land and the organizational structure involved in farming it. This stage of the model was accomplished with the land reform of the early 1950s, the primitive coops of the mid-1950s, and finally culminating in the Rural People's Communes in 1958. These changes put in place an organizational structure capable of mobilizing large quantities of surplus labor for large-scale projects involving restructuring of farm land and major irrigation works. While some of this labor was already available in the slack season, much more was needed to attack and transform nature on the scale widely advertised by the Chinese and in fact seen by our group in the model areas. This need for more labor provides a rationale for the first stage of agricultural mechanization—the processing of basic food grains by machine instead of by hand. The labor savings, as pointed out in previous chapters, are truly enormous. While this saved labor would be mostly female, the argument is not weakened a bit. Women work side by side with men in irrigation and farmland capital construction projects. A very substantial proportion of the total labor input in either type of project involves moving dirt and stone by baskets on shoulder poles, and we observed both women and men engaged in this task.

A second role of surplus labor generated at this stage of mechanization is in the provision of labor to extract and transport the basic raw materials of small-scale rural industries, especially coal and limestone for cement. The cement produced is then used to transform the physical aspect of agricultural land via irrigation works, drainage, and terracing.

A third role for this surplus labor, as indicated in the previous section, is to increase the amount of organic manure prepared and distributed to the fields. Since a very substantial proportion of the total input into the production of organic manure is human (both in a direct physical sense, but more important in terms of labor input), the generation of surplus labor permitted a substantial increase in the production of this vital yield-sustaining-and-raising input into Chinese agriculture.

The next stage of mechanization was to attack the most easily mechanized task in the harvest period—threshing. Although semi-mechanized threshing (pedal-operated threshers used in the field) had been a fairly standard feature of the double-cropped rice land in the south since liberation, wheat threshing is technically more difficult and awaited widespread rural electrification so that motor driven threshers on central threshing floors could be used.

The widespread mechanization of threshing (and it was not all that widespread in our own observations despite being in model areas) generates peak time surplus labor (and draft animals in many cases) that can be used to prepare land for a second crop and for its planting or transplanting. Obviously, multiple cropping was going on in China centuries ago and did not depend on mechanization of threshing for its existence. At the *margin,* however, peak time labor (and animals) saved from manual threshing can *increase* the extent of multiple cropping, and this is all the more true of a rapidly moving margin.

Two other inputs become critical at this stage; high yielding, fertilizer responsive seed varieties and the chemical fertilizer to put on them. Double-cropping is not doubly exhausting to the soil relative to single-cropping, because yields usually do not double, but there is no question that substantially more nutrients are required on a long-run basis, and it is very difficult to provide these strictly from organic manures. Locally available chemical fertilizer thus suddenly has a very high productivity, and in this context the small ammonium bicarbonate and ammonium nitrate plants make economic sense despite their high costs per nutrient ton. The costs are in terms of direct labor and raw materials, which are mostly only indirect labor. So once again, the desirability of labor *saving* mechanization in agriculture and processing becomes clear.

Some of the mechanization data that we collected in the regions we visited are presented in Table VIII-4. There are more than a few problems connected with the interpretation of the data in this table. For example, we were never able to get a very clear picture of precisely what was meant when the Chinese told us that an area was being 80 ot 90% machine plowed. Still it is clear that many key processes in China's advanced areas are being extensively mechanized. Furthermore, most, although not all of this development, has occurred during the past five to ten years.

Certain of the areas we visited were certainly way above the national average in terms of their current level of mechanization. Not surprisingly, the areas near the major industrial centers of Shanghai (including Wu-hsi) and Peking were the most mechanized. Areas deeper into the countryside such as Lin and Hsi-yang Counties were less mechanized at least in terms of numbers of tractors and percentage of area machine plowed, which were the most readily available although not necessarily the most meaningful statistics.

THE IMPACT ON FARM OUTPUT

The end result of all these efforts to increase the industrial inputs available to agriculture is, of course, a rise in farm output. In the case of certain inputs, water and fertilizer for example, the impact of increases on yields is direct. In other cases, labor saving machinery is the main example, increases free other inputs (i.e. labor) that can then be used to raise yields (by more weeding, etc.). In the areas we visited there is little doubt that the

Table VIII-4

MECHANIZATION LEVELS IN AREAS VISITED

Region	Food Processing by Machine	Threshers (No.)	% Crop Machine Threshed	Tractors (No.)	Per Capita	Machine Plowing (%)
Peking:						
Red Star Commune	Most	140	—	439	.0054	—
Shansi:						
Tachai Brigade	—	—	—	6	.0133	70
Shih-p'ing Brigade	—	—	—	5	.0028	33
An-p'ing Commune				27	.0027	18
Honan:						
Lin County	80%	—	—	700	.0010	60
—Brigade (Name unknown)	—	6	100	2	.0012	100
Hui County						
—Hsin-liang-ts'un Commune	—	—	—	—	—	50
Ch'i-li-ying Commune	100	—	100	80+	.0015	80
—Liu-chuang Brigade	—	—	—	4	.0033	—
Kiangsu:						
Wu-hsi County	Most	—	Most	3000+	.0033	90
—Yang-shih Commune	Most	—	Most	83	.0038	—
—Mei-ts'un Commune	Most	—	Most	124	.0040	90+
—Ho-lieh Brigade	—	14	—	20	.0048	—
Shanghai:						
Ma-lu Commune	Most	—	Most	—	—	98

— Indicates data not collected or otherwise unavailable.

Table VIII–5

GRAIN YIELDS IN REGIONS VISITED
(KG. OF UNHUSKED GRAIN/CULTIVATED HA.)

Region	Year 1949	1957 or '58	1965 or '66	1970	1971	1973	1974
Peking:							
Red Star Commune	750	—	—	—	—	—	6420
Shansi:							
Hsi-yang County	1050	—	1748	—	4808	4860	—
—Tachai Brigade	1050	—	5295	—	8220	7695	—
—Wu-chia-p'ing Brigade	—	2250[a]	1800	—	—	—	7650
—Shih-p'ing Brigade	—	1200[a]	—	—	6000	—	5250
—An-p'ing Commune	—	—	1155	—	—	—	3975
Honan:							
An-yang District	—	—	—	—	—	3000	—
—Lin County	1185	—	—	—	—	—	4800
—Ta-ts'ai-yuan Brigade	—	—	4000	—	6000	8250	—
—.....Brigade (Name not available)	1500	—	3000[b]	—	—	—	7170
—Hui County	735	—	1860	3030	—		
Ch'i-li-ying Commune	600	1253	3000+	—	—	—	8400
—Liu-chuang Brigade	1350–	—	3070	—	—	—	13,523
Kiangsu:							
Wu-hsi County	3600–	—	8875	—	—	—	11,025
—Yang-shih Commune	2510	—	8110	—	—	—	12,570
—Mei-ts'un Commune	3930	—	7958	—	—	—	10,680
—Ho-lieh Brigade	4050	8400	—	—	—	—	15,360
Shanghai:							
Ma-lu Commune	3150	4230	—	—	—	—	13,950

[a]The Wu-chia-p'ing figure is for 1956, the Shih-p'ing figure for 1960.
[b]This figure is for the period prior to the completion of the Red Flag Canal.

rise of rural small-scale industries had a great deal to do with the major increases in grain yields reported. As is apparent from the data in Table VIII-5, yields in these regions increased by from two to four and more times in the northern regions visited, and from 34 to 54% in the south between 1965–66 and 1973 or 1974. During this period the major changes involved the expansion of irrigation systems and increases in industrial inputs, a large portion of which came from rural small-scale plants. We lack sufficient data to specify precisely the contribution of each of these inputs to the rise in yields, and agricultural inputs are complementary in any case. That small-scale factories had a large impact, however, seems clear.

The number one question, of course, is whether the experiences in these counties are transferable to the rest of the country. Average grain yields in China are about 3300 kilograms per cultivated hectare[4] or substantially less than in the areas we visited. As our hosts pointed out, if the experience of these advanced areas is transferable to more backward regions, then China can anticipate major increases in farm output as this transfer occurs. Whether and how rapidly this transfer can or will occur, however, is not something that easily can be determined by twelve visitors in a four-week visit.

4. Official reports on total grain output put national output in 1974 at around 260 million and total cultivated acreage at 100 million ha., or a bit more of which about 78% is in grain.

Chapter IX

THE IMPACT OF
SMALL-SCALE INDUSTRY
ON CHINESE SOCIETY

Small- and medium-size industry have a potentially large number of effects on the social structure of the country and the countryside. Four of these potential effects need to be singled out. Though it is only a minor role in China, small-scale industry does have the possibility of absorbing some rural labor, which would otherwise be unemployed during parts of the year. The decentralization of intermediate size industry strengthens the network of cities through which economic innovations are diffused throughout the society. Small industries controlled by the commune greatly strengthen its administrative initiative and authority. Finally, though the effects are not as great as in large industry, small industry further weakens the role of the family, while strengthening the position of women.

LABOR ABSORPTION

Within the study of economic and social change in developing countries, there has long been a debate about the ability of small-scale rural industry to absorb surplus labor from the countryside. The proponents of the labor absorption theory argue that small plants located in the countryside not very distant from villages can solve part of the problem of chronic underemployment or hidden unemployment in village agriculture. Small industries using crude indigenous methods are necessarily more labor intensive. And not having a large investment in fixed machinery, which must be kept running year round, these small factories can vary their operations depending on the annual agricultural cycle. In the agricultural slack season, over the winter between the fall harvest and spring planning, small rural factories can absorb labor. During the busy agricultural season when there is a great demand for planting, harvesting, irrigating, and weeding, the small factories can release labor for agricultural work. This alternation in work is facilitated by the proximity of factories to villages such that workers never have to leave their village residences even when they are within the factory.

The critics of this theory question whether small industry can really absorb much labor. They note that since rural industry has only a limited market, it will be restricted in its growth. Cruder machines used in small industries may require slightly more labor, but most small industries are just as anxious as large industries to adopt more efficient machines which save time and labor costs. Industries of any type will expand only as they begin to adopt modern methods. If one is concerned about absorbing labor, that will best be done in agriculture. It is agriculture that has the almost infinite ability to absorb more labor.[1]

Though the Chinese adopt parts of the first position, it is the second position to which their practice is closest. The basic Chinese position is demonstrated most clearly in the practices of the national model for agriculture—the Tachai Brigade and the surrounding Hsi-yang County—which we visited. The model presented in Hsi-yang and Tachai is one of heavy labor absorption in agriculture rather than industry. The peasants are to be made to realize that their winters can be turned into productive activity if they will only dedicate themselves to what is called "field capital construction." That part of the year when there has been traditionally little employment in agriculture and in which many peasants have run off to the city to find menial labor or to do part-time work in factories is to be dedicated instead to building dikes and terraces, tunneling new waterways, making new dams to store water for the dry spring and early summer, and even rechanneling the courses of whole rivers. Within Hsi-yang County, for example, Shih-p'ing Brigade, which formerly had hordes of workers off in the city, has compelled these workers to come back and help rebuild the fields with subsequently dramatic increases in agricultural productivity.

Rural small industry has a role in this process of labor absorption in agriculture, but a more indirect than direct one. The indirect role is expressed in two ways. First, rural small industry is to provide the cement to

1. The debate about the labor absorption possibilities of small industry has been most vigorous over the role of small industry in India. See P. N. Dhar and H. F. Lydall, *The Role of Small Enterprises in Indian Economic Development*, Bombay: Asia Publishing House, 1961. Bert F. Hoselitz, ed., *The Role of Small Industry in the Process of Economic Growth*, the Hague: Mouton, 1968.

be used in dams and culverts, concrete beams and light poles to help in making new buildings and electric lines, scrap iron and steel to be used in pipes and support rods, fertilizer to increase output, as well as pumps, small tractors, and other machines to help in rebuilding the fields. Though some of these new agricultural inputs will be used to increase output throughout the year, many of them are particularly used in winter capital construction. In this way, small industry helps indirectly to soak up surplus labor in the winter.

Paradoxically, the problem of surplus labor in the winter is also linked to the opposite problem of a shortage of labor at certain other times during the year. In part, there has traditionally been no great incentive to bring more land under cultivation or to redo fields simply because villages did not have an adequate labor force to plant and harvest these fields. In those few weeks of planting and harvesting in the spring, summer, and fall, peasants go for days with only a few hours of sleep a night as they get up before day break and go to bed long after night fall. The second indirect contribution to the problem of leveling out of the demand for labor throughout the year, then, is to supply machines which help reduce the demand for labor during the busiest weeks of the year. With new tractors for plowing, power driven threshers, winnowers, and grinding mills, the labor demands are drastically reduced. Or, as they would sometimes put it, mechanization of agriculture through small industry helps get rid of the four stoops—in rice regions the stoops are for seeding, transplanting, weeding, and harvesting.

An example of how mechanization might save labor at certain critical junctures during the year while increasing labor at other parts of the year came at Ma-lu Commune outside Shanghai. This area, formerly growing two grain crops a year, has now begun to grow three. Mechanical threshing and especially mechanical transplanting of rice seedlings has been critical in this change to three crops. The commune now owns 180 transplanters and plans to add more. Now 60% of the rice is mechanically transplanted. In the future they plan to transplant even more mechanically, for without mechanical transplanting it would be impossible for the commune to make a success of the very important commercial crop of cotton. Commune cotton yields have been unstable, we were told, falling from a peak of 158 catties per mu in 1968 to 120 and 91 catties in 1973 and 1974. The instability in yield was said to be partly the result of their inexperience in growing cotton and of inadequate drainage during periods of unusually heavy rain in 1974. Unstable yields were also the result of insufficient labor. After they switched to growing three crops per year, there was a contradiction between the planting of cotton, which required a lot of labor, and the transplanting of one crop of rice, which had to be done at about the same time. The contradiction could be solved only by using more mechanical rice transplanters which release labor from rice cultivation for cotton cultivation.

Generally, in the Chinese model for rural development, small industry is but part of a package in which change in agriculture and extra human effort—particularly in the winter slack season—is the central focus. Small industry supplies the inputs which help make extra human effort pay off. Without the chemical fertilizer as well as the cement and pumps for greater irrigation, extra effort would not be rewarded with appreciably greater output. Without the new plowing and grain processing equipment, the extra output would not be easily handled with the existing labor supply.[2] The extra inputs from small industry, then, help inspire the peasants to greater effort throughout the year.

The nature of this model may help explain why the Chinese were so unconcerned with the question we kept raising about whether mechanization would not eventually put people out of work. The Chinese maintain that mechanization only frees people for more important tasks and that more and more work will remain to be done. In the short run, and at the presently low levels of mechanization in most places, they are undoubtedly correct in asserting that mechanization *creates* a demand for rather than *reduces* the demand for labor. In the long run, industry may well have begun to develop rapidly enough to absorb any displaced labor.

To this point we have been discussing only the indirect contribution of small industry to the absorption of rural labor. Small industry does absorb some labor directly, however. There are three types of variation in the manner and degree to which labor is so absorbed. First, there is a regional variation. Counties which have ample supplies of raw materials and ample markets by virtue of their location in prosperous regions or near cities are likely to support more industry. Second, there is a variation by type of enterprise. In most places, factories absorb rather little labor.

Other kinds of sidelines such as piggeries, orchards, gravel pits, and lamb herds run by the commune, brigade, or team absorb much greater amounts of labor. Third, and related to this second dimension, compared to factories, sidelines appear to be more seasonal. They have somewhat greater capacity to absorb labor during the agricultural slack season and to reduce this labor during the busy planting and harvesting seasons.

The three dimensions along which rural enterprises can vary greatly affect the results in Table IX-1. Three points need to be made about this table. First, though most of the data in the table come from our travel notes, also included are some data for Hsi-yang and Hui Counties, which we visited, plus some 1974 data for the July 1 Commune outside Shanghai, which we did not visit. We have included the last place as an additional illustration

2. For an eighteenth century statement of how a new innovation—the turnip—produced a similar compounding of inputs and increase in demands for labor, see C. Peter Timmer, "The Turnip, the New Husbandry, and the English Agricultural Revolution," *Quarterly Journal of Economics* 83 (1969): 385.

of the extreme development of small industry in a suburban commune. Both the Hsi-yang and July 1 data come from booklets bought on the trip. The second point about the table is that the level of employment for all factories and sidelines is that of the agricultural slack season or the maximum level of employment during the year. The third point is that the concept of rural labor force varies considerably from place to place, hinging on how the local village accountants choose to reckon work points for children, the aged, and others who work only part of the year.[3] In the places we visited, the labor force ran from a low of 31% to a high of 64% of the total population in the commune or brigade. Despite this improbable range, we have used the reported labor force figures. Where labor force figures were not reported, we have estimated the labor force as one third of the total population. This one-third is likely to come close to the total number of able-bodied, full-time working adults who are the ones eligible for work in small industry. In any event, varying estimates of the work force from one-third to one-half of the total population usually influences the results of column two by only a percentage point or two, which would not change the conclusions in this section.

The regions we visited tended to be those with somewhat more rural industry than the average county or commune. In Honan Province, where we spent a week, a member of the provincial revolutionary committee told us that Hui and Lin Counties, which we visited, were among the most industrialized in the Province. A ready source of limestone, coal, and other raw materials, such as are available in these two counties, which are backed up against the Tai-hang Mountains, helps support more than the average number of small industries. Likewise, Hsi-yang County in the hills of Shansi province has more than an average amount of coal to fuel small industry. To judge from visual impressions along the roadside, Hsi-yang also has far more tractors and other agricultural machines than the average county in north China. In south China, we spent most of our time around Wu-hsi and Shanghai. Both of these cities are in the rich Yangtze delta region, which today as in the past is one of the two or three richest agricultural regions in China. Both the general prosperity of the area and the proximity of several large cities is likely to create a greater demand for the products of small industry than would be found in other places. The July 1 Commune outside Shanghai was the most extreme case of a commune producing for an external market, with a spray paint factory and electric storage battery factory which subcontract with larger urban factories. Also outside Shanghai, Ma-lu Commune makes foodstuffs and medicine which are consumed in part

3. This assertion is based on our travel notes and a reading of accountant's manuals—for example, Hunan Province Revolutionary Committee, Agriculture and Forestry Bureau, *Nung-ts'un jen-min kung-she sheng-ch'an k'uai-chi* (Rural People's Commune Production Accountant), Canton: Kwangtung People's Press, 1974.

Table IX–1

INDUSTRIAL EMPLOYMENT AND INCOME IN DIFFERENT ADMINISTRATIVE UNITS

Unit and Type of Enterprise	No. of Enterprises	% of Total Labor Force	% of Total Income	% of Total Grain and Industrial Output Value[c]
Counties				
(factories only)				
Hsi-yang County (county and commune)	24	4[b]	13	—
Lin County (county and commune)	65	4[b]	—	52
Lin County (county only)	20	2[b]	—	31
Wu-hsi County (county only)	79	5	27	—
Hui County[a]	—	—	—	47
Communes				
(factories only)				
Hsi-yang County[a] (average per commune)	2.5	3	10	15
Lin County (average per commune)	3	2	—	29
Hsin-hsiang Ch'i-li-ying	5	4	—	—
Hui Hsin-liang	4	6[b]	—	—
Peking Red Star	6	11[b]	20	—
Wu-hsi Yang-shih	7	6	40	—
Wu-hsi Mei-ts'un	8	8	—	—
Wu-hsi City Ho-lieh	8	10	50+	—
Shanghai July 1	6	19	32	—
(factories and sidelines)				
Hsi-yang Tachai[a]	7	—	—	35
Hsi-yang Li-chia-chuang[a]	5	9	—	—
Shanghai Malu	10	8	—	—

Communes and Brigades
(factories and sidelines)

Hsi-yang An-p'ing (average per commune)	—	8	—	—
Wu-hsi County (average per commune)	42	—	37	—
Wu-hsi Mei-ts'un	61	25	—	46
Shanghai Ma-lu	63	28	40 +	—

Brigades
(factories and sidelines)

Ch'i-li-ying Commune (average per brigade)	2	—	—	—
Ch'i-li-ying Liuchuang	—	26	—	—
Ho-lieh, one brigade (factories only)	—	6	—	—
Mei-ts'un Commune (average per brigade)	2.5	18	—	—
Ma-lu Commune (average per brigade)	3.8	17	—	—

NOTE: Commune units are listed first by county and then commune name. Solely brigade units are listed first by commune and then brigade name. The division of enterprises into factories and agricultural sidelines is only approximate. For further details, see the Appendix to this chapter.

[a] 1973 data.
[b] Estimate based on the assumption that the labor force was one-third of the total population.
[c] Estimates based on the assumption that grain was valued at about .10 yuan per catty.

outside the commune. In the suburbs of Wu-hsi City, Ho-lieh Commune subcontracts parts with a city factory for a sophisticated table plane, while a brigade within the commune makes leather shoe uppers for a factory in the city. Outside Peking, Red Star Commune subcontracts screws for a city plant. Since these kinds of urban products have a much higher profit rate than agricultural products, these communes are doubly advantaged over places which have only a rural market.

Despite these advantages, most of the places we visited had only a small proportion of the total labor work force in factories. The relevant data appear in the top half of Table IX-1, Column 2. It is only in the extraordinary July 1 Commune outside Shanghai that employment greatly exceeds 10%. In the other suburban communes, employment in factories is around 10%. In the north, away from the major urban centers, factory employment never exceeds 4%. The various comments by our hosts as to where small industry would likely be prevalent, leads us to think that these figures for non-urban places in north China are more typical of the rest of the country. Given that they are in some ways demonstration sites, even they may be a bit high.

Small factories run by the county and commune, then, presently do not have the capacity to absorb much labor. For two reasons, we think that in most places they are not likely to absorb much labor for many years to come. First, in the plants we visited the emphasis was on efficiency and saving rather than absorbing labor. Plant managers were eager to point out the number of labor saving devices they had introduced during the year and the number they hoped to introduce next year. Second, since by government policy these plants are usully constrained to serving their local area, they will not have sufficiently large markets for much expansion. Or, as we were told at Ma-lu Commune outside Shanghai, industry cannot be allowed to grow much faster than agriculture. In a few places this kind of restriction has been formalized with a rigid ceiling on employment. In a 1973 visit to Lin County, Jon Sigurdson was told that by provincial decree the proportion of workers used by industries at county, commune, and brigade levels should not exceed 5% of the labor force in a county.[4]

It may be possible to absorb more labor in other kinds of ancilliary activities, but these are ones very closely related to the basic agricultural activity of producing rice, wheat, corn, and other grains. The bottom half of Table IX-1 Column 2 shows the proportion of workers engaged in non-industrial sidelines. Commune level sidelines include collectively run pig farms, animal breeding grounds, water conservation teams, transport teams,

4. Jon Sigurdson, "Rural Industrialization in China," in U.S. Congress, Joint Economic Committee, *China: A Reassessment of the Economy,* Washington: U.S. Government Printing Office, 1975, p. 412.

and the like. For example, at Liu-chuang Brigade in Ch'i-li-ying Commune outside Hsin-hsiang City, the collective enterprises include not only a tractor repair station, farm tool shop, flour mill, cotton gin, and popsicle factory, but also an electricity repair team, animal husbandry stalls for milk cows and draught animals, pig stalls, vegetable gardens, and a fruit orchard. These latter collective endeavors it would appear absorb more labor than the more "industrial" repair station, tool shop, mill and gin. As Table IX-1 suggests, these sorts of sidelines are greater in number and require the most labor at the lower brigade level. Any estimate of the typical amounts of labor so involved is hindered by two features of the data. First, the dividing line between mainline agricultural activities and sideline agricultural activities is vague, and often variable from place to place.[5] Second, there is a sparcity of data for brigades outside the very rich Yangtze delta region. In the delta region, brigade factories and sidelines employ one-fifth to one-fourth of all workers during the agricultural slack season. Also at the prosperous Liu-chuang Brigade at Ch'i-li-ying in the north, brigade sidelines and factories employ one-fourth of the population in the slack season. At other places, far fewer people may be so employed. In Hsi-yang County, for example, An-p'ing Commune has been so busy with the basic work of constructing dams and irrigation ditches as well as leveling fields that brigade and commune sidelines as well as factories remain relatively undeveloped. In 1975, ancillary activities employed no more than 8% of the total work force in the slack season. Sidelines run at the lowest level of production—the team— would add to this proportion somewhat. We suspect in most places, however, that sideline activities during the slack season tend more toward the 8% of An-p'ing than toward the 20 or 25% of the other places we saw. Even 8% additional rural employment provides some relief, but the major sources of slack season employment in places such as An-p'ing must continue to be in winter field construction or other similar activities.

The third dimension along which factories and sidelines vary is in the degree to which they can alternatively absorb and release labor depending on the season. As we saw in the third chapter, most of the labor employed in county plants is fixed. A few places such as the cement plant at Hui County have a large number of temporary quarry workers who still get work points in their home production team and who can be released in the agricultural busy season. Most, such as the nitrogenous fertilizer plants with expensive, continuous flow equipment, must keep a constant work force the year round. Commune industries have somewhat greater flexibility. Much is made of the principle that commune workers should be both peasants and

5. Based on a reading of travel notes, accountant's manuals, and the studies of village affairs referenced in Table IX-1.

workers at the same time (*yi kung yi nung*). Most still live at home and still get work points in their home production teams. Many stay at home to help with the planting and harvest during the busiest seasons of the year. Nevertheless, the total amount of labor in the fields by commune factory workers is not great. Not all workers go to the fields. Those who do go spend 10–30 days, or just long enough to help the production team through its most labor intensive periods. Most long lasting transfers, it would appear, are those transfers between grain growing and other agricultural sidelines. Grain mills, cotton gins, oil presses, and other food processing shops are perforce more systematically synchronized with the agricultural seasons, requiring their major labor inputs after the harvest. Other activities such as collective orchards, collective forests, collective repair teams, and the like also may be more flexibly scheduled to fit the annual cycle of employment at two places. At Liu-chuang Brigade in Ch'i-li-ying Commune, while 150 people (or 26% of the labor force) engaged in factories and sidelines during the slack season, only some 70 people (or 12% of the labor force) is engaged in these activities during the busy season for wheat and cotton, the two main crops in the area. Similarly at Hsin-liang Commune in Hui County, while 800 workers (or 6% of the labor force) is engaged in factories during the slack season, only 400 workers or 3% of the labor force is so engaged during the busy season. It would appear, then, that at the commune level and below, about half the labor force in non-grain growing functions can be shifted back and forth as the season demands, thereby fulfilling the specifications of some models of the proper function of rural industry. The numbers involved in most places, however, are small. As specified in the Tachai model for development, other peasants spend their winters in improving the fields for next year's planting. And contrary to the Tachai model, some other peasants spend their winters outside the village in private sideline activities such as working as transport workers in town or as private carpenters and other artisans who pocket much of their earnings.[6]

DECENTRALIZATION

An argument for small-scale industry, which is often paired with the employment argument, is that small industries avoid the problems of large cities. Without small industry, industry becomes concentrated in large cities, which are congested, filled with slums, and costly to run. If people could be

6. Discussions of slack season work outside the village, some of it more individualistically oriented, may be found in Jack Chen, *A Year in Upper Felicity*, New York: Macmillan, 1973, pp. 270–272, and Kwangtung Province, Agriculture Bureau, *Yi-nien san shou ta you ke wei* (To Have Three Harvests per Year is Eminently Possible), union serial number 16111.197, Canton: Kwangtung People's Press, 1973, pp. 3, 51.

kept in the villages and smaller towns, there would be less need for new housing and other social construction, and the people would enjoy a better life. People can be kept in their villages only if attractions in the form of industry are established there. Small industries can be more easily decentralized than large industries.

The critics of this position, while accepting the argument about the evils of overly large cities, suggest that small industry alone will not do the trick. Small industries cannot exist in isolation in the countryside. Many of the modern industries cannot be broken into such small pieces and shipped into the countryside. It would be better off if the decentralization began not with an immediate decentralization of small plants, but first with the dispersion of larger plants to intermediate-size cities. These cities in turn would help provide a suitable environment in which other small industries could survive.[7]

Again, though the Chinese accept much of the first argument, their practice is much closer to the second position—at least, if we can judge from the places we visited. In Chapter II, we have already dealt with the general problem of externalities and how this shapes the distribution of different types of industry. From that discussion, it should already be apparent that the Chinese have not suddenly decentralized all industry down to the level of the village. Many of those industries termed small in China are actually relatively large, sophisticated plants sited in county seats or intermediate regional centers. In this section, then, let us simply add a few observations on the growth of intermediate cities and then note the potential social consequences of this growth.

As early as the mid-1950s and most definitively in the 1958 Law on Migration, the Chinese made it clear that they did not want the largest cities such as Canton, Shanghai, and the like to grow. In the arguments for these restrictions on city bound migration, they made it quite clear that the reason they did not want large cities to grow is that urban growth created great costs for new schools, housing, and parks, which drained off funds that could better be used for new investment in industry.[8] Through tight controls over grain coupons, work permits, and the expansion of factories, the Chinese have drastically slowed the growth of the major cities, even reversing it in recent years with the sending down of many urban youth to the countryside.

Despite these restrictions on the very largest cities, however, it was our impression on the trip that many intermediate cities were being allowed to grow. For example, in Hsinhsiang City in north Honan Province where we

7. See Dhar and Lydall, *op. cit.*, pp. 20–24.
8. References to articles in the Chinese press can be found in William L. Parish, "Socialism and the Chinese Peasant Family," *Journal of Asian Studies* 34 (May 1975), pp. 625–26.

spent several days, there had been a tremendous growth in new factories in the last twenty years and a correspondingly great growth in population. One of our hosts gave the following figures:

	1949	1965	1974
Factories	5	130	180 +
Workers	300	70,000	100,000
Total population	57,000	320,000	420,000

The city still showed the signs of its recent growth. With cramped housing, dirt alleyways, and some mud brick houses, it looked much like an overgrown country town. The factories, which had responsibility for housing, had been so busy with building their plants that they appear to have gotten behind in the housing. The main strets were torn up as a new storm sewer system was being installed. And, in contrast to the beautiful tree-lined boulevards at the provincial seat of Cheng-chou just a few tens of kilometers to the south, the trees in Hsin-hsiang were just beginning to grow. Nevertheless, the spread of factories through fields, which were still farmed, already gave one a hint of the strong, well-laid-out industrial center that will eventually take shape there. Though our information on other cities is less precise, one of our guides in the province suggested that there were six or seven other middle size cities in Honan Province which were growing just as fast as Hsin-hsiang. Like Hsin-hsiang, each is the government headquarters for an administrative region which it serves.

While these intermediate cities were expanding rapidly, the provincial capital Cheng-chou maintained a constant 700,000–900,000 population since 1958. In the few parts of town that we saw, this constancy in population was apparent. The tree-lined streets and the well-developed housing blocks, many dating from the early 1950s, suggest a much more slowly growing and mature city. The pattern in Honan Province, then, is one of holding the largest cities constant in size, while expanding the size and functions of the intermediate regional centers.

Honan Province may be somewhat special; it is crossed by more rail lines than the average province. Movement of goods into and out of factories in regional centers may be easier here than elsewhere. Yet we did see enough other growing centers, and there are enough reports of new booming cities in the press, to suggest that the Honan pattern is a fairly general one.[9] In Hopei Province, the new provincial seat of Shih-chia-chuang where we stopped briefly, there are all the appearances of a boom town much like Hsin-hsiang. Also along the rail line in Hopei one passes through many medium-size cities, which are building new factories. Other travelers have

9. A collection of articles on new cities taken from the press appear in *Tsu-kuo hsin-hsing ch'eng-shih* (New Style Cities in Our Motherland), Shanghai: Shanghai People's Press, 1974.

remarked on the fast rate of factory construction along the railroad in other parts of the nation. In Kiangsu Province, the regional city of Ch'ang-chou was frequently mentioned to us, and in May and June, 1975, it was featured in *Peking Review* as a model of regional industrial development. From the train, it was obvious that this center was indeed growing rapidly. At least along the rail lines, then, there are many new regional cities which are building many new large factories and growing correspondingly in population.

There are two observations which should be made about this apparent pattern. First, the kinds of redistribution of industry that many western analysts have been looking for in China may have been the wrong one. Early in the 1950s, the Chinese talked about redistributing away from the coastal cities, such as Shanghai, where industry was located as a result of the intimate relationship between foreign contact and industrialization prior to 1949, to places further inland. Using provinces as the unit of analysis, western analysts have concluded that there has been very little coast to inland redistribution of industry. For example, industrial output in Honan Province has increased they conclude, but at no faster a rate than industrial output in Shanghai.[10] By looking only for the redistribution of industry among provinces, however, westerners may have missed a very important redistribution of industry within each province. If our observations are correct, industry has been moved from the largest cities in each province to the intermediate cities in that province, leading to a rather different pattern of economic activity within each region.

The second observation to be made is that the shifting of industry to intermediate cities, if this is a true pattern, may help promote economic development in China. Many developing societies as a result of their colonial past have only one or two large primate cities and then no intermediate cities in between the largest city and the smallest towns and villages in the countryside. Observations on Western cities suggest that this gap between types of cities may have very negative consequences on the spread on new innovations throughout a society. To take one example, in the United States, the street railway was first introduced in New York in 1851 and continued to be adopted in smaller cities in the U.S. through the 1880s.[11] The street rail did not spread throughout the country in a random pattern, but in a very orderly pattern which went down step-fashion through the cities by rank size. After the largest cities had adopted the street car, then the second

---

10. Charles Robert Roll, Jr., and Kung-chia Yeh, "Balance in Coastal and Inland Industrial Development," in U.S. Congress, Joint Economic Committee, *op. cit.*

11. Brian J. L. Berry and Frank E. Horton, *Geographic Perspectives on Urban Systems,* Englewood Cliffs, N.J.: Prentice Hall, 1972, pp. 87–92. For similar arguments in economic literature, see the books reviewed in Michael J. Rodell, "Growth Centers," *Economic Development and Cultural Change* 23 (1975): 525–31.

largest cities throughout the country adopted it, then the third largest, and so on. It was as though a city had to have a nearby big brother city adopt the new means of transport before it would try it. In the United States during these years, the distribution of cities by size was fairly regular or, more properly, it was lognormal such that when graphed on the proper paper, the cities were distributed in a straight line by size. In countries where such a lognormal distribution of cities does not obtain, it is sometimes suggested, the diffusion of innovations throughout the country will be inhibited. There will not be enough nodes of contact throughout the country for remote places to learn rapidly about new ideas and new ways of doing things.

In China, before 1949, the coastal cities such as Shanghai, Tientsin, and Canton, had grown much more rapidly than other cities. The biggest cities were all along the coast. Nevertheless, in the 1953 census, China still had a relatively regular (lognormal) distribution of cities.[12] The newest innovations were most likely to begin in the coastal cities, but there were still ample nodes spread throughout the country through which innovations might diffuse. The attempt to strengthen these intermediate cities with a new infusion of intermediate-size industries—such as the water pump plant, chemical fertilizer parts plant, and the like, which we saw at Hsin-hsiang City—indicates that the Chinese are working to keep these nodes of contact alive and to strengthen them even further. Their discussions about how these regional cities—often the centers of administrative districts—serve the surrounding county industries suggests that they are not too far away from the idea of a network of cities linked in a hierarchy for diffusing technology and new equipment.

RURAL ADMINISTRATION

We have noted that in rural small-scale industry at the commune and brigade level, the effects on employment are relatively modest. It needs to be separately noted, however, that the effects on rural finance can be considerably greater, and that this in turn may reshape the power of the different administrative units in the countryside. Since 1961, after the retrenchment from the Great Leap, the commune level of administration has had very few funds of its own. Except for salaries for clerks and officials and payments for other fixed expenses, which it gets from the county, the commune has had little in the way of funds which it could use as it saw fit. The brigade level of administration has had slightly more funds which it could get from the teams which constituted it—but still only slightly more. The most significant economic unit for the peasant has remained the production team, which is often a small village or just the neighborhood of a larger village.

12. Berry and Horton, *op. cit.,* p. 68.

There has been a long term ideal that the unit of economic sharing would be enlarged by combining small teams into larger economic units, organized first at the brigade and then later at the commune level. However, since the brigade and commune have had little to offer the peasant that he or she could not obtain at the team level among friends and relatives, there has been little reason to be enthusiastic about any larger cooperative units.[13]

Small industry could potentially change that lack of motivation. As noted in Chapter I, in great contrast to most county industries which are considered to be state owned or owned by all the people, the commune and brigade industries are considered to be owned by local collective units. The commune or brigade can then keep any profits which these industries generate and use them (within limits) in any way they choose. Thus, where small commune industries have flourished, the commune has more leeway for economic action than at any time since the 1958–1959 Great Leap. And this leeway, in turn, helps generate interest in the commune as a significant unit of administration and economic cooperation. In Tachai Commune, for example, where commune enterprises are still only moderately developed, the production of new farm tools and the generation of new income led to the following observation: "In the past some people were of the opinion that the commune was an empty shell—that economically it was flaccid. Today, they see that only by relying on the commune can one get on the road to prosperity."[14]

Columns 4 and 5 of Table IX-1 show the amount of income generated by industry and agricultural sidelines in the places we visited. In the average commune in Hsi-yang County, factories generate 10% of the total output value of the commune, or about 15% of the combined grain and industrial output value. Though 10% is not a great amount, it is generated by only 3% of the total labor force. This pattern appeared in every place we visited. In industry, the labor force generated from two to five times as much output as would a comparable group of laborers in agriculture.

Ten percent is of much greater significance to the commune level of administration than the small figure of 10 implies. The 10% is 10% of all output value, most of which is controlled by the brigades and teams which constitute a commune. For the commune, then, the 10% (or more properly, the profit from it) constitutes almost all of the income which properly belongs to the commune level of administration.

13. Other factors help inhibit the amalgamation of teams. Amalgamation would bring together people from different villages and surnames who are not accustomed to working together. Amalgamation would cause some teams to lose income. Amalgamated units also would be more difficult to manage.

14. *Hsiyang pien k'ai Tachai hua* (Hsiyang[County] Begins all Around Tachai Transformation), union serial number 3088.15, Taiyuan: Shansi People's Press, 1973, p. 151.

As we have noted, there is great variation from place to place in how much income commune and brigade industry generates.[15] Within Hsi-yang County, Tachai Commune has a somewhat longer history of commune-run enterprises. In 1972 its seven enterprises generated about a third of the total grain and industrial output value at both commune and brigade levels. In Lin County as well, commune industry generates about as much income as one-fifth of the total grain and industrial output value at commune, brigade, and team levels. In the richer areas near cities and in the Yangtze delta, commune industry generates an even higher percentage of the total income in a commune. In Wu-hsi County as a whole, the average commune has about 37% of its total income generated by commune- and brigade-run industries. In these places, the commune has already become a highly significant economic unit.

The significance of the commune as an economic unit is heightened by the greater profitability of commune enterprises as compared with brigade enterprises and the generally greater profit in industry as compared to agriculture. One example comes from Hsü-hsing Commune, which is in the suburbs of Shanghai and in the same county as Ma-lu Commune which we visited.[16] From 1965–1973, the twelve enterprises owned by Hsü-hsing Commune produced an annual accumulation or profit for the commune of 800,000 yuan. Together, the several brigades of the commune had no accumulation before 1970. As late as 1973, their combined annual accumulation of 220,000 yuan was still only about one-fourth that of the commune. The teams in the commune, depending mostly on agriculture, had a somewhat larger total annual accumulation of 500,000 yuan, but this sum had to be divided among considerably more units. Though this is an extreme example, a similar picture is repeated in other places. Commune industries are larger than those owned by the brigade. They sell a more sophisticated product to a wider market, including at times urban industries for which they do subcontracting work. These products bring in a reasonable profit.[17]

15. Data on all of Hunan Province, in south-central China, probably gives a fair representation of the average situation in most places. "Over 90 percent of the communes and 80 percent of the brigades in Hunan are now operating their own enterprises. Last year [1973], the total income of these enterprises amounted to 12.2 percent of the total three-level [commune, brigade, and team] income in the communes." (Hunan Radio, in British Broadcasting Corporation, *Summary of World Broadcasts*, FE/W799/A/6, 30 October 1974). The 12.2 figure is considerably below our commune and brigade figures and even below most of our figures for communes alone (Table IX-1). Among the places we visited, only Hsiyang County comes close to the province average.

16. Editing group, *Jen-min kung-she tsai yüeh-chin: Shanghai Shih Chiao-chü jen-min kung-she ta hsin ching-ven* (People's Communes Leaping Forward: New Experiences in Shanghai City Suburban People's Communes), Union serial number 3171.176, Shanghai People's Press, 1974, p. 116.

17. In 1973, the seven enterprises at Tachai Commune had a profit or accumulation rate of 24%. July 1 Commune outside Shanghai had the same rate in 1973. See Shansi Province,

Brigade industries in contrast, typically include only repair shops, grain mills, and brick kilns that sell only to agriculture at minimal to zero profit. Grain prices as well do not allow the profits in agriculture which they typically accrue to industry.

As a result, the income of the commune is steadily growing in many parts of the country. The countryside around Shanghai again presents an extreme example. In communes on the outskirts of Shanghai, the income at the commune level rose in proportion to total income from 28.1% in 1973 to 30.5% in 1974. That of all brigades rose from 15.2 to 17.2%, while that of teams dropped from 56.7% to 52.3%.[18] Though our hosts did not present figures in such detail,, in several of the places we visited it was also reported that commune income was growing faster than team income.

This growth of commune income gives the commune administrators much more influence over the life of the countryside. In the most developed places, they are using their new found income not only to reinvest in more sophisticated industry, but also to stimulate new programs in the units below the commune. This sort of development was particularly stressed in Wu-hsi County. There, Yang-shih Commune reserves 47% of its industrial profits for industrial expansion. Most of the rest is granted to the constituent production teams for their use in water irrigation and drainage projects, field leveling, and soil improvement. A small amount is used for health, education, and other cultural work in the countryside. To the extent that this sort of program of investment in lower level units is followed elsewhere, the lower level units cannot help but begin to pay more attention to the commune.[19]

Chinchung District Revolutionary Committee, Agricultural Mechanization Bureau, *Yung Tachai ching-shen kao nung-yeh chi-hsieh hua* (Use the Tachai Spirit to Carry Out Agricultural Mechanization), union serial number 16088.126, Taiyuan: Shansi People's Press, 1974, p. 11; Editing group, *Shanghai Ch'i-yi jen-min kung-she shih* (History of Shanghai July 1 People's Commune), Union serial number 11171.80, Shanghai People's Press, 1974, p. 181.

18. Chang Ch'un-ch'iao, "On Exercising All-round Dictatorship Over the Bourgeoisie," *Peking Review*, No. 14, 4 April 1975, p. 6. In this article, Chang—a member of the Politburo—elaborates on the theme of how communes will become accounting units. The book on July 1 Commune has a similar set of statistics on increasing commune level production over a longer period of time—pp. 174, 181.

19. Following the work of G. William Skinner, some western analysts have been struck with the idea of how communes frequently correspond to traditional market communities and with how this might facilitate the social and administrative role of the commune. We gathered explicit data on this question only at Wu-hsi where we were told that communes were bigger than the traditional market areas. In north China, the correspondence also seems rather imperfect, and more important markets have a greatly diminished economic role where we visited. In Hsi-yang County the private plots, which supply the rural free market, have been abolished, and as far as we could tell, all free markets have disappeared as well. Similarly throughout northern Honan, though private plots exist in name, they are all farmed collectively. There is then little basis for vigorous private marketing activities in these areas, even though the old temple fairs, which open only once or twice a year, continue to be active.

THE FAMILY AND WOMEN

Local industry also can weaken loyalty to the family and strengthen the position of women. There are both direct effects on the small number of workers in local industry and indirect effects on the much larger population which consumes the products of local industry. The direct effects include both the superior welfare benefits of industry and the superior technical knowledge and skills imparted by industrial work.

Welfare Effects

As indicated in Chapter III, there is great variation in welfare benefits according to the administrative level of industry. It is only in state-owned industry at the county level and above that welfare is likely to have any great influence on the family. Provincial and metropolitan industry located in the largest cities tends to provide medical care, generous retirement benefits, accident insurance, nurseries and kindergartens, and often housing as well. County-level industries tend to have minimal housing and few nurseries although they do have the standard health, accident, and retirement benefits—at least for the great majority of their workers who are regular, fixed workers. The families of workers remain in the countryside and the worker returns home weekly or even nightly.

In the county industries, then, there is closer contact with and somewhat greater dependence on the family for housing and child-care than in the largest urban factories. In the county factory, the male worker leaves his wife and children in his parents' home. Similarly, the female worker depends on her parents-in-law or other of her husband's kinsmen for child care while she is at work. Nevertheless, because of retirement benefits, health, and accident insurance, dependence on the larger family is still not so great as in commune and brigade factories and workshops.

With only one and one-half exceptions, the workers in commune factories visited were paid in work points through their home production team. In Peking's Red Star Commune, workers were paid fixed wages, and in Yao-ts'un Commune in Lin County, Honan Province, one-third of the workers got fixed wages. Elsewhere they got workpoints. Where we visited, commune industries only rarely had dorms for workers, and where they existed, dorms were only for overnight use by workers who lived too far away to commute daily. By design, then, the average commune and brigade industrial worker receives no more amenities than the average peasant. The amenities they receive through their home production team are sufficiently sparse to still make them rely heavily on parents, children, and other kin in the larger rural family.

In agriculture, the work point system, the welfare system, and restrictions on migration promote an emphasis on male children, early marriage, and large families. Because work points are based heavily on physical strength in field labor, able-bodied males tend to get ten points a day, while females get only seven points a day. Besides bringing more points into the family, the male will also remain permanently with the family—or at least in the same village—while most females will move out of the village at marriage. It is male children, then, who bring permanent laborers into the family. The private house, which requires many years of saving to build, keeps sons close to their parents. Since child care is frequently absent or is charged for in the village, the son depends on his parents for child care while he and his wife are at work during the day. The state rules on old-age support are quite explicit; it is the son who is responsible for the financial support of his parents in old age. It is only the aged without sons who are eligible for collective support. In addition, restrictive migration laws keep sons in the same village with their parents. Private plots and pigs allow the family to be a significant source of food and income. Together, these structural conditions maintain the rural family and the male line as an important focus of economic cooperation and loyalty.[20]

In brigade, commune, and some county industries which employ work-point workers, many of the same consequences can be expected to result. Young men and women in the factory continue to depend on their parents and parents-in-law for housing and child care. They not only support the husband's aged parents, but also look forward to support by sons in their own old age—an incentive to have one or two sons as soon as possible.

Technical skills.

Though the welfare effects of the smallest rural industries are likely to be limited, the lives of workers are likely to be affected by the extra knowledge and skills they acquire in the factory or workshop. There are three important differences between industrial and agricultural work. First, since in the factory skill is just as important as physical strength, females should get the same work points as men. Indeed it is often women who get the most skilled jobs, such as lathe operator, while men often predominate in the heavier, dirtier, and less skilled jobs in the factory. Second, the factory provides an opportunity for unmarried men and women to make acquaintance with potential mates. This is in contrast to agricultural laborers who have little chance to meet potential mates outside the village except through parental introductions. Finally, though we can only speculate about this, it seems likely that the learning of factory skills must give sons and daughters a sense of independence from their parents which could never be achieved otherwise. In agriculture one's skills are acquired only gradually under the

20. Parish, "Socialism and the Chinese Peasant Family," *Journal of Asian Studies,* May 1975, pp. 613-30.

supervision of parents. Except for tractor drivers, the skills are the same as one's parents and seldom exceed one's parents' skills. Working in a factory gives one a set of skills which are learned completely independent of parents. For women in particular, this must be a great liberating experience. At least, as we watched girls slap a wrench to the chuck on a lathe, we could not help but gain this impression. Even when fringe benefits are absent, work in small rural factories must lead to a number of changes in family loyalty and women's position in the family. In large county factories, which offer fixed wages, retirement benefits, and occasionally even child care and housing, the changes are likely to be even more dramatic.

Regardless of the level of industry, however, the direct effects of welfare and new skills can only be limited to a small percentage of the population. For, away from the cities and rich delta regions, industrial employment is no more than 5% of the rural labor force and often less. The limited scope of industrial employment holds particularly true for women in the countryside.

Women Workers.

The percentage of women employed varies drastically between light and heavy industry and slightly between large urban industry and smaller county industry—see Table III-2 in Chapter III. We visited six light industries making textiles, figurines, and optical equipment. In these six plants controlled by provinces and municipalities, women on the average constituted two-thirds (68%) of the work force. Percentages in each plant ranged from a low of 58% to a high of 85%.

As is true around the world and as was true in China before 1949, the percentage of women in heavy industry is much less. The heavy industries we visited made steel, tractors, engines, pipes, cement, chemicals, and fertilizer. Eight of these, located in cities and controlled by provinces or municipalities, employed on the average one-fourth (26%) females. The range was from 16–35%. We got statistics on female employment in thirteen heavy industries run by the county. In these thirteen, female employment averaged 18%. The range was from 5% to 31%. The one county-run light industry that we visited—a spinning and weaving mill—had a work force that was 70% female.

Though the difference between 26% female in higher administrative heavy industry and 18% female in county heavy industry is small, the difference runs contrary to our initial impression, which was that large, provincial, and municipal factories would have fewer females. Most of the higher administrative, urban plants were started and had acquired much of their work force in the early years of Communist rule in the 1950s. Most of the county industries were started since 1968 when, judging from the press, the emphasis on female employment and equal rights for women was stronger than before, and when these values were likely to be more widely accepted. It is with some surprise that we find female employment in county factories less than in big city factories. This situation may have come about because, contrary to our initial impressions, there has been relatively little infusion of women into industry in recent years. Our 1975 figures for female employment in large industry are not too different from what Barry Richman found in 1965.[21] Also, female employment in the more recently established county industries may be less because the difficulties of housing, commuting, and child care discourage employment there.

We have less data on female employment in commune industries. The few figures we gathered range from 20-37%. In Lin County of Honan Province, one administrator estimated that in the sixty-five enterprises run by both county and commune in the county, female employment averaged 30-40%.

Though we did not gather careful data on the subject, it appeared that females were much more common at the lower worker levels in factories than in higher technical and management levels. Barry Richman reports the same observation from his 1965 study of Chinese factories. At the Peking Internal Combustion Engine Factory, females constituted 34% of the total work force and a somewhat smaller 19% of all engineers. In our tours of factories, we met perhaps half a dozen female technicians—just as frequently in heavy as in light industry. We met senior female administrators, however, only at a small number of light industries in which they have historically constituted the majority of the labor force. Perhaps appropriately for an all male delegation, our principle factory host and briefer was only once—at Wu-hsi Silk Filiature—a female administrator.

Comparison with female employment in other societies provides one means of assessing the extent of female employment in China. We do not have national figures for China. Shanghai, according to one magazine report, has an industrial labor force which is 35% female.[22] The national average, which would include more county industries with fewer females and fewer of the housewife dominated street industries in which Shanghai seems to specialize, would be somewhat lower. Whatever the exact proportion, female employment in China is clearly much, much greater than that

21. Despite the overall constancy in female employment, a few places may have increased their female employment. Comparisons are clouded by the possibility that the 1965 data is for the total work force while later data is just for workers—there would be fewer women in the total work force. Nevertheless, it appears that at Shanghai Heavy Machine Tool female workers increased from 15-20% abetween 1965 and 1975. From another visitor's report, it appears that female employment at Wuhan Iron and Steel Corporation increased from 10-18% between 1965 and 1974. See Barry M. Richmann, *Industrial Society in Communist China,* New York: Random House, 1969, pp. 305, 754. Richard Lockwood, *Report on a Tour of Mainland China,* U.S.-China Friendship Association, December 1974, mimeo., p. 21.

22. Nadia Haggag Youssef, *Women and Work in Developing Societies,* Population Monograph Series No. 15, Berkeley: University of California, 1974, pp. 32, 64, 67.

in a few developing countries such as those of the Middle East, North Africa, India, and Pakistan where female employment never exceeds 10% of the non-agricultural labor force.[23] Chinese female employment is probably higher than in most other developing societies where females generally constitute 20–30% of those in manufacturing. One comparative example is Chile where in 1964 24% of those in manufacturing were female. The Chilean pattern of female employment by industry is similar to that in China but at a slightly lower level. The proportion of females in wearing apparel manufacture was 61%, in chemical products 22%, and in machinery manufacture only 4%. For its level of development, the proportion of women employed in Chinese industry is rather high.

In comparison to countries which are already industrially developed, Chinese female employment is not quite so high. In Japan in 1971, for example, women constituted 32% of the labor force in manufacturing.[24] By industry, the proportion of women in textiles was 64%, in chemical products 26%, and in machine building 16%. These percentages are similar to what one observes in China.

Chinese female employment is, thus, ahead of that in most developing countries. There is also some potential for Chinese female employment to eventually exceed that in industrially developed societies. Chinese female employment in industry is much greater than female employment in present industrially developed countries when they were at earlier stages in the process of economic development. With nurseries provided by many factories in the city and by grandmothers in the countryside, it appears that Chinese women are already less likely than those in industrially developed societies to drop out of the labor force once they have children. This apparently lower rate of turnover should in turn have a number of positive consequences for female seniority and income in the future. Already, Chinese women seem to get a very large proportion of skilled jobs, such as lathe operators, overhead crane operators, and the like. With uninterrupted work careers, they should be able to hold onto these jobs and parley them into prestige and income, which is every bit the equal of those earned by men.

Indirect Effects.

For women in the countryside, the direct effects of industrial employment are still muted by the small proportions of both men and women so employed. For the average rural woman, the indirect effects of industry—of which there are two—are far more important. The first indirect effect is a result of local industry supplying most of the machinery to agriculture, such

23. See *Peking Review,* No. 27 (1975), p. 17.
24. Rodosho Fujin Shonen Kyoku, ed., *Fujin Rōdō no Jijō* (Female Labor Force Situation), Tokyo: Okurashō Insatsu Kyokyu, 1973, p. 13.

as threshers, electric motors, milling machines, transplanters, and, increasingly, hand tractors. Local industry and mechanization go together. We saw a large number of women driving hand tractors in only one brigade, but women can and do operate other machinery in the village. As this machinery reduces the physical strenuousness of farm labor, some of the old differences between male and female farm labor should begin to disappear. Though the male dominance on tractors will continue to interfere, it should become more and more possible to grant the same daily workpoints to women as to men. Yang-tui Brigade outside Shanghai reports that in recent years because of mechanization and the greater equalization of male and female exertion in the field, the average differential in male and female work points has been reduced. In 1965 females received on average one-third fewer work points per day, but by 1973 received only about one-tenth fewer work points than men. It was reported, as a result, that more women joined work in the fields and that they worked more vigorously.[25]

More women are spending more time in collective field labor throughout China because local industry is freeing them from some of their most burdensome household tasks. This is especially true in north China where women have traditionally done less field work than in south China. In north China, spinning mills run by the commune and county are relieving women of the onerous task of spinning cotton into thread. One has only to read Jack Chen's diary of life in a village in northern Honan Province in 1969–1970 to realize what a saving mechanical spinning would be. In Jack Chen's story of life in one family, the whir of the wife at her spinning wheel is continually heard in the background. With her duties of making clothes, sewing shoes, feeding the pig, cooking, and tending children, there is little time for the wife to join labor in the fields.[26] Now in some places the women can take their raw cotton to a nearby spinning mill for processing. In Lin County at the county spinning and weaving mill, there is a fee of one yuan per catty for turning raw cotton into thread. Some communes had their own mills. Throughout this county of some 700,000 population, we were told, mechanized spinning was saving 800,000 work days per year. The women still weave at home, but the time-consuming task of spinning for four or five days to supply one day's weaving is avoided.[27]

Also, the mechanization of rice husking and flour grinding saves women much time. A county official in Kiangsu Province described the husking of rice in the days before mechanized milling. According to the official, in the old days, there were two methods of processing rice by hand. One was by

25. Editing Group, *Jen-min kung-she tsai yüeh-chin,* pp. 143–48.

26. Jack Chen, *A Year in Upper Felicity,* New York: Macmillan, 1973.

27. Chu Li and Tien Chieh-yun, *Inside a People's Commune: Report from Ch'i-li-ying,* Peking: Foreign Languages Press, 1974, p. 87.

hand operated and the other by pedal operated mortar and pestle.[28] The hand operated version, he said, would process only about 5 kilograms of grain in two hours, and the pedal operated version was only slightly better, processing 25 kilograms in three hours. Assuming that these figures refer just to the unhusked weight of the rice, feeding a family of five on a diet of 1200 kilograms of rice annually would require processing of about 1800 kilograms of unhusked rice, involving 720 or 216 hours, depending on which of the above methods was used to prepare the grain for cooking. Even though these rough figures refer only to rice processing, the magnitude of female labor released by the transition to mechanized grain processing is clearly substantial. With possibly one exception, we saw no hand- or pedal-operated grain processing devices on our trip. At the places we visited, women were taking their grain to a brigade or commune mill where for a fee of .005 yuan per catty, they were given back an equal weight of flour and bran or polished rice and husks.[29] When officials report that women are working outside the home much more than ever before, there is ample reason to believe them.

Similarly, in some places women are saved the task of chopping grass and vegetables into fodder for the family pig. Electric choppers supplied by the local machinery plant have begun to take over their job.[30] This leads to a cycle in which agricultural production increases in all spheres. In Lin County, we were told, the ability to chop more fodder faster means that more pigs can be raised. More pigs means more manure to be used in compost for the fields. More compost means more grain and more fodder. Small industry and greater mechanization, then, are part of a larger complex of events that leads not only to more output and a greater demand for labor, but also to more involvement by women in directly productive tasks outside the home and potentially to their own liberation.

Our conclusion about the effects of small industry on Chinese society are, thus, very similar for both its labor absorption effects and for its effect on women. There is a direct effect on both. Small industry absorbs a certain small percentage of the labor force from the countryside, and in commune and lower industries some of this labor force is alternatively absorbed and released according to the seasons. Also a small percentage of women are drawn into these industries, giving them new economic power and authority *vis-à-vis* their family of birth as well as family of marriage. Nevertheless, for both the effect on employment and on women, the strongest effects of small industry are indirect. Indirectly, small industry helps supply the goods which make it profitable for more labor to be absorbed in winter field capital

28. For illustrations of devices of this sort, see Rudolf P. Hommel, *China at Work*, New York: John Day, 1937, p. 100.

29. This is the fee at the head brigade in Ch'i-li-ying Commune, Honan Province.

30. In Tachai Brigade, for example—Wen Chin, *et. al., Tachai Hung Ch'i* (Red Banner Tachai), Peking: People's Publishing House, 1974, p. 214.

construction. Likewise, small industry supplies the new machinery, which relieves women of the tasks which have formerly kept them within the home, and thereby indirectly helps them to change to tasks with greater outside economic reward and prestige. The direct effects may eventually become quite important, but for the time being it is the more subtle indirect effects which have the greatest influence on rural society.

APPENDIX TO CHAPTER IX

In constructing Table IX-1, a number of details had to be left out and a number of compromises had to be made in classifying enterprises as between factories and sidelines, between commune and collective, and the like. The material below lists some of the details which help in interpreting Table IX-1.

Hsi-yang County:

Of the 24 factories managed by the county level of administration, 13 were owned solely by the state and 11 were collectively owned. Though the distinction was never satisfactorily explained to us, the 11 collectively owned—including agricultural implement repair, weaving, hemp and tile making—appear to be light industries staffed almost solely by commune members who continue to be paid only in work points through their home production teams. In the county, 50 + non-agricultural enterprises were both owned and managed at the commune level of administration. In 1973, most communes had commune level collective farms, forests, and animal husbandry fields, which were counted among the sidelines. Of the 20 communes in the county, 17 had implement repair stations in 1973. Some had aluminite plants, small coal pits, and refractory plants. Li-chia-chuang Commune and Tachai Commune were among the most industrially developed in the county. In 1973, Li-chia-chuang had a coal mine, refractories pit, implement repair and construction station, tractor station, and water control construction team. Within this commune, Shih-p'ing Brigade had no enterprises of its own in 1975, but simply delegated 10% of its labor force to work in commune enterprises. The seven Tachai enterprises were an agricultural implement repair and construction shop, refractory plant, aluminite plant, small coal pit, animal breeding grounds, commune farm, and a motorized transport team. They had been developed serially, one helping the other get started. In 1975, An-p'ing Commune had no factories of its own, but only brigade brick factories, brigade coal pits, and collective agricultural sidelines.

Sources: Travel notes; Shansi Province, Chinchung District Revolutionary Committee, Agricultural Mechanization Management Bureau, *Yung Tachai ching-shen kao nung-yeh chi-hsieh hua* (use the Tachai Spirit to Carry Out Agricultural Mechanization), union serial number 16088.126, Taiyuan: Shansi People's Press, 1974, pp. 2, 11-12. *Hsiyang pien k'ai Tachai hua* (Hsi-yang County Begins all around Tachai Transformation), union serial number 3088.15, Taiyuan: Shansi People's Press, 1973, pp. 141, 145. Shansi, Hsi-yang County Revolutionary Committee, "Experiences in constructing the Hsiyang County seat," *Architecture Journal* (Chien-chu hsüeh-pao), No. 3 (1975), p. 6.

Lin County:

As in Hsi-yang County, industry is divided among state, collective, and commune industries. Following the emphasis of Lin County officials, Table IX-1 groups collective with commune enterprises. A more precise delineation is as follows: There are 19 collective enterprises employing 1.1% of the labor force and generating 20% of the combined value of grain and industrial output at the three levels of commune, brigade, and team. There are 26 commune enterprises employing 0.7% of the labor force and generating 9% of the combined grain and industrial output. There are 15 communes in the county.

Wu-hsi County:

The 1520 enterprises run by communes and brigades are divided among 30 communes for an average of 42 per commune. The 7 industries at Yang-shih Commune include powdered metallurgy (mostly bushings), farm machinery (including large electric transformers), cement products (telephone poles, etc.), electro-plating, plastic products, and a brick kiln. Meitsun Commune has 8 commune enterprises, including a musical instrument plant, brick kiln, grain mill, and farm implement repair and construction, employing 8% of the labor force. It also has 53 brigade enterprises in 21 brigades employing 18% of the work force in the slack season.

Wu-hsi City:

Ho-lieh Commune industries include a workshop making shoe uppers as well as a farm implement shop making not only parts for rice transplanters and pond aerators, but also parts for a sophisticated table plane, which must be subcontracted with a city factory.

Hui County:

The gross value of output from industry in this model county doubled between 1972 when 48 plants produced 28,120,000 yuan worth of output and 1973 when county industry produced 56,000,000 yuan or 47% of the combined value of industry and grain output in the county (see *People's Daily,* 4 April 1973, and Rewi Alley, "In an ancient kingdom . . . ," *Eastern Horizon,* Vol. 13, no. 6 [1974], p. 43). Hsin-liang Liang-ts'un Commune has a cement plant (100 tons per day), phosphate fertilizer plant, brick kiln, and farm implements shop.

Hsin-hsiang County:

Chiliying Commune has a farm machinery plant, phosphate fertilizer factory, spinning mill, tractor station with repair shops, and transport team with four trucks. In 1973, there were 38 small factories in the brigades or one per brigade. These included farm tool shops, flour mills, and other farm processing shops. In 1975, some 70 collective enterprises, including sidelines, were reported for an average of almost two per brigade. At Liu-chuang Brigade, collective enterprises include a tractor repair station, farm tool shop, flour mill, cotton gin, popsicle factory, electricity repair team, animal husbandry stalls (for milk cows and draught animals), pig stalls, vegetable garden, and orchards. In the busy planting and harvesting season only some 70 people (12% of labor force of 574) are engaged in these enterprises. In the agricultural slack season, 150 people (26%) are so engaged. Since only about a dozen men were in the farm tool shop when we visited, and no one was at the tractor repair station, it would appear that the great majority of workers are in non-industrial sidelines. Sources: Travel notes; Chu Li and Tien Chieh-yun, *Inside People's Commune: Report from Chiliying,* Peking: Foreign Languages Press, 1974, pp. 50, 80.

Peking:

Red Star Commune industries include a powdered milk plant, farm implement repair and construction, paper mill, grain mill and oil press, and screw factory. The number of workers grew from some 2000 in about 1973 to 3000 in 1975. Source: Science for the People, *China: Science Walks on Two Legs,* New York: Avon Books, 1974, p. 33.

Shanghai Suburbs:

At Ma-lu Commune, the commune exhibition room reports 10 workshops at the commune level and 53 workshops in brigades. A book on the commune reports 16 enterprises at the commune level. The reported output figure includes not only implement construction, carpentry, the making of soy bean sauce, Chinese medicine, and fodder, but also collective pig farms, milk cows, and the like. Source: Editing Group, *Shanghai chiao-ch'ü nung-ye hsüeh Tachai* (Shanghai Suburban Agriculture Studies Tachai), Union serial number 3144.96, Shanghai: Agricultural Press, 1974, p. 57.

July 1 Commune "industries" include a spray paint factory and an electric storage battery factory, which subcontract with urban factories, a farm implement factory, a general factory, a repair team and a rural bridge team. Source: Editing group, *Shanghai Chi-yi jen-min kung-she shih* (History of Shanghai July 1 People's Commune), union serial number 11171.80, Shanghai People's Press, 1974, p. 179.

Chapter X

EXPANDING KNOWLEDGE AND TRANSFORMING ATTITUDES

ATTITUDES TOWARD TECHNOLOGY

It is a truism that economic development requires many and varied technological skills, but it may not be so obvious that the diffusion of these skills involves much more than simply learning how to do some specific task. Technological diffusion also involves certain attitudes, the recognition of logical-mechanical systems as wholes, and the ability to deduce inter-relationships among the various elements of the system.[1] Although China's historical record of technological innovation is rich and diverse, this outlook was traditionally less emphasized than the holistic and analogical patterns of thought which dominated Chinese culture until quite recent times. It was only in the latter part of the nineteenth and the twentieth centuries that the technological outlook began, piecemeal at first, to gain currency in China. Last to be reached were the rural areas, where poor communications and low levels of literacy reinforced the inertia of customary ways and attitudes.

We were frequently told of two kinds of attitudes, which must be transformed in order to promote rural development. The first was an attitude of fatalism, of the impossibility of change. The way things always have been is the way things always will be. Moreover, to tamper with nature or the

---

1. This ability is movingly described in Richard McKenna's novel, *The Sand Pebbles* (New York: Harper and Row, 1962). See pp. 146-148, 190, and especially 252-256 (page references are to the Fawcett/Crest paperback edition.

236

traditional ways is to risk dire consequences. References to change in this attitude were often expressed to us as follows: "Formerly we were the subjects of nature (of landlords, of machines, etc.), but now we are the masters of nature."

The second attitude was a kind of superstitious awe of advanced technology, and of those with knowledge of it. Many peasants felt that machines were simply beyond their comprehension or control. To be able to cite a book in which it was written that something must be done in such-and-such a way often conferred a nearly unchallengeable authority on both the process and on the expert who was capable of reading about it.

Much effort has been expended to eliminate or change these attitudes, and it seemed to us that small scale rural industry has an important role in this process, partly as cause and partly as effect. The existence of local industry is one indication of the changes that have already taken place, while at the same time, it provides a mechanism for further change.

During our visit to China, we heard on several occasions a series of parallel phrases which express at least part of the Chinese attitude toward small-scale industry. The phrases are (1) *"ts'ung hsiao tao ta* (from small to large),"* (2) *"ts'ung tien tao mien* (from key points to general application),"* and (3) *"ts'ung t'u tao yang* (from indigenous to modern)."* The first two phrases are fairly straightforward: small-scale industry is intended to grow in size and scope. The third phrase is both more complex and more revealing.

The term *yang* has a checkered history in China. Literally, it means "ocean, sea." Hence by connotation it has come to mean "coming from overseas: foreign, as opposed to native." That it was used during the nineteenth and early twentieth centuries in the names of modern products, which China was at that time unable to produce herself (e.g., *"yang-huo*—foreign fire—matches,"* *"yang-yu*—foreign oil—kerosene")* seemed to many Chinese a humiliating reproach to Chinese backwardness. In this way, there has taken place a partial merging of the ideas of "modern" and "foreign, alien," a conceptual and psychological conjunction that is reflected in a certain ambivalence toward modernization. To the extent that *t'u* means "native, indigenous," it is identified with the Chinese people and is at least potentially good; to the extent that it also suggests backwardness and primitiveness, it is to be eliminated or transcended. On the other hand, where *yang* means "modern, developed, strong," it is a goal to be achieved; but when it suggests "foreign, alien, westernized," it risks revisionism, the restoration of capitalism, and a continued implication of inferiority by comparison with technologically more developed societies.

To some extent, the "red and expert" issue shares a similar polarity and a similar ambivalence. Expertise is prized, but there is a lingering suspicion, at least, that experts tend to be expert in foreign technology: they think the only way something can be done is the way it is done in foreign countries and described in foreign books, which they accept as authoritative. Consequently, they are divorced from the masses, whose ruder methods they look down upon as unsuitable. In this stereotype, the experts want large-scale, urban enterprises, full of the most advanced technology and imported machinery. The perfect "red" is, of course, the antithesis of all this: one with the masses, confident in their ability and their methods, unintimidated by the presumed superiority of the technological mandarins and their foreign mentors. There is thus some degree of consonance between "red" and "native" on the one hand, and "expert" and "foreign" on the other.

Central to the resolution of this contradiction is technological assimilation and accessibility: technologies which are felt to belong naturally in one's immediate environment, not as wonderful and exotic phenomena; and technologies which are capable of being thoroughly understood and mastered by those at all levels who work with them. "Most of the machinery in this plant was made and installed by ourselves." "Our own staff, in teams made up of old workers, cadres, and technicians, have produced 104 innovations in the past six months." Such phrases, which we heard over and over again, bespeak an important role in assimilation and accessibility for local small-scale industry.

The products of such industry have immediate and obvious utility. The production process, from beginning to end, is short enough and straightforward enough to be understood by most workers willing to make the effort. Yet these industries employ machines, machine tools, and processes of substantial complexity. Innovations, even minor improvements, show that the technology and the production process is well understood, and they evince the satisfactions that come with understanding and mastery.

When a young worker has spent several years in a commune or county industry which makes, say, tractor parts, has helped to make the machine tools which make the parts, has been part of a mobile team that goes to the fields during the busy season to make repairs on the spot—when all this has been done, he or she is both competent and confident. If we now imagine that this worker now goes on to a large modern factory, to a university, or to a technical training institute, he or she may well be able to approach a combination of the best features of "red" and "expert," of *t'u* and *yang*.

TRAINING AND THE DIFFUSION OF SKILLS

When one turns from these rather general attitudes toward technology to rural industry itself, one is immediately aware of its importance as a technological training ground. At commune and brigade levels, workers are drawn directly from the peasant population—indeed, they are *both* peasants *and* workers in that they continue with few exceptions to live in their rural homes, their income is figured in work points rather than in regular wages (as in industry at county and higher levels), and many are dispatched to the fields during periods of peak agricultural activity. This training function is essential, therefore, to the development of a competent labor force.

Although this training function is carried on in all of the "five small industries," it was particularly obvious in the machine shops which existed in every commune and many brigades which we visited. In most cases, some mix of three kinds of work was being done. First, there is the manufacture, usually in batch rather than in continuous flow, of some product or part: water pumps, electric motors, implements, bearings, gears, etc. Second, is the building of machine tools or other capital goods which provide expanded and diversified capacity. We saw lathes, shapers, and pneumatic hammers being built at commune level; in a commune in Hui County (Honan), we saw a ball mill being made for the cement plant the commune was constructing. Third, one sees assembly and repair, with larger jobs being done at commune level and more routine maintenance and repair at brigade level.

All three activities develop or enhance competence in the use of machine tools, semi-precision instruments, and design work. We saw many examples of apprenticeship training being done among younger workers, frequently women, who staff these machine shops. For example, in Liu-chuang Brigade (Ch'li-li-ying Commune, Honan), older workers were obviously instructing young women lathe and shaper operators, who were simply learning how to work the machines and were not making parts. It might be observed in passing that this sort of equipment, and this sort of competence allows considerable flexibility, desirable in the absence of machine standardization, and easily obtained spare parts: to a considerable extent, one can make one's own.

On-the-job training and education is but one aspect of technological diffusion. In writing about the interdependence of enterprises, Jon Sigurdson described a series of linkages which conformed closely to the patterns we observed.[2]

> Links between county-run enterprises within the county: (1) Transfer of skilled manpower; (2) training of manpower; (3) transfer and delivery of equipment; (4) learning the spirit of self-reliance—in order to economize on funds and equipment.
> Links with county-run enterprises outside the county: (1) Learning indigenous production technology; (2) learning how to make indigenous equipment; (3) establishing co-operative relations for the future.

2. "Rural Industry—A Traveler's View," *China Quarterly*, 50 (April–June 1972), 326.

Links with higher level enterprises: (1) Learning modern production technology; (2) obtaining ideas for modifying design; (3) establishing donor-recipient relationship, involving further training, on the spot assistance and delivery of equipment.

So often were these contacts mentioned that we began to refer to them as the practice of "sending out and inviting in." A small-scale plant will frequently send its own technicians to larger and more developed plants or to technical institutes to learn about some process which the smaller plant intends to adopt or to improve. Conversely, larger and more developed plants are often asked to supply technological talent to help a smaller plant with its problems. There is thus both a consumer and a supplier function: an enterprise consumes technology from higher levels and supplies it to lower levels. That this flow is sometimes not without problems was suggested by a responsible person in a county-run plant in Honan who said that other factories were often too busy to provide needed assistance. On the other hand, a technician in a Wu-hsi county enterprise remarked that they often sent personnel to Shanghai, fifty miles away, for technical consultation. When asked how this was arranged, he replied, "We just get on the telephone, and tell them we're coming." These may represent two extremes; perhaps, also, "sending out" is easier than "inviting in."

As Sigurdson indicates, the flow can be lateral as well as vertical, between enterprises on the same, or nearly the same, level. Among the places we visited, the clear champion in this regard was the county-run fertilizer plant in Hui County (Honan).[3] The walls of its conference room were literally covered with banners and mirrors expressing thanks for assistance rendered. We spotted only two from commune-level fertilizer plants (one in Honan, one in Shensi near Yenan), but many from county-run plants in Honan, Shansi (2), Shensi, Shantung (2), Anhwei, Peking municipality, Tientsin municipality, Chekiang, and Yunnan. This last one was particularly impressive since the plant went into production only in 1970.

At the county level, the consumption and supply of technology seem about balanced; lower down there is more consumption than supply, while at higher levels the responsibility for supplying technology is greater. In the large plants we visited, technological training appeared to be quite systematized and regularized. In a Cheng-chou textile mill employing 5600 workers, there were at the time of our visit about 3000 middle school youths in the plant for a three-to-four week period of labor.

3. This plant was featured in a recent issue of *Peking Review*: No. 32 (August 8, 1975), 16-19. It is noted, among other things, for having constructed nitric acid absorbing towers out of quarried granite rather than of the conventional stainless steel, at a savings of 80 tons of steel.

Worker institutes, called "7/21 Worker Universities (*Ch'i erh-i kung-jen ta-hsüeh*)" after Chairman Mao's Directive of July 21, 1968, existed at two plants we visited. The first, at the Hsinhsiang Cotton Textile Plant, had been established in 1974, with forty students currently enrolled. Much more well-established was the 7/21 School at the Shanghai Machine Tools Plant, where such an institute was first established in China. The full course lasts for three years of combined study (both political and technical) and work, the proportions of which were not clearly explained. Since 1968, three classes have gone through the school: 52 in the first; 98 in the second (of whom 40 came from other factories); and 109 in the third class, now in session (60 from other factories). There are 26 instructors, four assigned from universities, and the rest drawn from the plant's own staff. After completion of the course, most students return to their parent plant as technicians and planners among other things. Since almost half of the second and third classes will be returning to other, presumably smaller and less advanced plants, the role of the Shanghai Machine Tools Plant in technological diffusion is a significant one.

THE ROLE OF EDUCATED YOUTH

The role of educated youth in rural development generally and in local industry in particular is not easy to determine with confidence. What follows, after a few general comments to put the issue into some perspective, is not in any way an overall assessment of the movement, but only a description of what we saw and heard about educated youth (some of this data is presented in tabular form). Although we tried to ask about this subject wherever we went, we were not always successful in obtaining answers, nor was it usually possible to ask as many questions as we might have wished. Readers should therefore use this material with caution, realizing that the data is fragmentary, may not be typical, and has not been systematically compared with the literature on the subject. At the end of this section, we shall draw a few tentative inferences from what we learned.

"How you gonna keep 'em down on the farm" is a line from an American song that would translate easily into the languages of most developed or developing societies: rural youth wants to move to the cities, and urban youth wants to stay there. Indeed, the urbanization of modern skills is so widespread a phenomenon in developing societies that it seems natural, almost inevitable. Yet there is increasing recognition of the serious imbalances which may result from such a trend. The urban sector cannot absorb so many young skilled and unskilled workers, technicians, and intellectuals, with consequent unemployment (or underemployment), wasted abilities, and the explosive discontents that come from blighted hopes. The cities tend to be overcrowded anyway, especially in countries with large rural populations, and this migration further increases the demands placed on all urban services: food, housing, sanitation, transportation, and police among others.

Meanwhile, the departure of large numbers of rural youth deprives the countryside of their labor and their potential leadership, for it is among the most able and energetic that the migrants are usually found. This widens the gap between rapidly modernizing cities and increasingly stagnant hinterlands. Once it begins, such a pattern tends to be self-sustaining, unless strong counter pressures are brought into play.

Chinese leadership is fully aware of this problem, whose effects were already being seen by the 1930s at the latest. Since 1949, there have been periodic but only partially successful efforts to control rural-to-urban migration and to return surplus population from the largest cities (especially Shanghai) to the rural areas whence it came. Mao Tse-tung, in particular, has always felt greater affinity for rural China than for her cities, which he mistrusts as potential sources of revisionism and bourgeois values. In addition, he is committed to closing the gap, as much as possible, between rural and urban China. Finally—and this is very important—he wants the youth of China, the "revolutionary successors," to train themselves in self-lessness, dedication, and service. These traits, he feels, can best be inculcated by the poor and lower-middle peasants.[4]

A campaign aimed at these various goals is the sending to the country-side of educated youth (literally, *"shang-shan hsia-hsiang chih-shih ch'ing-nien,* or educated youth going up to the mountains and down to the villages," also more conventionally called "sent-down youth" or "rusticated youth"). This movement takes as its point of departure the call issued by Mao Tse-tung in December 1968: "It is highly necessary for young people with education to go to the countryside to be re-educated by the poor and lower-middle peasants."

It is said that since late 1968 over 10,000,000 educated youth have volunteered or been assigned to work in the countryside. Much has been written in China and elsewhere about this movement; indeed, from written materials it appears to be one of the most significant ongoing social movements since the Cultural Revolution (many Red Guards having been among the first sent to the rural areas).

Considering the magnitude of the movement and the amount of publicity it has received, there was what seemed to us a rather low level of

---

4. Chinese sources explain that "poor and lower-middle peasant" is "a term denoting class status and not present economic status." It is selectively descriptive (of those occupying this class stratum in the old society) and normative (referring to those who exhibit the attitudes and values said to be hallmarks of this stratum).

interest in our questions about educated youth. These questions were usually answered without very much elaboration or encouragement to continue along this line. Only once, at the large and self-confident Red Star Commune near Peking, did we speak directly to a person identified as a sent-down youth; on a few other occasions, an educated youth was pointed out to us. It should, perhaps, be noted in passing that virtually all of our information came from areas to which educated youth might be sent, not from the cities whence they might have come.

We quickly discovered that a distinction is often (but not always) made between two types of educated youth. The first are "sent-down youth," coming from the cities or towns for their first prolonged stay in the country. The second are "returned youth (*hui-hsiang chih-shih ch'ing-nien*)," coming back to their native place. The identity of these returned youth is a little unclear. A few may have returned from service in the PLA, but the majority are probably either young persons who had gone into the cities and towns seeking wage labor (what was called in one brigade, *"p'ao ch'eng-shih kao fu-yeh,* going off to the cities to get sideline jobs"), or rural youth who had received some of their middle school education in town.[5] The subject of returned youth seemed to arouse marginally more interest than that of sent-down youth, probably because the former are naturally identified as members of the locality, whereas sent-down youth are outsiders.

We were given no very specific information concerning the nature and amount of education possessed by educated youth, except that most had graduated from middle school (graduates of universities and technical institutes have passed beyond this classification). Graduates of either lower or upper-middle school may be sent (or returned) to the countryside, and this may occur up to as much as several years after graduation if a higher priority work assignment has not been obtained.[6] Hence, educated youth may range in age from about 15 to the early 20s.

Without exception, we were told that educated youth were first assigned to a brigade and team (*"ch'a-tui,* inserted into a team") and required to perform ordinary farm labor.[7] After a substantial period of re-education by the poor and lower-middle peasants, usually said to be two or three years,

5. This might be because some levels or kinds of schools are not operated by the commune, requiring that students be sent elsewhere. In other cases, family ties might be utilized to enable a youngster to continue his education in the city.

6. In Shanghai, we were told, middle school is now a unified four-year course, with no distinction between lower and upper middle schools.

7. Quite frequently and with unconcealed symbolism, this labor involves the handling of nightsoil and manure. Mao is cited: ". . . in the last analysis, the workers and peasants were the cleanest people and, even though their hands were soiled and their feet smeared with cow dung, they were really cleaner than the bourgeois and petty-bourgeois intellectuals." (*Talks at the Yenan Forum*)

educated youth are eligible for reassignment. We did not learn very much about how this reassignment takes place, or how many educated youth are affected by it, but the options seem to be these:

> 1. Reassignment away from the commune or brigade; we saw or were told of (a) return to factory work in the city, (b) entry into the People's Liberation Army, (c) successful application to higher education.

> 2. Reassignment within the commune or brigade; this was the most commonly mentioned option, with teacher, barefoot doctor, technician, and accountant the most frequently cited jobs. Less frequently mentioned were factory worker, tractor driver, cadre, Party member.

> 3. Continuing assignment as an ordinary farm worker.

In post-Cultural Revolution China, one can apply for admission to higher education only after a period of work on the production front. Applications must contain recommendation and endorsement by the unit in which the individual has served and by the relevant Party branch. This is unquestionably a major factor in motivating young persons to go to the countryside and to work hard while there.

For many educated youth, therefore, the stay in the countryside is a temporary though prolonged sojourn. Others, however, become permanent members of the local unit: it is said that they *"lo-hu,* settle a household,"* often by marrying a native or another educated youth. *Lo-hu* is not always done voluntarily, and may sometimes be required for the second option above. Since the commune or brigade makes the assignment and pays whatever additional training costs may be involved, its leaders wish to select those who will remain within the local system. Partly for these reasons, returned youth may be deemed a better risk than sent-down youth.

In the areas we visited—none of them in the remoter areas of China—most of the sent-down youth came from a few nearby urban areas, including county-level towns. This pattern, often noted in the Chinese press, seems to be quite common in the more traditionally settled areas of China. The reasons for adopting it are easily inferred:

> 1. Youth coming from the same (or nearby) cities have much in common, and can provide companionship and support for one another.

> 2. Being sent to a nearby area makes for a relatively quick adjustment and avoids the very great difficulty of learning to communicate effectively in a strange dialect. Climate, food, and local customs are also less strange than in a more distant area.

> 3. Family ties can be more easily maintained, with correspondingly readier acceptance of the assignment by the youth and by his or her family.

Only in Wu-hsi County (Kiangsu, 50 miles west of Shanghai) were we told of work teams made up primarily of educated youth, although we know from material published in China that this practice is quite common.[8]

The process by which educated youth are assigned to particular communes and brigades was not described to us, but we caught some glimpse of the considerations which might be involved from the point of view of the receiving units. Red Star Commune, we were told, welcomed the assignment of sent-down youth because the labor situation there was "very tight." Precisely the opposite was true of Liang-ts'un Commune in Hui County, Honan. Here, where land reclamation was the major preoccupation of the commune, it was said that land was scarce, and no additional population was wanted; hence there were no sent-down youth in this commune.

It has already been noted that one of the movement's goals is the re-education of educated youth by the poor and lower-middle peasants. In Chinese publications, this is by far the most salient goal. But it is also thought that another goal is to increase the supply of educationally skilled manpower in the countryside, thus facilitating rural development.

In the areas we visited, it is difficult to say what the payoff may be for rural development. It was little dwelt upon by our Chinese hosts, except in general terms. There may be several reasons for this. First, the number of educated youth is very small in the units we visited. Only in Red Star Commune, which may be as atypical in this as in several other respects, did the number exceed 1% of the total population; in most units, it was much less than that. Second, upon arrival, most educated youth have little to offer beyond their intelligence and literacy; for the first two years or so, during which they are performing manual labor, neither their intelligence nor their literacy may be put to use. In most cases, educated youth will not have had enough work experience before rustication to have acquired specialized skills. On the contrary, for farm work they are initially less capable and softer than their local peers. They may require the guidance and supervision of peasants who might otherwise be working. After a learning and toughening period, they probably become as effective as peasant youngsters, but if they then leave the countryside to be replacd by others, the process must begin again. Even for those who *lo-hu* permanently, reassignment will require further training and experience. There is little doubt that in the long run, those educated youth who remain in the country will become potentially important contributors to rural development. But their impact is delayed, and it may be further attenuated by small numbers and dispersion. Finally, as local educational facilities are gradually developed and improved, more and more rural areas will be able to home grow their own educated manpower, at least to the middle-school level.

8. See, for example, *China Reconstructs,* XXIV:7 (July 1975), p. 2–13.

To return to a point made earlier, our delegation visited units in traditionally settled regions of China. Several—above all, Ta-chai and Lin-hsien—were models of rural development, to be emulated elsewhere in China. Others (e.g., Wu-hsi) were clearly prosperous and able to take care of themselves. One might expect that it is precisely in such areas that educated youth would have the least to offer, and it may be for these reasons that relatively few such youth have been assigned to them. In the remoter areas—in Heilungchiang (often chillingly called the *"pei ta-huang,* the great northern wilderness"), in Yunnan, Kansu, Sinkiang, and in the poorer regions of China proper—the experiences and the role of educated youth may well be very different from those in the areas we saw.[9]

THE ROLE OF THE PRINTED WORD

In recent years, the spread of technology has been greatly facilitated by numerous publications of new books by both national and provincial presses. Judging from the number of browsers and purchasers in bookstores, these books are avidly consumed by people trying to keep up with new technical information. There are a few highly specialized books for senior engineers. There are translations of foreign technical books, and journals dedicated entirely to translations of foreign technical articles. But many, if not most, of the new books are meant to popularize technology for workers, peasants, and educated youth.

An example is the 108-page booklet on carbonization processes in small-scale nitrogenous fertilizer plants.[10] Subtitled "Reading material for Workers," this book provides flow charts, formulas of chemical reactions, graphs of differences in chemical reactions under varying pressure and temperature conditions, detailed drawings of the internal construction of valves and chambers, as well as maintenance and repair procedures. Printed in 30,500 copies in December 1971 and selling for only 0.28 yuan, this book is part of a series of six paperbacks meant to be used by workers in after-hours study classes (at the Wu-hsi Electro-chemical Plant, these voluntary classes were said to meet three times per week—once for political study and twice for technical study).

There are similar series for other industries. For small cement plants there is a series of eight booklets covering basic knowledge, raw materials,

9. At Fu-tan University in Shanghai, an extensive correspondence course program has recently begun, with 16,000 students enrolled. Most are sent-down youth from Shanghai. Provinces with large numbers of corresponding students are Heilungchiang, Anhwei, Kiangsi, and Yunnan.

10. Light Industry Bureau, Hopei Province, *T'an-hua [Carbonization]*: Small-scale Nitrogenous Fertilizer Plant Production, Reading Material for Workers (Peking: Fuel Chemistry Industry Press, 1971), 108 pp. Union ser. no. 15063.2039.

grinding, firing, equipment, chemical analysis, inspection, and raw cement. The first book in the series, basic knowledge for cement production, was printed in 42,750 copies in 1972; it contains 76 pages and sells for 0.20 yuan.[11] There are other collections of books for agriculture. They cover a wide array of topics: how to raise and prevent diseases among pigs, ducks, chickens, horses, cows, bees, silkworms, and fish. There are books on different grains, their scientific cultivation, test and control plots, and cross-breeding for new strains of plants. There are books on fertilizer application, and books explaining agricultural machinery and its maintenance.

We bought three books on fertilizer application. Though meant for a popular audience, two of these books go into great detail as to the nitrogen, phosphate, and potassium content of various kinds of fertilizer. The advantages, disadvantages, and appropriate application procedures of different fertilizers are discussed. Included are not only the more common chemical fertilizers, but also a very large number of organic fertilizers. One booklet, published in Kwangtung Province, lists the composition of almost 150 potential organic fertilizers, including manure and urine of humans and twelve different animals, various kinds of pressed oil cakes, water plants, vegetables and grasses, silt from rivers and ponds, as well as cured compost.[12] The Kwangtung fertilizer book, with 109 pages and selling for 0.26 yuan, was first published in 50,000 copies in 1974, then republished in another 50,000 copies in 1975. With a total of 100,000 copies, the book could reach every brigade and many work teams in Kwangtung Province.

Many of these books are published for rural administrative personnel, but because in many rural areas the standard of education is now seven years—five years of primary school and two years of lower middle school— many local youth can read these books as well. Equally important, perhaps, these books are aimed at educated youth sent to the countryside after completing seven, nine, or even twelve years of education in the city. This may explain the large stock of such books in city bookstores. By being able to read about and put into practice new technical know how, these urban youth with usually superior education may be given a more meaningful role in the countryside.

In addition to these narrowly technical books, there are a large number of books meant to popularize the leadership, economic, and ideological experiences of advanced production units. These popularizing agricultural

11. Editing group for small cement technology compendium, *Shui-ni sheng-ch'an chih-shih* [*Cement Production Knowledge*], (Peking: Chinese Construction Industry Press, 1972), 8 vol. Union ser. no. 15040.3003.

12. Kwangtung Province, Agricultural Bureau, Technical Materials Editing Group, *Fei-liao chih-shih wen-ta* [*Questions and Answers on Fertilizer Knowledge*], (Canton: Kwangtung People's Press, 1974), 109 pp. Union ser. no. 16111.206.

Table X-1

DATA CONCERNING EDUCATED YOUTH (COLLECTED BY THE SMALL-SCALE RURAL INDUSTRY DELEGATION)

Unit	SDY*	RY*	Origins (SDY)	Comment
Hopei Province, Peking Municipality				
Red Star Commune (also known as the Sino-Korean Friendship Commune; 10 management districts, 129 brigades, 17000 families, 82000 persons	5600		Peking only	SDY currently comprise ca. 7% of the total population. A total of 7200 SDY have served in the commune since 1968, but no information was obtained concerning length of service, rotation, etc. SDY are assigned directly to labor in the brigades; after a period of about two years, they may be reassigned. "Several tens" of SDY were said to be employed in commune industry.
Shansi Province, Hsi-yang County				
Hsi-yang County; population ca. 200,000	ca. 500		"Mostly Peking, Tientsin"	Ta-chai Brigade, the national model in agriculture, has no SDY.
An-p'ing Peoples Commune; 26 brigades, 2700 households, over 10,000 persons	0	1500		Of these, about 120 have been educated beyond upper middle school. About 200 RY have been assigned to units outside the commune.
Shih-p'ing Brigade (Li-chia Chuang Peoples Commune); 8 work teams, 480 households, 1970 persons	0	ca. 100		
Agricultural Machinery Plant (county managed); 310 workers	20 +			SDY are nominated by the brigades to which they are assigned; none come directly from the city to the factory. No information on the tasks performed by SDY in this factory

Honan Province, Lin County			
Lin-hsien; 15 communes, 487 brigades, 3932 work teams, about 700,000 persons	ca. 1000		All are first assigned to labor in the brigades and work teams, after which they may be reassigned as teachers, technicians, etc. Assignment decisions are made at the brigade level.
Ta-ts'ai-yuan Brigade (Ch'eng-kuan Peoples Commune); 340 households, 1700 persons	0	About 10 per year	Both barefoot doctors in the brigade are FY.
East is Red Agricultural Machinery Plant (county managed); over 300 workers	A few		Head technician (mid-30s) is a native of Manchuria.
Lin-hsien Cotton Weaving Factory; 186 workers	0	0	
Honan Province, Hui County			
Kao-chuang Peoples Commune; 21 brigades, 218 work teams, 31,500 persons	78		These SDY are assigned to one or the other of only two brigades in the commune. After a period of labor assignment, they may be made barefoot doctors, teachers, etc., in other brigades.
Hsin Liang-ts'un Peoples Commune; 27 brigades, 220 work teams, 42,000 persons	0	Some	Reason given for the absence of SDY was that the land-to-population ratio was low in this commune; additional population was therefore unwanted
Hui-hsien Chemical Fertilizer Plant; 536 workers	15		
Honan Province, Hsin-hsiang County			
Ch'i-li-ying Peoples Commune; 38 brigades, 298 work teams, 9500 families, 55,000 persons	Over 300	Mostly from Hsin-hsiang City and Cheng-chou	First assigned as labor, then eligible for reassignment as accountants, technicians, etc.

Table X-1 Continued

Unit	SDY*	RY*	Origins (SDY)	Comment
Kiangsu Province, Wu-Hsi County				
Wu-hsi County; 36 communes, population over 900,000	Some (of 8000)	Most (of 8000)	Some from Chen-chiang, Ch'ang-chou; a few from Nanking	I.e., total of both SDY and RY is about 8000. Educated youth are re-educated by the poor and lower middle peasants; they participate in agricultural production, class struggle, and scientific experiment. More than 500 educated youth have been selected to serve in leading organizations at various levels; over 1500 have become agro-technicians, barefoot doctors, teachers, accountants, etc.
Mei-ts'un Peoples Commune; 22 brigades, 104 work teams, 7475 families, 30,817 persons	180 combined total			After re-education by the peasants, they become cadres, agro-technicians, tractor drivers, barefoot doctors. Some have been sent to the university.
Shanghai Municipality, Chia-ting County (Chia-ting County)				
Ma-lu Peoples Commune; 14 brigades, 144 work teams, 7020 families, 28,000 persons	About 500		Mostly from cities in Chia-ting County; a few from Shanghai	First tempered in labor, then may be reassigned to other tasks.

*SDY: Sent-down youth   see text for definitions.
 RY: Returned youth

models usually run to at least 100,000 copies in the first printing. One 190-page book on the July First Commune outside Shanghai had 100,000 copies in its first printing in June 1974 and was then reprinted in 200,000 additional copies three months later.[13] Through these books, other local leaders learn about the proper mix of water control, field reconstruction, mechanization, leadership techniques, and ideological study, which will hopefully bring success throughout China.

SUMMARY

What we witnessed in China was an extensive, flexible, and varied system for acquiring, adapting, and utilizing standard technologies. By and large, these are not high technologies by international standards, but many such technologies would be inappropriate or of little use in the countryside. Furthermore, higher technologies require (take for granted) a broad foundation of basic technology and a labor force skilled in its use. This the Chinese are in process of creating. When one reflects on how far the Chinese have come since 1949, progress is impressive indeed.

Partially as a result of the emphasis placed on local small-scale industry, a technological infrastructure, previously lacking, is now coming into existence. It is easy for persons from technologically developed nations, where a literate and technically competent labor force has long been taken for granted, to forget how long and painful was the development of this labor force in their own society. This can lead, quite unintentionally, to the application of inappropriate assumptions, comparisons, and judgments.

13. History of Shanghai July First People's Commune, *op. cit.*

Chapter XI

CONCLUSION

In the summer of 1975 China's rural, small-scale industry program had entered into a new expansionary phase centered on farm mechanization. At least that was clearly the case in the areas we visited. Everywhere we went factories were equipping themselves for the production of new (for them) machinery from hand tractors to rice transplanters. At the same time the previous stage in these industries' development, that centered on cement and chemical fertilizer, was in no way being abandoned. Factories in these sectors are being expanded in scale and many of their processes mechanized. The day will probably come when these enterprises can no longer be called "small-scale," but they presumably will continue to be located either in the countryside or in small county towns scattered across the length and breadth of China.

The prime motive force for this extensive development lies within the counties and communes themselves. Provincial and central government planners sometimes provide financial aid and more frequently technical assistance, but it is the interests of the localities that drives the program forward. High transport costs and bureaucratic bottlenecks inherent in central planning both stand in the way of the supply of local needs, and the way around these barriers is to do it oneself.

The ideas for the various parts of the small-scale industry program, of course, did not spring full blown and unprompted from the heads of local farmers and cadres. In fact, for the past decade and more, the major thrust of the Chinese Communist movement has been based on the view that attitudes must be transformed by education including moral example before people will see and take the correct road. Thus the Tachai Brigade is not primarily an example of land levelling and drainage technology, but of the spirit of what human beings can do for themselves if they are sufficiently determined. And millions of Chinese, particularly the young, are brought to Tachai to study this experience firsthand.

Nor does the technology for the small-scale program originate in rural areas although adjustments in this technology are constantly being made by local people. Research institutes at the province and higher levels, large-scale urban factories, and other similar organizations are the original sources of the basic techniques. The Chinese are not busy reinventing the wheel over and over again in each county. The more advanced counties instead learn from these higher level units; they in turn then pass their experience on to other localities.

Are these enterprises efficient? Much, of course, depends on what one means by the word efficient. In an idealized world where transport and commercial systems are highly developed, many of China's small-scale operations might not make much economic sense. But China is a developing country and like most developing nations, although not always for the same reasons, China's distribution system is anything but efficient.

The issue, therefore, is whether these localities should wait until the state puts up a large chemical fertilizer or farm machinery plant or go ahead on their own relying primarily on local resources. If these local resources could be readily transferred to a major urban center, the efficient decision might well favor the larger urban plant. But these rural plants use local outcroppings of coal, local limestone, and, most of all, local labor many of whom continue to live in their old village homes. The cost of transferring many of these resources would be high and possibly even prohibitive. Basic to the Chinese idea of efficiency, as well, is the concept of dynamic efficiency. Many small-scale plants at the moment may be high-cost producers, but their costs come down as they learn better how to manage operations and expand output.

We, for the most part, saw some of China's best small-scale plants, and therefore we are not in a position to judge what is happening in the country as a whole. Nor were we able to collect enough price and cost data to do a full blown cost-benefit analysis. But in the areas we visited, most small-scale enterprises appeared to be producing items for which there was a ready local market. In fact, there were frequent indications that local demand exceeded the available supply at the going price. It also appeared to be the case that at these prices most enterprises made a profit, often a quite large one. If the opportunity or social cost of many of the inputs into these enterprises were used instead of the higher actual wages and raw material costs paid, it is likely in most cases that net social benefits would be higher than reported profits. Whether the net social benefit would have been even higher if these resources had been concentrated in large-scale plants cannot be determined with the data available to us, but it seems unlikely.

For the most part, the technology being used in the small-scale enterprises we visited was not unique to China. There were, to be sure, both major and minor exceptions. No one else in the world produces ammonium bicarbonate for use as a fertilizer. And Chinese farm machinery designs make greater use of cast iron and less of sheet steel than those elsewhere. Generally, however, it is not the techniques themselves that the Chinese are adding to the world's storehouse of knowledge, but the fact that these techniques can be adapted to rural conditions on a widespread scale.

How good are the products coming out of these enterprises? In many cases the quality of output by industrialized nation standards is low, but that comparison is not particularly relevant. More significant is that these products seem to meet a real need at China's current level of development. One does not require high quality cement in the dominant forms of rural capital construction currently underway in China. And if ammonium bicarbonate would involve more bother than it is worth for American farmers who have access to higher quality materials, Chinese farmers don't have comparable access to supplies of urea and the like, and ammonium bicarbonate does significantly increase the amount of nitrogen in the soil.

Rural China's economy at present is not being transformed solely or primarily by rural small-scale industry. County and commune level irrigation works (except for well digging) still involve the mobilization of great amounts of labor combined with relatively little machinery. Even fertilizer still comes more from organic than from industrial sources. And a majority of activities in the field from transplanting to harvesting are still done by hand. But rural small industry is playing an important if supplementary role in raising Chinese farm yields and in feeding the Chinese people. In areas such as those which we visited where these industries have been highly developed, Chinese grain yields are comparable to those in the most advanced agricultural regions in the world, including Japan. It is reasonable to assume that this combination of high yields and well-developed local industry is not a coincidence.

The Chinese, of course, are interested in transforming more than food output, and rural small-scale industries play an important role in the broader effort at social transformation as well. Millions of peasants throughout the country are acquiring through these factories a familiarity with modern technology that will serve them in many ways, not just in those connected with agricultural production. And the peasants involved are not just men.

Large numbers of women are participating in this education in modern technology

Rural industries also tend to narrow the gap between rural and urban experience in other ways. Factory workers continue to live in rural villages and draw wages not too different from their farming relatives. These workers thus tend less to think of themselves as a class apart and above their rural compatriots as has so often happened in all developing countries including China.

Rural small-scale industries, needless to say, are not the solution to all of China's economic and social problems either now or in the future. Their essential role is really an interim one, to help bridge the gap in both economic and social terms between China's current rural-oriented reality and a future in which China will be both industrialized and urbanized. In fact rural industries will often be the base from which new urban centers will arise. As rural small industries gradually expand in scale and number they will not be moved into existing urban centers. To the contrary, urbanization will be brought to them.

Appendix A

PEOPLE MET

The following list is arranged geographically according to the sequence of visits on our itinerary:

Peking
Hsi-yang County, Shansi Province
Lin County, Honan Province
Hui County, Honan Province
Hsin-hsiang Area, Honan Province

Cheng-chou, Honan Provicne
Wu-hsi
Shanghai
Canton

Under the geographical headings, we first list the names of our local hosts, i.e. those people responsible for planning and/or implementing our local itineraries. Then we list in alphabetical order the units visited, and the people met from each of those units. All names of individuals appear with surname first. Titles and names of organizations are given in Chinese characters on first appearance only. In many cases we were unable to get the Chinese names.

Before beginning with the list, there are two groups of people whom we would like to single out for special appreciation. First there are the eight people who escorted us throughout most of the trip as the representatives of our official host organization, the Scientific and Technical Association of the People's Republic of China (STAPRC):

Ms. Cheng Li
郑 力

Staff Member, Bureau of Foreign Affairs, STAPRC
中国科学技术协会外事局工作人员

Ms. Chiang Chien-wei
蒋见微

Professor, Peking Foreign Language Institute and Interpreter
北京外语学院

Mr. Fan Kuo-hsiang
范国祥

Division Head, Chinese Foreign Affairs Institute
中国外交学会处长

Mr. Fu Feng-kuei
付丰圭

Professor, Peking Foreign Language Institute and Interpreter

Mr. Huang Te-yi
黄德一

Responsible Person for the Office, Economics Research Institute, Chinese Academy of Sciences
中国科学院经济研究所办公室负责人

Mr. Li Ch'eng-jui
李成瑞

Research Fellow, Economics Research Institute, Chinese Academy of Sciences
研究员

Mr. Li Wei-min
李为民

Staff Member, Bureau of Foreign Affairs, STAPRC

Mr. Shen Ken-sheng
沈根生

Staff Member, Bureau of Foreign Affairs, STAPRC

257

Second is the group of six representatives of national units concerned with small-scale industries who made presentations to the group in Peking:

Mr. Ch'ieh K'e-ming 且克明	Ministry of Metallurgy 冶金部
Mr. Liu Chien-hsun 刘建勋	Chinese Silicate Society 中国硅酸盐协会
Mr. Liu Kung-ch'eng 刘公成	Chinese Silicate Society
Mr. Liu Tsun-san 刘尊三	Ministry of Hydroelectric Power 水利电力部
Mr. T'ang Chung-nan 唐仲南	Ministry of Petrochemical Industries 石油化工部
Mr. Tu You-ts'ai 杜郁哉	First Machine Building Ministry 第一机械工业部

PEKING AREA

Local Hosts (in addition to the people mentioned above):

Mr. Chang Wei 张 维	Secretary General, Secretariat, STAPRC 韦记处总韦记
Mr. Ch'en Chia-chen 陈家振	Chinese Foreign Affairs Institute
Mr. Chu Yung-hang 朱永行	Office Director, Bureau of Foreign Affairs, STAPRC 办公室主任
Ms. Hsiao Chen-yung 肖振荣	Staff Member, STAPRC
Mr. Wang Jen-ch'uan 王任全	Division Head STAPRC

Capital Iron and Steel Factory 首都钢铁工司

Mr. Ch'ang Lun-k'ai 常伦楷	Scientific and Technical Section 科技处
Mr. Kao Chien-p'ing 高迠平	Office Director

Peking Internal Combustion Engine Factory 北京内燃机厂

Mr. Chai Chin-hsueh 翟进学	Office Director
Mr. Fu Ch'ang-ch'uan 付长泉	Staff Member
Ms. Kao Yu-chen 高玉珍	Engineer 工程师
Mr. Li K'e-tsuo 李克作	Vice Chairman of the Revolutionary Committee and Chief Engineer 革命委员会付主任，总工程师

Peking West City Area Optical Instruments Factory 北京西城区光学仪器厂

Mr. Chang Lan-t'ing	Chairman of the Revolutionary Committee 革命委员会主任

Red Star (China-Korea Friendship) People's Commune
(no names)

HSI-YANG COUNTY, SHANSI
山西西阳县

Local Hosts

Mr. Chao Wei-cheng
赵维政

Office Director, Hsiyang County Office of Industries and Communication
西阳县工业交通办公室主任

Mr. Chia Lai-heng
贾来恒

Vice Chairman of the Revolutionary Committee of Tachai Brigade
大寨大队革命委员会付主任

An-p'ing People's Commune Water Conservancy Works 安平人民公社

Mr. Chang Ju-ch'eng
张如诚

Chairman of Revolutionary Committee

Hsi-yang County Chemical Fertilizer Factory 西阳县化肥厂

Mr. Chang Ch'i-cheng
张起争

Chairman of the Revolutionary Committee

Hsi-yang County Farm Tools Factory 西阳县农具厂

Mr. Wang Yun-wu
王运物

Chairman of the Revolutionary Committee

Hsi-yang County Tractor Factory 西阳县拖拉机厂

Mr. K'ang Ch'an-chen
康蝉镇

Vice Chairman of the Revolutionary Committee

Tachai Cement Factory 大寨水泥厂

Mr. Pu Hung-yi
卜鸿叉

Tachai/Hsi-yang Exhibition Hall

Mr. Chao Sun-liang

Head of Exhibition

Shih-p'ing Brigade, Tachai Commune 石坪大队

Mr. Ch'en You-t'ang
陈有堂

Chairman of the Revolutionary Committee

Wu-chia-p'ing Brigade

Mr. Po Lai-liang

Chairman of the Revolutionary Committee

LIN COUNTY HONAN
河南林县

Local Hosts

Mr. Ch'in Hsueh-tseng
秦学增

Staff Member, Lin County Office of Foreign Affairs
林县外事局办公室工作人员

Mr. Fang Ts'un-chi
方存吉

Vice Director, Lin County Office of Foreign Affairs

Mr. Hsueh

Chief of An-yang Subregion Bureau of Industries

Mr. Feng Hsiu-ch'ang

Staff Member, An-yang Subregion Office of Foreign Affairs

(no name)	Chief of the An-yang Subregion Office of Foreign Affairs
(no name)	Staff Member, Honan Province Office of Foreign Affairs
Mr. Suo Ping-fu 索丙伏	Responsible Person, Lin County Bureau of Industries 林县工业局负责人

Lin County Chemical Fertilizer Factory 林县化肥厂

| Mr. Lu
芦 | Vice Chairman of the Revolutionary Committee |

Lin County Cotton Textile Factory

| Mr. Sun En-hsi
孙恩喜 | Vice Chairman of the Revolutionary Committee |

Lin County Flourescent Light Factory

| (no name) | |

Ta-ts'ai-yuan Brigade Grain Mill, Ch'eng-kuen Commune 城关公社大菜园大队

| Mr. Ma Yung-hsi
马用喜 | Chairman of the Brigade Revolutionary Committee |
| Mr. Ma Tung-sheng
马东生 | Vice Chairman of the Revolutionary Committee |

Tung-fang-hung Agricultural Machinery Factory 东方红农机械厂

| Mr. Kuo Lin-ying | Vice Chairman of the Revolutionary Committee |

Yao-ts'un People's Commune Agricultural Machinery Factory
姚村人民公社农业机械厂

| Mr. Li Lin-sen
李林森 | Chairman of the Revolutionary Committee |

HUI COUNTY, HONAN
辉县

Local Hosts

Mr. Fan Shao-ch'ing 范少卿	Deputy Head, Bureau of Industries, Hui County Revolutionary Committee
Mr. Li Ts'an 李 灿	Permanent Member (Member of the Standing Committee), Hui County Revolutionary Committee 常委员会常委
Mr. Sung Ying 宋 英	Responsible Person, Office of Foreign Affairs, Hui County

Hsiang-yang Tunnel

| Mr. Chu T'ien-hsiang
朱天祥 | Deputy Head, Hui County Bureau of Communications
交通局付局长 |

Hsin-liang-ts'un, Liang-ts'un People's Commune 梁村公社新梁村

| Mr. Wang Hai-lung
王海龙 | Vice Chairman of the Revolutionary Committee |

Hui County (Pai-ch'uan) Cement Factory 辉县(百泉)水泥厂

Mr. T'ien Shu-wen   Chairman of the Revolutionary Committee
田树文

Hui County Chemical Fertilizer Factory 辉县化肥厂

Mr. Chao Ch'iang   Vice Chairman of the Revolutionary Committee
赵　强

*Kao-chuang People's Commune Agricultural Machinery Manufacturing
and Repair Factory* 高压公社农机修造厂

Mr. Sung   Vice Chairman of the Revolutionary Committee
宋

HSIN-HSIANG AREA, HONAN
新乡区

Local Hosts

Mr. Keng Wan-t'ai   Staff Member, Bureau of Foreign Affairs,
耿万太   Hsin-hsiang County

Mr. Yuan Che-hua   Responsible Person, Bureau of Industries,
元折华   Hsin-hsiang Area Revolutionary Committee

*Ch'i-li-ying People's Commune Agricultural Machinery Manufacturing
and Repair Factory* 七里营人民公社农机修造厂

Mr. Chang Hsiang-wen   Vice Chairman of the Revolutionary Committee
张祥闻

Ms. Chao Hsueh-mei   Chairman, Women's Federation of the Com-
赵学梅   mune
          妇女协会

*Hsin-hsiang Region Chemical Industry Equipment
and Accessories Factory* 新乡地区化工机械备件厂

Mr. Li Hua-ch'un   Vice Chairman of the Revolutionary Committee
李化纯

Mr. Shih Chien-ch'ing   Vice Chairman of the Revolutionary Committee
史竝青

Mr. Wang Hsi-wen   Vice Chairman of the Revolutionary Committee
王细文

Hsin-hsiang City Cotton Textile Factory 新乡市绵织厂

Mr. Chao Chin   Vice Chairman of the Revolutionary Committee
赵　勤

Ms. Huang Chü-lan   Vice Chairman of the Revolutionary Committee
黄菊兰

Mr. Wang Ch'ing-chieh   Vice Chairman of the Revolutionary Committee
王清杰

Hsin-hsiang City Water Pump Factory 新乡市水泵厂

Mr. Chang Kuan-fu   Vice Chairman of the Revolutionary Committee

*Liu-chuang Brigade Agricultural Machinery Manufacturing and Repair
Factory*(Ch'i-li-ying Commune) (七里营人民公社)刘庄大队农机修造厂

Ms. Chang Hsiu-chen   Vice Chairman of the Revolutionary Committee
张秀贞

Mr. Shih Lai-ho   Chairman of the Revolutionary Committee
史来贺

CHENGCHOW, HONAN

Local Hosts

Mr. Chang Shen 张 申	Permanent Member (Member of the Standing Committee) of the Revolutionary Committee of Honan Province
Mr. Chao Jen	Vice Director, Office of Foreign Affairs of Chengchow City
Mr. Ch'en Ping-chih 陈丙之	Office Director, Foreign Affairs, Honan Province
Mr. Huang K'e-kang 黄克刚	Responsible Person, Honan Province Scientific and Technical Association 河南省科学技术协会
Mr. Ma Hsieh-ch'eng 马血成	Responsible Person, Honan Province Scientific and Technical Association

Cheng-chou (State Owned) Cotton Spinning Factory 国营郑州第三棉纺厂

Mr. Chang Chung-chieh 张仲杰	Deputy General Engineer 付总工程师
Mr. Chao Shun-yi 赵顺义	Chairman of the Revolutionary Committee
Mr. Lu Ch'ing-shun 卢清舜	Office Director

Cheng-chou (State Owned) Textile Machinery Factory 国营郑州纺织机厂

Mr. Shen Kuo-lin 沈国霖	Permanent Member (Member of the Standing Committee) of the Revolutionary Committee
Mr. Sun Yen-hai 孙言海	Vice Chairman of the Revolutinoary Committee
Mr. Wang Wen-chieh 王文杰	Permanent Member (Member of the Standing Committee) of the Revolutionary Committee

WU-HSI, KIANGSU PROVINCE
无锡

Local Hosts

Mr. Chu	Staff Member, Wuhsi City Office of Foreign Affairs
Mr. Hua Ting-yuan 华丁元	Chief of the Bureau of Industries, Wuhsi County
Mr. Wei	Interpreter
Mr. Wu Ying-hsiung 吴应雄	Office Director, Wuhsi County Bureau of Industries

Ho-lieh People's Commune Agricultural Machinery Manufacturing and Repair Factory and Ho-lieh Brigade 河坼人民公社农机修造厂

Mr. Liu Wei-hua 刘维华	Chairman of the Revolutionary Committee, Ho-lieh Brigade
Mr. Wu Te-ch'ang 吴德昌	Vice Chairman of the Revolutionary Committee, Ho-lieh Commune

Mei-ts'un People's Commune and Agricultural Mahcinery Factory

Mr. Liu Teng-feng	Chairman of the Revolutionary Committee

Wu-hsi City Local (state-owned) 1 Silk Filature
  Factory 国营地方无锡第一纺丝厂
   Ms. Hua Chin-fen   Vice Chairman of the Revolutionary Committee
     华劲奋

Wu-hsi City Clay Figurine Factory
   Mr. Li Chien-wei   Chairman of the Revolutionary Committee

Wu-hsi County Electric Motor Factory 无锡县电机厂
   Mr. Yu Ch'ang   Chairman of the Revolutionary Committee
     于 昌

Wu-hsi County Electro-chemical Factory 电化厂
   Mr. Kao Han-ch'uan   Vice Chairman of the Revolutionary Committee
     高汉全

Wu-hsi County Iron and Steel Factory 钢铁厂
   Mr. Ch'en Hsing-hsiang   Secretary of the Revolutionary Committee
     陈兴祥   秘韦
   Mr. Sun P'an-ta   Member of the Revolutionary Committee
     孙益大
   Mr. Ting Ching-fu   Chairman of the Revolutionary Committee
     丁景福

Wu-hsi County Tractor Factory 拖拉机厂
   Mr. Miao Chin-fu   Vice Chairman of the Revolutionary Committee
     缪近福

Yang-shih People's Commune Agricultural Machinery, Concrete Products
and Power Metallurgy Factories 杨市
   Mr. Chao   Office Director, Commune Bureau of Industries
   Mr. Ch'en Jui-chung   Director, Commune Bureau of Industries
     陈瑞中
   Mr. Huang   Staff Member, Bureau of Industries
     黄

SHANGHAI

Local Hosts
   Mr. Chu Kang   Staff Member, Revolutionary Committee of
     祝 刚   Shanghai City #1 Bureau of Machinery and
                      Electricity
                      上海市机电一局
   Mr. Ho Kao-sheng   Staff Member, Revolutionary Committee of
     贺高生   Shanghai City #1 Bureau of Machinery and
                      Electricity
   Mr. Hsieh Ku-ch'un   Staff Member, Revolutionary Committee of
     谢谷君   Shanghai City #1 Bureau of Machinery and
                      Electricity
   Mr. Huang Hsing-sheng   Vice Chairman of the Revolutionary Committee
     黄星生   of Shanghai City #1 Bureau of Machinery
                      and Electricity
   Mr. P'ang Fu-li   Permanent Member of the Revolutionary
     庞夫力   Committee of Shanghai City

*Chia-ting County Agricultural Machinery Manufacturing
and Repair Factory* 嘉定県农业机械修造厂
(No names)
Futan University 复旦大学
    Mr. Chang Yu-fu   Office Director
Ma-lu People's Commune 马陆
    Ms. Chao Ching-chen   Vice Chairman of the Revolutionary Committee
    赵静珍
Shanghai Machine Tools Factory 上海机床厂
    Mr. Chou Ting-tseng   Secretary, Office of the Revolutionary Com-
    周定增   mittee
    Mr. Kuo Le-chin   Director, Office of the Revolutionary Committee
    郭乐金
    Mr. Lin Chi-k'ang   Worker-Technician
    林积康   工技人
Shanghai Shaped Steel Tubing Plant 上海异型钢管厂
    Mr. Chang Chih-jan   Vice Chairman of the Revolutionary Committee
    张志然
Shanghai (Bumper Harvest) Tractor Factory
    Mr. Ch'eng   Chairman of the Revolutionary Committee
Ts'ao-yang New Village and Vacuum Pump Processing Factory 曹杨新村
    Ms. Yu Ts'un-jen   Vice Chairman of the Revolutionary Committee
                          of the Village

CANTON AREA

Local Hosts
    Mr. Chang Ch'iang   Vice Director, Bureau of Water Conservancy and
    张　强   Electric Power of Kwangtung
                         广东省水利电力局
    Mr. Han Chien   Vice Director, Kwangtung Province Bureau of
    韓　健   Science and Technology
                         广东省科技局
    Mr. Li Han-ch'ing   Division Head, Kwangtung Scientific and Tech-
    李汉卿   nical Association
                         科技协会处长
Hsun-te County, Kan-chu-t'an Hydroelectric (Tidal and Flood) Station
顺德県甘竹滩水电站
    (no name)
Fo-shan Ceramics and Porcelain Factory 佛山陶瓷厂
    (no name)
Nan-hai County Cement Factory of the Fo-shan Region 佛山地区南海県水泥厂
    Mr. Feng Ch'ing   Technician
    冯　青   技术人员
    Mr. Hu Chung-hsin   Vice Chairman of the Revolutionary Committee
    胡忠信
    Mr. Wang Ch'eng-chu   Chairman of the Revolutionary Committee
    王承聚

Appendix B

DAILY ITINERARY

June 12, 1975—Thursday

PM   Arrive Peking Airport (from Tokyo)

        Greeted by Ambassador Bush and Mr. Perrito of U.S. Liaison Office

        Meet greeting committee representing our host organization, the Chinese Scientific and Technical Association STAPRC)

        Trip to Peking Hotel

        Sightseeing at Imperial Palace

        Pre-supper discussion on itinerary

June 13—Friday

AM   Presentation on Chinese National Economy and Rural Small-scale Industries: Mr. Li Ch'eng-jui, Research Fellow, Economics Research Institute, Chinese Academy of Sciences

PM   Red Star (China-Korea Friendship) People's Commune:

        Briefing by Commune Head

        Walking tours of:
           a) farm machinery repair and production shops
           b) food processing shops, including corn milling, fodder chopping, and flour milling

        Banquet given by our hosts at Peking Roast Duck Restaurant: main host Mr. Chang Wei, Vice President of Tsinghua University and Secretary General of the Secretariat, STAPRC

June 14—Saturday

AM   Capital Iron and Steel Factory

        Briefing by Mr. Kao Chien-p'ing, Officer Director

        Walking tours of:
           a) pig iron smelting plant
           b) steel plant
           c) rolling mill
           d) canteen

        Question period

PM   Presentations on Small Industries by the following experts:

        Mr. Tu You-ts'ai: First Machine Building Ministry

        Mr. Liu Chien-hsun: Chinese Silicate Society

        Mr. Liu Kung-ch'eng: Chinese Silicate Society

        Mr. T'ang Chung-nan: Ministry of Petrochemical Industries

        Mr. Liu Tsun-san: Ministry of Hydro-electric Power

        Mr. Ch'ieh K'e-ming: Ministry of Metallurgy

Evening   Films on Sandstone Village (Sha-shih-yu) and agricultural machines

June 15—Sunday

AM   Great Wall

PM   Sightseeing at Ming Tombs and Reservoir; Friendship Store and Bookstore

June 16—Monday

AM   Peking Internal Combustion Engine Factory

Briefing by Mr. Li K'e-tsuo, Vice Chairman of Revolutionary Committee and Chief Engineer

Walking visits to:
   a) foundry
   b) forge
   c) diesel engine shop
   d) gasoline engine shop
   e) canteen
   f) nursery

PM   Peking West City Area Optical Instruments Factory

Briefing by Mr. Chang Lan-t'ing, Chairman of the Revolutionary Committee

Walking visits to:
   a) metal processing shop
   b) optical meters shop
   c) magnifier shop

10:15—Train for Hsi-yang County in Shansi

June 17—Tuesday

AM   5:30—Arrive at station and bus to Tachai Brigade in Hsi-yang County

Briefing and itinerary remarks by Mr. Chia Lai-heng, Vice Chairman of Tachai Brigade Revolutionary Committee

Walking visit of Brigade

PM   Tour of Tachai Hsi-yang Exhibition Hall

Briefing by Mr. Chao Sun-liang, Head of Exhibition

Wu-chia-p'ing Brigade

Briefing by Mr. Po Lai-liang, Chairman of the Brigade Revolutionary Committee

June 18—Wednesday

AM   Briefing on Hsi-yang County Industries by Mr. Chao Wei-cheng, Office Director, Office of Industries and Communications, Hsi-yang County

Walking tour of exhibition

Hsi-yang County Tractor Factory

Briefing by Mr. K'ang Ch'an-chen, Chairman of the Revolutionary Committee of the Factory

PM   Hsi-yang County Chemical Fertilizer Factory

Briefing by Mr. K'ang Ch'an-chen, Chairman of the Revolutionary Committee of the Factory

Walking tour of factory

Tour of Hsi-yang County Farm Tools Factory led by Mr. Wang Yun-wu, Chairman of the Revolutionary Committee of the Factory

Evening   Two movies on Tachai

June 19—Thursday

AM   Walking tour of Tachai Cement Factory

         Briefing by Mr. Pu Hung-yi, Chairman of the Revolutionary Committee

         Tour of Shih-p'ing Brigade

         Briefing by Mr. Ch'en You-t'ang, Chairman of the Revolutionary Committee

PM   Tour of water conservancy works of An-p'ing People's Commune, including Shih-t'ing Reservoir and Dam

         Briefing by Mr. Chang Ju-ch'eng, Chairman of the Revolutionary Committee of the Commune

June 20—Friday

AM   Leave Tachai

         Tour Ch'in-shan Reservoir construction

         Train to Lin County, Honan

         Two-hour rest at Shih-chia-chuang Guest House while changing trains

PM   8:15—Arrive Anyang

         Briefing at railway station by Mr. Hsueh, Chief of the Bureau of Industries of the Sub-region of An-yang, on local industries

         1½-hour car ride to Lin-hsien City

June 21—Saturday

AM   Briefing on Lin County by Mr. Fang Ts'un-chi, Vice Director, Office of Foreign Affairs of Lin County

         Tour of Red Flag Canal Exhibition

PM   Red Flag Canal including:
         a) Main trunk
         b) Ch'ing-nien Tunnel
         c) Nan-ku Tunnel Reservoir
         d) Sluice gate dividing branch channels

Evening Movie on Red Flag Canal

June 22—Sunday

AM   Water conservancy projects

         Tour of Red Flag Canal and Hero Canal confluence

         a) Briefing
         b) Power station of confluence

         T'ao-hua Aqueduct-Bridge of #1 Branch Canal, Red Flag System

         Small power stations on 12th Branch Canal

         Spontaneous visit to threshing floor

PM   Program cancelled because of rain

June 23—Monday

AM   Briefing on Lin County industries by Mr. Suo Ping-fu, Responsible Member of Lin County Office of Industries

         Lin County Chemical Fertilizer Factory

         Briefing by Mr. Lu, Vice Chairman of Revolutionary Committee of the Factory

         Walking tour

Lin County Cotton Textile Factory

Briefing by Mr. Sun En-hsi, Vice Chairman of the Revolutionary Committee of the Factory

PM   Tung-fang-hung Agricultural Machinery Factory

Briefing by Mr. Kuo Lin-ying, Vice Chairman of the Revolutionary Committee

Tour

Lin County Fluorescent Light Factory

June 24—Tuesday

AM   Agricultural Machinery Factory of Yao-ts'un People's Commune

Briefing by Mr. Li Lin-sen, Chairman of the Revolutionary Committee Walking tour

Ta-ts'ai-yuan Brigade of Ch'eng-kuan People's Commune

Briefing by Mr. Ma Yung-hsi, Chairman of the Revolutionary Committee

Tour of food processing and peasant home

PM   Depart by car for Hui County and Hsin-hsiang City

Briefing at Hsiang-yang Tunnel by Mr. Chu T'ien-hsiang, Director of the Communication Bureau of the Revolutionary Committee of Hui County, on county projects

Travel to Pai-ch'uan

Briefing on Hui County industries by Mr. Li Ts'an, Permanent Member of Hui County Revolutionary Committee

Arrive at Yu-pei Guest House in Hsin-hsiang City

June 25—Wednesday

AM   Power operated pumping station and aqueduct in five stages, Hui County

Hui County (Pai-ch'uan) Cement Factory

Briefing by Mr. T'ien Shu-wen, Chairman of the Revolutionary Committee

Hui County Chemical Fertilizer Factory

Briefing by Mr. Chao Ch'iang, Vice Chairman of the Revolutionary Committee

PM   Kao-chuang People's Commune

Agricultural Machinery Manufacturing and Repair Factory

Briefing by Mr. Sung, Vice Chairman of the Revolutionary Committee

Yang-yao River Underground Dam and Well

Hsin-liang Village of Liang-ts'un Commune

Briefing by Mr. Wang Hai-lung, Vice Chairman of the Revolutionary Committee

June 26—Thursday

AM   Ch'i-li-ying Commune

Briefing by Mr. Chang Hsiang-wen, Vice Chairman of the Revolutionary Committee

Commune Agricultural Manufacturing and Repair Factory

Ch'i-li-ying Brigade

    Exhibition of Chairman Mao's 1958 visit

    Performance by Brigade amateur troupe

Liu-chuang Brigade

    Agricultural Machinery Manufacturing and Repair Factory

    Livestock pens

    Family visits

    Briefing by Ms. Chang Hsiu-chen, Vice Chairman of the Revolutionary Committee of the Brigade

June 27—Friday

AM   Hsin-hsiang City Water Pump Factory

    Briefing by Mr. Chang Kuan-fu, Vice Chairman of the Revolutionary Committee

    Walking tour

    Hsin-hsiang City Cotton Textile Factory

    Hsin-hsiang Region Chemical Industries Equipment and Accessories Factory

    Briefing by Mr. Shih Chien-ch'ing, Vice Chairman of the Revolutionary Committee

PM   Travel to Cheng-chou by train

    Itinerary briefing at train station

June 28—Saturday

AM   Cheng-chou (state owned) #3 Cotton Textile Factory

    Briefing by Mr. Chao Shun-yi, Chairman of the Revolutionary Committee

    Yellow River Exhibition/VanSlyke to Museum

    Trip to Hua-yuan-k'ou where Chiang Kai-shek broke the dikes of the Yellow River in 1938

Evening   Banquet hosted by Chang Shen, Permanent Member of the Revolutionary Committee of Honan Province

    Depart for Wu-hsi by train (9:15)

June 29—Sunday

PM   1:15—Arrive in Wu-hsi

    Staying at #5 Hotel in suburbs

    Tour of surroundings

Evening   Performance by local Red Guards

June 30—Monday

AM   Briefing on Wu-hsi County by Mr. Hua Ting-yuan, Chairman of the Bureau of Industries of Wu-hsi County

    Wu-hsi County Iron and Steel Factory

    Briefing by Mr. Ting Ching-fu, Chairman of the Revolutionary Committee

PM   Yang-shih People's Commune Industries

    Briefing by Mr. Ch'en Jui-chung, Director of the Commune Office of Industries

       Concrete Products Plant

       Powder Metallurgy Plant

       Agricultural Machinery Manufacturing and Repair Factory (transformers)

July 1—Tuesday

AM   Wu-hsi County Tractor Factory

       Briefing by Mr. Miao Chin-fu, Vice Chairman of the Revolutionary Committee

       Wu-hsi County Electric Motor Factory

       Briefing by Mr. Yu Ch'ang, Chairman of the Revolutionary Committee

PM   Wu-hsi County Electro-chemical Factory

       Briefing by Mr. Kao Han-ch'uan, Vice Chairman of the Revolutionary Committee

July 2—Wednesday

AM   Wu-hsi Clay Figurine Factory

       Briefing by Mr. Li Chien-wei, Chairman of the Revolutionary Committee

       Mei-ts'un People's Commune

       Briefing by Mr. Liu Teng-feng, Chairman of the Revolutionary Committee

       Tour of fields and Agriculture Machinery Factory

       Tour of consumer testing store

PM   Boat ride on Lake T'ai

Evening Revolutionary ballet *Yi Meng Ode*

July 3—Thursday

AM   Wu-hsi City Local (state owned) Silk Filature Factory

       Briefing by Ms. Hua Chin-fen, Vice Chairman of the Revolutionary Committee

PM   Ho-lieh People's Commune and Ho-lieh Brigade

       Tour of Agriculture Machinery Factory, hospital, and Brigade enterprises including fish raising, silk worms, pigs

       Briefing by Mr. Wu Te-ch'ang, Vice Chairman of the Revolutionary Committee of the Commune and Mr. Liu Wei-hua, Chairman of the Revolutionary Committee of the Brigade

       Train to Shanghai

July 4—Friday

AM   Shanghai Industrial Exhibit

       Sightseeing from top of Shanghai Hotel

PM   Shanghai (Bumper Harvest) Tractor Factory

       Briefing by Mr. Ch'eng, Chairman of the Revolutionary Committee

Evening Banquet given by Mr. P'ang Fu-li, Permanent Member (Member of the Standing Committee) of the Revolutionary Committee of Shanghai

July 5—Saturday

AM   Shanghai Shaped Steel Tubing Plant

       Briefing by Mr. Chang Chih-jan, Vice Chairman of the Revolutionary Committee

PM   Futan University Tour

          Briefing by Mr. Chang Yu-fu, Office Director, Revolutionary Committee

          Group departs for shopping

          Dwight Perkins stays to deliver lecture on American economy

Evening   Song and dance performances

July 6—Sunday

AM   Shanghai Machine Tools Factory

          Briefing by Mr. Kuo Le-chin, Office Director, Revolutionary Com-
          mittee and Mr. Chou Ting-tseng, Secretary of the Revolutionary
          Committee

PM   Ma-lu People's Commune

          Briefing by Ms. Chao Ching-chen, Vice Chairman of the Revolutionary
          Committee

          Chia-ting County Agricultural Machinery Manufacturing and Repair
          Factory

          Dinner given by group for traveling and local hosts

July 7—Monday

AM   Ts'ao-yang New Village of the P'u-t'uo District

          Briefing by Ms. Yu T'sun-ren, Vice Chairman of the Revolutionary
          Committee

          Visits included:
            a) Vacuum Pump Processing Factory
            b) nursery
            c) kindergarten

PM   Plane to Canton

Evening   Itinerary discussion

          Lecture on Chinese Economic Planning by Li Ch'eng-jui

July 8—Tuesday

AM   Kan chu-t'an (rapids of Hsun-te County)

          Hydroelectric Tidal and Flood Station

            Briefing and tour

          Lunch at Kan chu-t'an

PM   Fo-shan Ceramics and Porcelain Factory

          Sightseeing at Fo-shan Ancestral (Taoist) Temple

Evening   Acrobatics

July 9—Wednesday

AM   Nan-hai County Cement Factory of the Fo-shan Region

          Briefing by Mr. Hu Chung-hsin, Vice Chairman of the Revolutionary
          Committee

PM   Free for shopping or rest

Evening   Banquet

July 10—Thursday

AM   Train from Canton to border

Appendix C

LEVELS OF ADMINISTRATIVE CONTROL IN INDUSTRY

Chinese factories vary greatly in structure according to the administrative unit that controls them. Administrative control ranges all the way from central ministries attached to the government in Peking all the way down to brigades or teams at the level of the village. Below the central government, there are 29 provinces—or, more precisely, 26 provinces and 3 provincial level cities (Peking, Shanghai, and Tientsin). Each province includes some six or seven special districts, which are sometimes termed administrative districts or prefectures. Hsin-hsiang City, which we visited, was the administrative center for a special district. Below the district is the county. There are a total of some 2000 counties throughout the country. Below the county are some 50,000 communes, 750,000 brigades, and 5 million production teams. The commune is a township size unit. The brigade is a large village or several small villages combined into a single administrative unit. The team, around which most agricultural production activities are organized, is a neighborhood of a large village or simply a small village.

Table C-1 indicates the average population of sub-county administrative units in the counties and communes we visited. There are two observations which can be made from this table. First, except in Hsi-yang County and Wu-hsi City, the places we visited were considerably more populous than the average county and commune in the nation. The greater number of people in these units, we might speculate, along with greater proximity to urban centers and abundant raw materials, helped make them capable of supporting factories more readily than the average county. Second, the population figures in the brigade column show that in only two places—Hsi-yang County and Peking's Red Star Commune—were brigade populations below the national average. Significantly it was only in these two places that there was wholesale adoption of the brigade as the basic production and accounting unit in the countryside. In other places, the basic unit for collective production and accounting remained the team. At a number of our stops in north China, there was mention of the necessity of eventually moving to the broader and hence more socialist brigade level of accounting. Though our figures are representative of brigades in only a few places, they suggest that whether a place moves to the brigade level for production and accounting depends as much on the size of the brigade as on such nebulous factors as people's ideological commitment or "socialist consciousness."

In Chinese industrial administration, there are multiple distinctions between small and large industries and between collective and state industry. So as to help clarify these distinctions, Figure C-1 presents a simplified schema of state administration. The level of administrative control determines how profits are distributed.

272

Table C-1

NUMBER AND AVERAGE POPULATION OF SUB-COUNTY ADMINISTRATIVE UNITS

	County Population	Communes		Brigades		Teams	
		No.	Popul.	No.	Popul.	No.	Popul.
National Averages[a]	350,000		14,000		900		140
Counties							
Hsi-yang County	210,000	20	10,000	411	500	—	—
Hui County	560,000	26	20,000	505	1000	3669	150
Lin County	700,000	16	16,000	187	1100	3032	176
Wu-hsi County	900,000	36	25,000	—	—	—	—
Communes							
Wu-hsi City, Ho-lieh Commune			15,002	7	2143	82	183
Wu-hsi County, Yang-shih Commune			22,000	12	1833	198	111
Wu-hsi County, Mei-ts'un Commune			30,817	12	1401	304	101
Shanghai City, Ma-lu Commune			28,000	14	2000	144	194
Hsin-hsiang City, Ch'i-li-ying Commune			55,000	38	1447	298	185
Peking City, Red Star Commune			82,000	129	636	—	—

[a]Based on the assumption of a total population of 850 million which is 80% rural.

Factories above Line A in Figure C-1 are in the state sector. Those below the line are in the collective sector. State factories are considered to be owned by the state or "all the people." Though there may be some deviation from the strictest sense of the principle, in principle the county, special district, and province have no a priori claim to the funds their factories generate. These funds are remitted to the national budget, and may if the planners so desire be transferred out of the administrative unit which generated them for use in some other administrative unit. This cannot happen with funds generated in the collective sector. After taxes, the profits from commune and brigade enterprises are retained within the unit which generated them. Though the use of these funds may be subject to some planning supervision from the county, the commune and brigade own these funds and can reserve them for their own use. Though teams are rarely large enough to have factories, any enterprises they might control would be subject to the same principles.

Somewhat more difficult to generalize about are the "collective enterprises" which we were told about at Lin County, and which we later read about for Hsi-yang County.[1] At Lin County we were told that these factories were run by the county but were staffed by people from communes. They appear to be spinning, weaving, tile making, and other light industries with many workers paid largely

1. See Shansi Province, Hsi-yang County Revolutionary Committee, "Experiences in Constructing the Hsi-yang County Seat," *Architecture Journal* (*Chien-chu hsüeh-pao*), No. 3 (1975), p. 6.

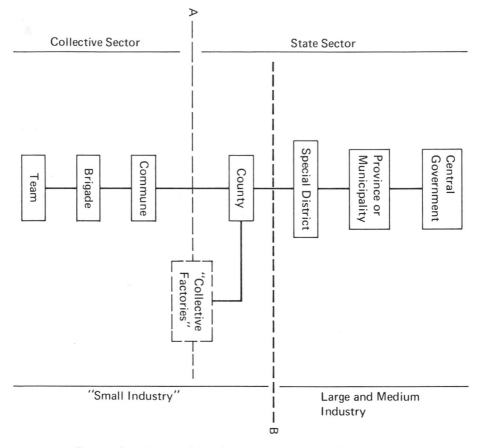

FIGURE C-1. Levels of Administration and Types of Factories.

through work points in their home production team. It may be that the financial situation of these collective industries is similar to that for collective industries in cities. In cities, the street factories run by housewives for the purpose of assembling toys, radios, or whatever also are called collective factories. Half of their profit goes to the state. The other half is retained by the factory for reinvestment in the factory or for the support of social services in the neighborhood. The collective factory in the countryside also appears to be a kind of in-between organization with some of the same attributes.

Besides the division between collective and state sectors, there is a division between small and larger industries. Though one occasionally finds exceptions in the press, those industries below Line B in Figure C-1 are generally considered to be small factories. With the exception of street industries in cities, those industries above Line B are generally considered medium or large industries. Large industries are exclusively in the state sector. Small industries include plants both in the collective and in the state sector.

Appendix D

BRIEFING ON CHINESE PLANNING BY LI CH'ENG-JUI (JULY 7, 1975)

(The following account is based on notes taken during the briefing, not a verbatim transcript—some errors, therefore, may have crept into this summary, but they are not believed to be serious.)

DRAWING UP THE PLAN

I. BASIC PRINCIPLES

The basic principles guiding the planning effort include self-reliance and maintaining independence, keeping the initiative in our own hands, taking agriculture as the foundation and industry as the leading factor, and walking on two legs.

The key method of planning, as directed by Chairman Mao, is that planning should be "from the masses to the masses," a principle that will be elaborated on at length in what follows.

II. THE ORGANIZATION OF STATE PLANNING

The main organization concerned with drawing up the plans is the State Planning Commission, which is subordinate to the State Council. Organizations similar to the State Planning Commission are attached to the revolutionary committees at the different levels (e.g. province, subdistrict, county, etc.). Some of these organizations are called planning committees, others planning bureaus, but they amount to the same thing. Every central ministry (Machine Building, Water Conservation, etc.) has a similar organization.

At the grass roots level (communes and factories), there are planning personnel or organizations. Bigger enterprises generally have a planning section, but smaller enterprises have only a few personnel. Communes have one or two people in charge of planning although they usually perform other tasks as well. The names of these grass roots organizations vary (are not unified).

III. KINDS OF PLANS

There are a great many different kinds of plans among which are plans for

—industrial production
—agricultural production

—capital construction
—transport and communications

—internal commerce
—foreign trade
—state budget
—allocation of goods
—manpower use

—education and culture (includes only the provision of material support, not the content of the films, etc. which is the responsibility of the relevant departments)
—health care

We draw up both five-year and annual plans. As can be seen from Premier Chou En-lai's report of January 1975, the State Council is now working on the Fifth Five-Year Plan for 1976–1980.

IV. PLANNING PROCEDURES (THE MAIN FOCUS OF THE BRIEFING)

There are three stages in drawing up the plan.

Stage 1: The State Planning initially draws up a sketchy and tentative plan (either five-year or annual). That plan includes only key targets for major products or items. This plan is completed in the latter half of the year and passed down through the revolutionary committees of the different administrative levels eventually reaching the individual enterprise or other grass roots unit. This plan is drawn up on the basis of historical experience together with surveys of requirements and potentials, and its purpose is to give grass roots units a clearer view of the goals of the state.

Stage 2: When revolutionary committees at the various levels receive the tentative plan, they put it into a more concrete form by adapting it to their local conditions; then they present the plan to the broad masses of workers or commune members for widespread discussion. The best of the suggestions by the masses are incorporated in the plan, and the revised plan then is forwarded to the next higher level. This discussion by the masses is of particular importance in making changes that bring the plan into closer conformity with reality.

Stage 3: When the plan has been passed up through the various levels to the top, the State Planning Commission calls meetings attended by responsible members from the various provinces and municipalities and also from the various ministries of the central government. The major task of these meetings is to achieve a comprehensive balance between production and needs and between accumulation and consumption. The initiative of the masses in Stage 2 has many advantages, but it does create problems, because all want to speed up production in their own area. When it comes to investment in the chemical industry, for example, province leaders argue for large state investments in their own provinces, and someone must decide who is to get the investment, because the accumulated funds of the state are limited. The final decision is made on the basis of implementing the policy of the central government and the principle that a locality should subordinate its local interests to those of the state as a whole. In this way, comprehensive balance is achieved.

This tentative plan is then forwarded by the State Council to the Central Committee of the Chinese Communist Party with whose approval it becomes a draft plan and is forwarded to the National People's Congress for formal approval. When the National People's Congress is not in session, the draft plan goes to the Standing Committee of the NPC. With the plan formally approved, it is passed back down to the provinces and municipalities and eventually to the grass roots organizations.

Premier Chou En-lai has stressed the importance of mass discussion throughout the planning process as illustrated by the two following examples from industry and agriculture. Many, for example, thought that the K'ai-lan Mine, opened by the British ninety years ago, was an aging mine with limited potential. But the older miners knew there was still a lot of potential left. In the past, mining had been done on the basis of seeking profits and only easily mined coal was dug out. The older miners, however, worked to meet the needs of the state and not for profit, and they knew where there was more coal. After several thousand surveys, therefore, they revised the old plans, and K'ai-lan's output was greatly increased.

V. KEY RELATIONS THAT MUST BE HANDLED BY PLANNING

Centralization and Decentralization.

At the time of liberation we (the Chinese people) didn't have much experience, so we copied the model of the U.S.S.R. Under the Soviet system everything was centralized, and Liu Shao-ch'i even coined the slogan that all things including tiny screws should be centralized. But experience showed us that deciding everything in Peking was faulty. Chairman Mao called instead for bringing two initiatives, the central and the local, into full play. Local places were encouraged to develop their own industries subject to higher approval. The central authorities would determine major items and policies, the output levels of major products, the distribution of industries between different localities, retail prices of key commodities, and the ratio between ministries [presumably the distribution of funds between ministries]. Other matters such as products locally made and consumed can be decided by local authorities, but they must report their efforts to the State Council (examples of such products include matches, hand tractors, and pumps to meet local needs).

In capital construction, the central authorities determine the level of funding of major items, while local authorities can decide minor items and report them to the State Council.

The Role of Ministries Under the State Council.

The Ministry of Metallurgy is in charge of all metallurgical enterprises and the situation is similar with other ministries. At the same time, however, there is also a metallurgy (and agriculture, etc.) bureau under the revolutionary committee of each province. The problem is that when an enterprise is under the dual control of a province and of a central ministry, to whom should it listen? The Soviets advised us that the ministries should have the whole say, and the provinces should only be responsible for implementation.

Chairman Mao, however, said that planning should center around the localities, although his instructions were not carried out until the Cultural Revolution. Now we place our emphasis on the localities. The province, for example, now decides the location of iron and steel works. The ministries can put forward suggestions for reference to the revolutionary committees of the provinces, but these must be discussed and approved by the provincial revolutionary committees before implementation. Major items must be reported to the State Council.

Thus power of decision-making lies largely with the provincial revolutionary committees, but the ministries do have a role. They can make suggestions and are responsible for technical guidance. If new technology becomes available, the ministry has the duty to popularize it, to organize meetings to swap technical experiences, and the like.

Since we switched our emphasis to the localities, we have increased the pace of socialist construction. Local authorities have a better understanding of how things run than does the center. As a result, we now have better implementation of the principle of taking agriculture as the foundation and industry as the leading factor. This change also has accelerated the development of small-scale industry. For example, during the drought of 1972, the worst in 100 years, Hopei Province went ahead with a tremendous effort to organize machine shops in local places to turn out diesel engines, pumps, and steel pipes. After several years, the province achieved big gains in the number of power driven wells.

Since the Cultural Revolution and particularly since 1972, we have made much headway in water conservancy development. Drought, in a sense, has provided us with a motivating force. To mention another example, in the spring of 1975, there was drought in the north and too much rain in the south. But even though it rained for 15 days prior to our [group's] arrival in Wu-hsi, we saw no flooded fields—all had been drained.

Decentralization leads to big battles to overcome local difficulties. Waging such battles in the past was difficult because we had to listen to the ministries in Peking.

IMPLEMENTATION AND INSPECTION

In implementation we again rely on the masses. At the start of the year, national, enterprise, and commune plans are all put forward to the masses for suggestions on how they can best be fulfilled. The masses are encouraged to have a clear understanding of the goals for the year because, as the plan is being carried out, new problems crop up. Due to unanticipated natural disasters and the like, some units fail to fulfill the plan, and the masses are mobilized to get at the route cause. The Soviets said, "the plan is law," but we have changed that. Where appropriate, we make adjustments in the light of changed circumstances.

Chairman Mao has urged all to endeavor to carry out the plan. But when imbalances occur, efforts must be made to achieve a new balance. Basically there are two methods of overcoming imbalances; the positive method is for the lagging sector to catch up with the faster growing sector. The other method is for the slower growing sector to slow down the others. We take the positive attitude, and when the textile industry grew too fast for the level of cotton output, we encouraged cotton to catch up.

Sometimes plans don't correspond to reality. China is a large and complicated country, and thus precise planning is out of the question. What we try to do is correct the imbalances once they arise.

Appendix E

PRICE DATA

Although price data were generally not included in the short introductions or "briefings" given by our hosts, our group made a concerted effort to collect price data for basic industrial materials and products. As the following data (all expressed in *yuan,* the Chinese currency unit) show, we were more successful in obtaining price data in the north than in the south. Our observations suggest the following:

1. There is considerable standardization of prices for some manufactures (e.g. power tillers, electric power for industrial use), but wide regional price variation for coal and perhaps for other bulky materials as well.

2. There is widespread concessional pricing for agricultural users of energy, specifically electric power and diesel fuel.

Red Star Commune

Wheat sold to state .284/kg. + about 20% for above quota—Rice about the same

Tractors—large 54 and 75 h.p. from Loyang—10,000-20,000 yuan; 12 h.p. walking tractor 2000+ yuan

Lathe bed   (make fixtures on spot) 8000

Fodder from grain mill—sold at 220/ton

Ex-factory price of wheat flour calculated at 264-314/ton

Peking International Combine Engine Plant

75 h.p. gas engine—price 2500, cost 1300

45-65 h.p. diesels (different data from 2 informants):

(A) 4500 to 1970, 3200 thereafter

(B) Cost 3200, Price 3600-4000 (based on size)

Steel—cheapest 400/ton (probably mild steel)

Steel for Camshaft—800-900/ton

Alloy—much higher

Cast iron—120/ton

Power—.08/kwh

Aluminum from Penki—3000/ton

Peking West City Area Optical Instruments Plant

Wheat Flour—.37/kg.

Tachai

Fertilizer prices paid by Tachai Brigade (yuan per catty): nitrogenous, 0.15; phosphate, 0.06

Power—for ag. use—.03/kwh.; industrial use—.06/kwh.

Tractor—10 h.p. crawler from county plant—3600; 20 h.p. from Tientsin—4000

Cotton Wadding—.68 yuan per chin (3rd grade)

Wu-chia-p'ing Brigade—State purchase price for grain virtually unchanged 1965-74. Increase only several 1/100 or 1/1000 of yuan per catty.

Tachai—State purchase price rises about 50% for above quota grain sales

Cotton Cloth—(1) Colored printed, plain, mostly cotton: .37, .49/price, 80 x 33 cm; (2) Plain cotton—.37, .4; (3) With more synthetic fiber—.79, .89, 1.12 (ration coupon required in proportion to cotton content); (4) Silk—1.71

Hsi-yang County Agricultural Machine Plant

Diesel fuel—.28/kg. for agricultural use

Hsi-yang County Fertilizer Plant

Ammonium nitrate 265/ton state price 260-65; production cost 200/ton; Coal—10/ton, 10-12

Agricultural Machine Plant

Lumber—ordinary grade 170-180/m³

Cast Iron—360/ton (pig iron for casting)

Department Store

Blue cotton cloth 1.32/meter (cloth about 30″ wide)

Hsi-yang C. Tachai Cement Plant

Cement (apparently #400 with 30-40% slag added): price—38 yuan/ton, cost—30

Coal: cost—3.5/ton

Lin County, Honan

Hydro plants: Price of electricity paid to producer by state—.035 yuan/kwh same at 2 plants; price fixed by the state

Chemical Fertilizer plant

Coal Costs 30 yuan/ton delivered, including 10 yuan/ton for transportation over distance of about 40 km.; coal is anthracite and bituminous

Power from RFC hydro plant costs .048 yuan/kwh.; thus state buys power at .035, sells at .048 for a markup of 37.1%

Bags for packing ammonia bicarb (25 kg.) cost 0.30 yuan a piece

Ammonia bicarbonate fertilizer: ex factory price—180 yuan/ton; cost—130

Cotton Textile Factory

Processing fee for spinning cotton provided by local growers: 1 yuan/yarn is 16 count

Tung-fang-hung Agriculture Machinery Plant

12 h.p. diesel engine for power tiller: produced by Anyang Diesel engine plant—800 yuan; this is a model 195 diesel engine: 130 kg., 2000 rpm

Threshers, price 400 + yuan; 4.5 kw engine; handles 1200 kg./hour for wheat

Power Tiller, 12 h.p. now in trial production; sells for 2000 + yuan; this price is uniform throughout the province, therefore there can be no problem of new product overpricing at the plant level in this case

Drill Press made by Szechuan White 518 Plant costs 8000 yuan

75 kg. air hammers produced serially by this plant (about 50 per year) sell for 6000 + yuan; these are not precision machines: they are used to flatten round metal bars heated in a furnace

Cast iron used by the plant comes from the local small ironworks in two grades, which cost 150 and 140 yuan/ton

Model CQ6137 lathe, work dimensions maximum 370 x 850 mm., produced here and sold to brigades and communes for 4000 yuan

Coal is purchased for .03 yuan/kg. or 30 yuan/ton

Ch'eng-kuan Commune

Flour Mill; milling charge is based mainly on power consumption

Hsin-hsiang C. Ch'i-li-ying Commune agricultural machine station

Batch production of power tillers; engines purchased for 700 yuan from Hsin-hsiang ti-ch'ü #2 diesel engine pl.; engine is model 195 12 h.p. diesel, 150 kg., 2000 rpm.; same engine used in Lin C., slightly less expensive here

Ch'i-li-ying: processing fee at flour mill 0.01 yuan/kg.

Commune machine shop produces seeder, price fixed "by the brigade" at 35 yuan

Commune grain storehouse: price for grain sold to the state is 0.13 yuan (presumably per catty)

Briefing at production brigade: grain milling fee is .01 yuan per chin (contradicts above? different mill?); no fee for cotton ginning because all cotton is sold to the state

Selling price for grain: Q. Has it gone up since 1962? A. Basically no, but there have been readjustments

Wu-hsi County Iron-Steel Plant

1974 gross output value was "over 9 million yuan"; output consisted of 10,000 tons each of steel ingots and rolled steel (reinforcing bars and angle irons); value of both products was included in calculating overall gross output value; therefore average price of all products was approximately 9 million/20,000 = 450 yuan/ton

Therefore assuming that angle irons were produced in small quantity (we saw none being produced or on hand) and/or that their price is similar to that of reinforcing rods, the price of steel ingots may be calculated at 400 yuan/ton

Electric power—average cost .07 yuan/kwh

Conversations in Wu-hsi

Moped (motor bicycle) about 250 yuan

Power tiller about 2000 yuan

Wu-hsi Clay Figurine Plant: Gross value: 37 million yuan for 7 million figurines, so the average ex-factory price is about 0.43 yuan

Shanghai Shaped Steel Tube Plant

1974 gross output value 15 million yuan; processed 9000 tons of all metals, therefore the average price of their output is 1667 yuan/ton; output seems to consist mainly of steel tubes, but also includes aluminum, copper and brass

Shanghai Ma-lu Commune

Machine shop manufactures diesel engines for which the price is 550 yuan/set; this is model 1E65F air-cooled 1 cylinder diesel, 3.5 h.p., 2000 rpm., weighing 38 or 42 kg. depending on the materials used

Shanghai Chia-ting County Agricultural machine repair and manufacturing plant

Producing rice transplanters (1260 units "so far" this year); price (without engine) is 1000 yuan per set

Ma-lu Commune

Grain and cotton purchase prices have not risen in recent years

Visit to street committee

Price data obtained in family visits:
rice: 16.5 fen/catty (Grade 1); 14 fen (Grade 2)
pork: 0.9 yuan/catty

eggs: 0.8 yuan/catty

telephone call: 0.03 yuan (charge is for being summoned when the call comes through—you order it in advance

flour: .17 yuan/catty

sugar: 1.5 yuan/catty

3-4 catties of tomatoes cost 0.1 yuan

1 catty of coal ("mei"—presumably refers to coal-dust balls used for cooking) costs 0.9 yuan

Hsun-te County hydropower station

Price of electricity: .07 yuan/kwh (forgot to ask if price is same for all use)

Foshan City, Shihwan-chen Art Pottery Works

1974 gross value of output was 1.5 million yuan for 1.3 million pieces, so average ex-factory price of ceramic figures is 1.15 yuan

#85 gasoline (used by Mercedes-Benz)—sign on the pump: 1 (obviously liter) = 1.42 yuan

Officials of agricultural machinery research institute gave the price of diesel fuel for agricultural use as 0.25 yuan/kg. (close to the Tachai price of 0.28) and said that gasoline costs 3 or 4 times as much as diesel fuel (this implied gasoline price is less than the pump price; however it too may be a concessional price for farm use)

Appendix F

NOTES ON PRODUCTION OF MACHINERY

Chinese-made motors, machine-tools, tractors, pumps, and other types of equipment are almost invariably marked with tags giving the name of the producer, year, and often, the month of manufacture, serial number, and specifications. Systematic observation of these labels in the factories and communes which we visited enabled our group to compile a substantial file of manufacturers whose products were used in the units which we saw. The following remarks are based primarily on data compiled in this fashion. In the course of our brief visits, we were not able to survey all or even most of the machines in use. Nonetheless we collected a substantial volume of data which can give considerable insight into the production of machinery and equipment in the People's Republic.

OUTPUT VOLUME

Our findings, summarized in Table F-1, show clearly that an enormous number of plants are presently engaged in machinery production. In addition to the large and well-known plants in Shenyang, Shanghai, Ta-lien, Peking, Loyang, Ch'ang-ch'un, Chinan, etc. whose products we expected to encounter and frequently did encounter, we observed during our brief visit products emanating from hundreds of lesser plants, including some in localities so obscure that our Chinese hosts could not tell us in which province they were located. Not surprisingly, the products of these smaller factories included many small and relatively simple items. At the same time, howver, we encountered substantial quantities of rather sophisticated products, including automatic lathes, pre-set gear hobbing machines, and piston pumps, produced by these lesser-known plants.

We were impressed by the spread of machinery manufacture to medium and small-scale plants in both urban and rural areas. It would appear that American studies of China's industrial growth have failed to comprehend the depth and dispersion now evident in China's machinery sector, trends which have probably developed rapidly during the past 10–15 years. By focusing their attention on developments at a few large-scale plants, foreign observers have almost certainly underestimated the recent expansion of machinery manufacture, perhaps by a large margin.

The extent of development in machine-building outside the well-known major centers is best illustrated by observations in Honan province, where our group spent the largest block of time (nine days of 28). Of the areas which we visited, Honan entered the Communist era with by far the weakest industrial base. Since then, Honan has been among China's more rapidly industrializing provinces, with its estimated share of national industrial gross output rising from 1.4% in 1952 to 2.7% in 1965 and 3.3% in 1971.

Table F-1

IDENTIFIED PRODUCERS OF MACHINERY BY PRODUCT TYPE AND LOCATION

| Province | Number of Plants Noted as Producing: | | | | | |
	Machine Tools	Engines	Electrical Motors & Equipment	Meters & Instruments	Other	Total No. of Plants Noted
Chekiang	1	1	—	—	2	4
Fukien	—	—	1	—	—	1
Heilungkiang	1	—	1	—	—	2
Honan	44	2	15	3	17	81
Hopei	3	—	2	—	2	7
Hunan	1	—	1	—	1	3
Hupei	2	—	1	—	1	4
Kiangsi	1	—	—	—	—	1
Kiangsu	30	4	4	5	16	59
Kirin	2	—	1	1	2	6
Kwangtung	7	—	8	1	7	23
Liaoning	6	—	—	1	2	9
Peking	8	1	3	1	5	18
Shanghai	20	4	4	5	39	72
Shansi	9	1	—	1	5	16
Shantung	5	—	—	1	4	10
Shensi	3	—	—	—	3	6
Szechuan	2	—	—	—	2	4
Tientsin	2	1	2	5	5	15
Yunnan	—	—	1	—	—	1
Others (unidentified location)	3	—	—	1	4	8
Totals	150	14	44	25	117	350

NOTE: No enterprise was counted more than once in compiling this table. Firms which manufactured machine tools for self-consumption were counted under "machine tools" rather than under the category appropriate to their major product. Thus Cheng-chou Textile Machinery Plant and Hsi-yang Agricultural Machinery Plant are both counted as producers of machine tools rather than under the "other" category.

Our Honan data indicate that the province now possesses a substantial base for machinery production. We found direct evidence of 81 plants producing a wide range of products including trucks, buses, large and small electric motors, power generating equipment, small diesels, agricultural pumps, ball mills for cement plants, meters, parts for flour mills, compressors, large and small tractors, scales, wire-drawing machines, threshing machines, cranes, textile machinery, and a wide range of machine tools.

Furthermore, our findings indicate wide dispersion of machine manufacture, especially in the northern part of the province which we visited. Nearly half of the 74 plants we identified were located outside the province's major cities of Cheng-chou, K'aifeng, Loyang, Hsin-hsiang, Shang-ch'iu, Anyang, Chou-k'ou, and Hsu-ch'ang.

While many of these plants are probably quite small, some appear to have achieved substantial size. The best-documented example is the Anyang Diesel Engine Plant, which supplies 12 horsepower diesels to power tiller producers in Lin and Hsin-hsiang Counties and perhaps elsewhere. Engines made by this plant in April 1975 included the following serial numbers: 2715; 2722; 3036—indicating an annual output rate of at least $(3036-2715)$ x 12 h.p. x 12 = 46,224 h.p., which may be compared with 1965 output of about 65,500 h.p. at Wu-hsi Diesel Engine Works, one of China's major manufacturers of diesels.

A brief visit offers little basis for judging the timing of this growth and dispersion of machinery manufacture in Honan. Some products are certainly new: Lin County's Tung-fang-hung Machine Plant was just beginning to produce power tillers, and the generators installed at a hydropower project in Lin County and made at the provincial water control bureau's machine plant in Cheng-chou were marked 001 and 002, indicating that local manufacture of turbines and generators may have begun in 1973. On the other hand, the discovery that Hsin-hsiang City, with one of the largest concentrations of machinery plants, already had 70,000 industrial workers in 1965 (and 100,000 in 1974), suggests that a considerable portion of the presently visible development may be 10–15 years old.

Despite this uncertainty, the implications of our observations regarding the present status of Honan's machinery industry are unambiguous. Honan now possesses a network of machinery producers, both large and small, numbering in the hundreds of enterprises. Machinery manufacture is not limited to the large urban centers, but has spread to smaller cities and towns throughout the northern portion of the province. These plants now turn out a wide range of industrial and agricultural equipment, most of which appears destined for use within the province.

Honan's machine industry is not one in which externally supplied machines are installed and used to produce equipment locally. With the exception of the Cheng-chou Textile Machinery Plant, a national-level factory equipped with first-class domestic and imported machine tools; and the Hsin-hsiang Chemical Fertilizer Equipment Plant, at least 80% of the equipment observed in the machinery plants and machine shops we visited was made in Honan province.

Evidence from other areas as well as Honan suggests that this provincial integration extends to planning, design, and technical advice as well as production of machinery. Outside the major plants associated with the First Ministry of Machine-building, the technical and administrative horizons of machine producers were primarily local and provincial. Except in Wu-hsi, which reported close relations with nearby Shanghai, local machinery producers seemed to have fewer contacts with national administrators and outside suppliers, advisors, or trainees than did their counterparts in the fertilizer, cement, textile, and ceramic industries (the latter two groups often exporting part or all of their output).

To what extent have other provinces matched the achievements of Honan, an area of above-average industrial growth, in building a wide-ranging and largely self-supporting machinery industry? Our findings, summarized in Table F-1, clearly point to the presence of similar networks of machinery manufacture in Peking

Municipality, which has organized a group of 200 farm machinery producers to supply its needs in that field, and in Kiangsu Province. Our Shansi and Kwangtung data suggest similar conclusions, but the special national role of Hsiyang County in Shansi and our limited observations in Kwangtung make this statement rather speculative.

What of other provinces? Lacking first-hand evidence, we can only speculate on the basis of general information provided by our hosts and from various publications. These give the impression that the type of development we saw in Honan is taking place, perhaps on a smaller scale, throughout China. We were told that all provinces except Tibet now produce tractors either individually or, in some cases, through cooperation among two or more units. Furthermore, this is not mere assembly, but includes manufacture of engines and other parts. We saw tractors from Peking, Shansi, Honan, Kiangsu, Shanghai, Tientsin, Liaoning, Kirin, and Kwangtung, and agricultural machinery handbooks list numerous other producers. Motor vehicle production is similarly widespread: in addition to the large Changch'un plant, we identified sedans, trucks, buses, minibuses, and motorcycles from Shanghai, Nanking, Yangchou, Wu-hsi, Cheng-chou, Wuhan, Peking, Tientsin, and Canton. The presence of farm machinery repair and manufacturing plants in over 95% of China's counties indicates widespread use, if not manufacture of machine tools, as does the widespread availability of such inexpensive pamphlets as "Basic Lathe Knowledge," published in an edition of 255,300 by the Yunnan People's Press in 1973.

All this evidence of massive volume and dispersion of machine manufacture and use suggests that great changes have occurred in China's machinery sector since the 1950s, when modern machine production was dominated by the larger, primarily coastal urban areas.

PRODUCT QUALITY

It is difficult to judge the quality of equipment at a glance. Nevertheless, sufficient material was collected to indicate the serviceability of the machinery which we saw and to demonstrate that major advances have occurred in raising quality standards. In particular, it was possible to ascertain that small and medium-sized plants are now producing machine tools and diesel engines which compare favorably with models produced by major urban manufacturers 15 to 20 years ago.

Chinese machines appear to be tough, sturdy, and durable. We saw machine tools dated 1962, and locomotives made in 1958. Nearly all the machinery at the Cheng-chou #3 Cotton Textile Plant was original equipment dating from the commissioning of the plant in 1954. Tractors are used for about 2000–2500 hours annually—about six hours daily (mostly for transportation)—lending support to published reports that Japanese farm machinery samples could not withstand the demands made on it by Chinese users. Some of the plants we visited offer impressive guarantees to their customers: Peking Internal Combustion Engine Works guarantees its gasoline engines for 100,000 km. If the engines break down within this limit— about 1% do—the factory provides a replacement and pays damages. Wu-hsi Tractor Plant offers free repairs and refunds to dissatisfied customers.

Many smaller machinery plants now turn out models of similar design to machines currently produced at some of China's largest machine tool plants. Although comparisons of precision and durability between samples from large and small plants are unavailable, it is worth noting that successful production of C620 series lathes now manufactured in many county plants was regarded as a major advance at China's largest machine tool factories during the latter part of the First Five-Year Plan period (1953–57). Similarly, gear-cutting machines, a much more sophisticated product, again, are now made by small as well as large plants.

Diesel engines currently produced by small plants are clearly superior to earlier products of China's largest plants in terms of weight and cost. Data in Table F-2 show that today's diesels typically weigh less and cost less than comparable products of the years 1956–57.

INTEGRATION OF PRODUCTION

The small and medium-scale machinery producers which we visited appeared to be no less vertically integrated than any but the largest of China's machinery manufacturers. Lin County's Tung-fang-hung Machinery works, for example, purchased the engine, ball-bearings, standard parts (this may indicate such items as steering-wheel, seat, shift lever), tires, rubber and plastic parts for its 12-h.p. power tillers, and made the rest, including chains and gears. Shanghai's much larger (Bumper Harvest) Tractor Plant, with 4 times the work force of the Lin County plant, had a similar degree of integration, relying on outside suppliers for the engines, tires, gearboxes and probably other parts as well. The Wu-hsi County Tractor Plant, a plant of intermediate scale, relied on outsiders for its engines and about 30% of the remaining parts.

Our observation of machine tool production, mostly for self-consumption, indicated even smaller reliance on outside assistance—indeed self-suply for machine tools may have been a response to inability to obtain external supplies. Except for the Red Star Commune, which had purchased lathe beds, small-scale machine tool production, as at the Wu-hsi Tractor Plant and the Tung-fang-hung Plant in Lin County, appeared highly integrated.

Further evidence of substantial integration in small and medium-scale machinery production comes from the modest scale of spare parts production at the large machine plants we visited in Peking and Shanghai.

Table F-2

CHARACTERISTICS OF CHINESE DIESEL ENGINES, 1956-57 AND 1975

Plant	Horse-power	Weight kg.	Kg./h.p.	Cost of Production yuan	Cost/h.p. yuan
A. Data for 1956-57					
Chi-nan (Shantung)	—	—	—		84[a]
Shanghai Diesel Plant	—	—	—		89[a]
Wu-hsi (Kiangsu) Diesel Plant	—	—	—		91[a]
Wu-hsi (Kiangsu) Diesel Plant	40[b]	1202[b]	30[b]		
Wei-fang (Shantung)					117[a]
Wei-fang (Shantung)	10[b]	260[b]	26[b]		—
Nan-ch'ang (Kiangsi)	12[a]	600[a]	50[a]		—
Nan-ch'ang (Kiangsi)	16[a]	580[a]	36[a]		—
Tientsin Internal Combustion Plant	small		60[b]		—
Unspecified	300[c]	1300[c]	4.3[c]		—
Unspecified: past	—	—	—		200+[d]
present (1956)	—	—	—		150−[d]
advanced units, 1956	—	—	—		110[d]
B. Data for 1975 (Collected by Rural Small-scale Industries Delegation)					
Large Plants					
Peking Int. Combustion	45–65			3200–4000	60–70
Old Model	55	550	10	—	—
New Model	60	340	5.7	—	—
Wu-hsi (Kiangsu) Diesel	12	130	10.8	—	—
Medium-small Plants					
T'aiyuan (Shansi)	10	126	12.6	—	—
Anyang (Honan)	12	130	10.8	800[e]	67
Hsin-hsiang #2 (Honan)	12	150	12.5	700[e]	58
Tzu-ch'i (Chekiang)	3	39	13	—	—
Wu-hsi County Plant (Kiangsu)	4	40	10	—	—
Ch'ang-chou (Kiangsu)	12	130	10.8	—	—
Shanghai Power Machine Plant	35	310	8.8	—	—
Shanghai Ma-lu Commune	3.5	38–42	11.4*	550	157

— indicates data not available to delegation.
*Indicates midpoint of data range.
[a]*Chugoku shiryo geppo* (China Materials Monthly) 114 (1975), pp. 17, 42.
[b]Wang Hsin-min, "Opinions on Developing Our Country's Production of Diesel and Coal-gas Engines," *Chi-hsieh kung-yeh* (Machinery) 5 (1975), p. 5.
[c]*Jen-min jih-pao* (People's Daily, Peking), October 30, 1956.
[d]*Ibid.*, May 13, 1956.
[e]Indicates prices paid by purchasers.

Index